On the Fault Line

On the Fault Line

*Race, Class, and the
American Patriot Movement*

Carolyn Gallaher

ROWMAN & LITTLEFIELD PUBLISHERS, INC.
Lanham • Boulder • New York • Oxford

ROWMAN & LITTLEFIELD PUBLISHERS, INC.

Published in the United States of America
by Rowman & Littlefield Publishers, Inc.
A Member of the Rowman & Littlefield Publishing Group
4720 Boston Way, Lanham, Maryland 20706
www.rowmanlittlefield.com

P.O. Box 317, Oxford OX2 9RU, United Kingdom

British Library Cataloguing in Publication Information Available

Library of Congress Cataloging-in-Publication Data

Gallaher, Carolyn, 1969–
    On the fault line : race, class, and the American patriot movement /
Carolyn Gallaher.
        p.   cm.
    Includes bibliographical references and index.
    ISBN 0-7425-1973-2 (cloth : alk. paper) — ISBN 0-7425-1974-0
(pbk. : alk. paper)
    1. White supremacy movements—United States.   2. Patriotism—Political
aspects—United States.   3. Whites—United States—Politics and government.
4. Whites—Race identity—United States.   5. Whites—Kentucky—Politics and
government.   6. United States—Rural conditions.   7. Kentucky—Rural
conditions.   8. Working class—United States—Political activity.   9. United
States—Race relations—Political aspects.   10. Racism—Political aspects—
United States.   I. Title.

E184 .A1 G16   2002
322.4′2′0973—dc21   2002013414

Contents

Figures

Acronyms and Abbreviations

AAA	Agricultural Adjustment Act
AAM	American Agricultural Movement
ACLU	American Civil Liberties Union
ADL	Anti-Defamation League
BATF	Bureau of Alcohol, Tobacco, and Firearms
CCK	Citizens for a Constitutional Kentucky
CPK	Constitutional Party of Kentucky
DEA	Drug Enforcement Administration
EPI	Environmental Perspectives, Inc.
FBI	Federal Bureau of Investigation
FmHA	Farm Home Administration
GLBT	Gay, Lesbian, Bisexual, and Transgendered
IRB	Institutional Review Board
KC3	Kentucky Coalition to Carry Concealed
KRBA	Kentuckians for the Right to Bear Arms
KSM	Kentucky State Militia
LBL	Land Between the Lakes
NAFTA	North American Free Trade Agreement
NRA	National Rifle Association
ONDCP	Office of National Drug Control Policy
SPLC	Southern Poverty Law Center
TBK	Take Back Kentucky
TVA	Tennessee Valley Authority
UN	United Nations
UNESCO	United Nations Educational, Scientific, and Cultural Organization

Acknowledgments and Preface

I could not have written this book without the support and help of numerous people. Primary among them are the patriots, legislators, and community activists whose voices make up a good portion of this book. I am especially grateful to the patriots who granted me interviews and, in so doing, gave me a window into a social movement that is often crudely caricatured and largely misunderstood. Indeed, all of the patriots interviewed for this book were warm and courteous to me. Some invited me into their homes for interviews, others bought my lunch in the course of an interview, and all were patient with my sometimes clumsy attempts to understand patriot ideology. Many patriots even shared deeply personal information with me about family problems. While I have not included such information in this book—it is largely irrelevant to the analytic questions herein—these personal stories helped me see my informants first and foremost as ordinary people with the same sorts of problems we all have.

People often ask me two questions when they discover I spent five years on and off researching the Patriot Movement. The first question is always "What was it like hanging out with militia guys?" I usually reply that there was "never a dull moment." I found patriots' candor, which was the rule rather than the exception, especially refreshing. Most of the people I interviewed for this book had a cynical view of politicians and ingenious ways of describing their political shenanigans, whether in Kentucky, where I did my research, or in Washington D.C., the "heart of darkness" for patriots. Indeed, there were times when I roared laughing at patriots' sarcasm and wit.

The second question people ask me is why I chose to research the Patriot Movement. Generally, people want to know if I am "one of them," although few are bold enough to ask me outright. I am not a "patriot," nor do I espouse a patriot worldview. Moreover, I abhor certain aspects of patriot politics, especially its links to white supremacist organizations and its antagonism toward traditional "others." I am sympathetic, however, to patriot disenchantment with government and with some of their positions (such as Kentucky patriots' calls to legalize industrial hemp), even while I remain skeptical of the packaging these positions come in. Also, I find the Patriot Movement a fascinating site of analysis. My reasons are both academic and personal.

In 1996, when I was doing background research for an article I was writing on the religious right, I recall being surprised at the dearth of information on right-wing groups, especially when compared to the relative abundance of work on left-oriented movements. As a progressive, I fully support the study of left-wing movements, but I believe it is equally important to understand the workings of the right wing, since its leaders routinely blame progressives for all of the major problems of our day. Crudely put, I believe the left needs to know its foes as well as the right does. It is also worth noting that the right has been enormously influential in the twentieth century. Some scholars would even argue that it has had more influence than the more ballyhooed impact of the sixties counterculture. While such assertions are difficult to measure, they certainly deserve our attention. Also, empirical studies on right-wing social movements can certainly prove useful in clarifying our understanding of the extent of right-led social change.

I am also interested in understanding the right because of personal circumstances. I grew up in Lynchburg, Virginia, a small town in the Bible Belt that was dominated by the televangelist Jerry Falwell. My growing up was simultaneous with the rise of the new right, which I experienced all around me. Indeed, it was hard to escape it, given where I lived and went to school. Like many of my peers, I rebelled against the new right's social agenda. I was young, female, and curious about all manner of things. When I was in my early teens, the politics put forward by the religious right seemed boring, and I found them increasingly chafing as I grew older. Everyone, it seemed, was doomed to hell. While you can leave your hometown, it is difficult to fully escape its effect on you. This is especially the case when you love many aspects of your background, even as you feel alienated from large parts of it. Eventually, with some critical time and distance from my hometown, I became interested in applying an analytic eye to my own past. In particular, I was curious why so many people in my hometown, and places like it across the United States, were attracted to the religious and far right. And I felt compelled to understand if the rise of the right was inevitable or if some alternative was possible. As an optimist, I choose to believe in alternatives, and in this book I explore one of them: a class-based politics. I am aware, of course, that any number of progressive alternatives exists and should be explored as well.

Patriots may very well disagree with the perspectives I put forward in this book. My hope in writing it, however, is to explore alternatives to regressive solutions and do so in a way that addresses the actual issues patriots raise. In so doing, I hope to challenge the left to consider progressive solutions for patriot anxiety with globalization. The white, working-class, often rural males who make up the Patriot Movement can and should be mobilized as strongly as other traditional left-wing constituents have been these past thirty years. The decline in unions—the traditional outlet for white workers—makes the need for their mobilization all the more immediate. Moreover, that the Patriot Movement exists at all is testimony to the dangers of not doing so. I also write this book (meager contribution though it may be) so that mantras like that of Margaret Thatcher's now famous quip, "There is no alternative," will never ring true.

In addition to the patriots who allowed me into their movement, I would also like to thank numerous people who helped me during the course of my research for, and my writing of, this book. John Paul Jones, Priya Rangan, and John Pickles were instrumental in helping me delineate my initial research question and in pushing me to hone my analytic perspective. A special thanks is due to the Kentucky "junta"—Mary Gilmartin, Vinny Del Casino, Stephen Hanna, and Susan Mains. They listened to my stories, gave me excellent advice, read bits and pieces of my work, offered helpful suggestions, and most importantly, made me laugh. Paul Paolucci served a similar function, in addition to giving me rousing commentary over beer about marxism and poststructuralism. I would also like to thank Dick Gilbreath for making the high quality maps in this book, and for doing so on fairly short notice.

In Washington, D.C., I am grateful to all of the students in my Militia Movements course, held in the fall of 1999. Their enthusiasm for the subject made me smile and gave me inspiration. I would also like to thank special friends and colleagues in Washington who saw me through the latter portion of this work. Sohini Sarkar, Phil Brenner, Cathy Schneider, Mustapha Pasha, Ed Comor, Randy Persaud, Mark Hager, Richard Gordon, and Rebecca DeWinter probably now know more about the Patriot Movement than they had ever hoped to (my apologies to all of them!). Their support and humor are much appreciated.

I am also indebted to the staff at Rowman & Littlefield. My editor, Brenda Hadenfeldt, has been especially spectacular. In addition to giving her full support to my project, she addressed all of my concerns and queries promptly and with care. She also kept the production process for this book running smoothly and on time. I would also like to thank April Leo for her work in the production phase of this work and Dave Compton for his copyedits on my manuscript. Both proved to have a much-needed eagle eye for detail, something I sometimes lack.

Finally, and most importantly, I would like to thank my parents, Morris and Carrie Gallaher, for their love and for instilling in me a concern for the underdog, whoever and wherever he or she may be.

August 13, 2002

1

February 27, 1997:
Garrard County, Kentucky

A BIG TENT

On Wednesday, February 26, a friend called me late in the evening. Almost breathless, he said, "Have you seen today's paper?" "No," I responded, "it's been a busy day." I was surprised by the immediacy in his voice. Tom was normally a laid–back sort of fellow. "What are you doing tomorrow night?" he asked. "I have no idea," I responded. "Well, I think you should save your evening." That's when he told me that the local paper had run an interview with the commander of the Central Kentucky Militia, Charlie Puckett. He and a local veterinarian named James Laughlin were sponsoring a People's Constitutional Town Hall Meeting in Garrard County, about an hour from Lexington, where I was then living (figure 1.1). Puckett and Laughlin had told Cheryl Powell, the reporter on the story, that they hoped it would be the first of many such meetings (Powell 1997).

So began my trek into the Patriot Movement. As a new scholar of the movement, I had initially planned to conduct my research in Montana. Those who followed the movement at the time knew that Montana was a hot spot. One of the cofounders of the Militia of Montana, John Trochmann, had managed to obtain lots of publicity after the Oklahoma City bombing two years prior and he was fast becoming the movement's de facto spokesperson. He had appeared on *This Week* with David Brinkley, been interviewed by several newspapers and magazines, and had even testified before a special committee in Congress about the movement (U.S. Senate 1995a).

Trochmann, his brother, and a nephew founded their militia in 1994 in Noxon, a small city of 450 people on the far western edge of the state. Although remote by most standards, Noxon is centrally located on the land-

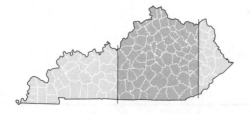

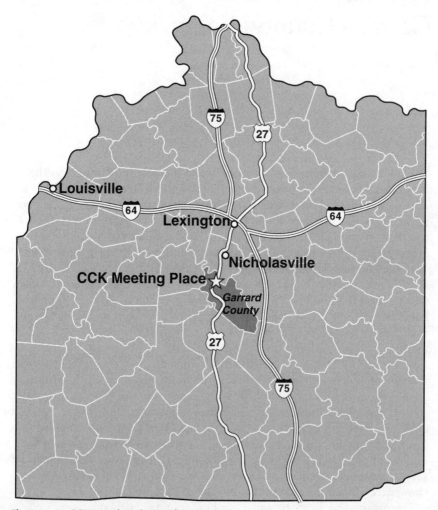

Figure 1.1   CCK Meetings in Local Context

scape of the extreme right (figure 1.2). First and foremost, it is close to Ruby Ridge, Idaho, where in 1992 white supremacist Randy Weaver engaged U.S. marshals and agents with the Bureau of Alcohol, Tobacco, and Firearms (BATF) in a bloody standoff that eventually led to the death of Weaver's wife and fourteen-year-old son and two marshals. Noxon is also close to Richard Butler's Aryan Nations compound in the Idaho panhandle.[1]

While I wasn't ready to give up on Montana just yet, the prospect of studying the movement closer to home had its appeal. At the very least, I decided that attending the meeting would allow me to experience the movement firsthand. Given that the meeting was not a militia meeting per se, I also decided that attending it would expose me to the movement's more "mainstream" face. While hard-core militias make up the core of the movement, they often rely on above-ground umbrella groups to funnel in members and to provide a more moderate face. Such groups have innocuous names, such as the Iowa Society for Educated Citizens or Nebraskans for Constitutional Government, that belie the far-right substance of their agendas (Davidson 1996). After several meetings, Puckett and Laughlin began calling their gathering forums for Citizens for a Constitutional Kentucky (CCK) and they eventually created a loose group around the name and a mailing list obtained at early meetings. Town-hall formats are also common, which establishes the impression that such groups are for *all* citizens. Renowned right–wing scholar Sara Diamond (1996, 202) argues that it is this "kinder, gentler, periphery" that buffets hard-core extremists and ultimately sustains the movement.

I left Lexington the next night at 6 P.M. Tom offered to come with me. I was grateful. I imagined the meeting would be packed with young men in camouflage and would include few to no women. Although I was not worried about my safety (the meeting had been advertised in the local paper after all), I couldn't help thinking I would stand out like a sore thumb. I figured that with a male at my side I might at least appear less conspicuous.

Garrard County, about a forty-five-minute drive from Lexington, is in the heart of Central Kentucky. Seventy percent of the total population is classified as rural and tobacco dominates the local economy (Raitz 1998; Watkins 1998). Garrard County is also politically conservative. It has voted Republican in the past eight presidential elections. Neither Tom nor I knew exactly where we were going. The directions in the paper said to look for a flashing marquee on the side of the road just after crossing the Kentucky River. We passed the river but there was no sign in sight. It was getting dark and neither of us saw much in the way of lights. Just as we were beginning to wonder if we had missed some crucial part of the directions, Tom saw the marquis in the distance. We turned left at the sign, almost missing the narrow gravel driveway, and drove up a winding drive to the top of a hill. At the top was a rectangular structure. It had sheet-metal siding, no windows, and two small

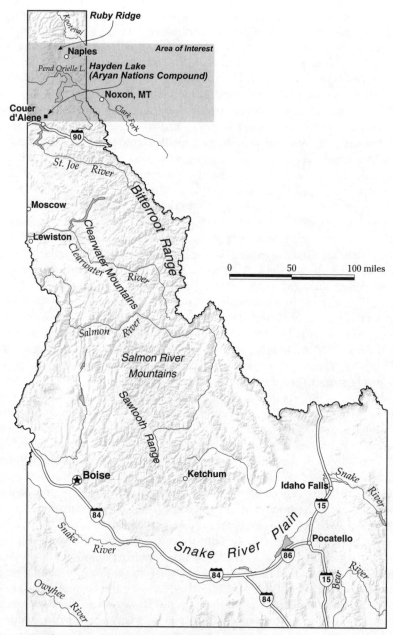

Figure 1.2   The Extreme Right in the Pacific Northwest

doors. There were about twenty cars parked in the lot in front of the building. A few had bumper stickers with common patriot mantras such as "Out of My Cold Dead Hands!" and "Join the Army, Serve the UN, Join the Militia, Serve your Country." Tom and I parked and got out of the car. As we approached the building, I saw about ten men standing outside one of the two small doors, smoking and talking in low voices. They nodded as we walked by, but said nothing, turning back to their hushed conversation as we brushed past them on our way into the building.

The inside of the building matched the frugality of its outside. The floor was concrete and the walls were made of unfinished plywood. Lights were strung up on the walls and were plugged into various outlets around the baseboard. On the right there was a small concession stand. A man was selling hot dogs and cokes. On the left were two long wooden tables covered with pamphlets, newsletters, and bumper stickers. Between the two tables was a narrow doorway. I peeked inside and saw a much larger room with a wooden stage at the far end and about a dozen rows of wooden benches extending to the doorway where I stood. There were about twenty-five people sitting down, scattered across the room, and several men in the front of the room wearing suits and ties, talking among themselves as they readied the podium. One of the men immediately caught my eye. He was tall and lanky and wore a large, black cowboy hat. His face seemed to match his frame—long and angular with deep lines.

I wasn't sure if the room was officially open yet, so I turned back to find Tom. He was walking toward me, holding a large hot dog smothered in chili. He smiled at me guiltily. "I haven't had my dinner yet," he explained. I was too nervous to eat, but I had to admit the dog looked good. We walked over to the far corner, trying to get out of the middle of the cramped space. We were standing close to the table furthest from the entrance. As Tom took a big bite out of his hot dog, I looked over and was surprised to see several books on industrial hemp as well as hats and T-shirts for sale that were made from hemp. Currently, federal law prohibits the growth and sale of domestically grown hemp, while recent restrictions make foreign-grown hemp difficult to import as well. Hemp was a major cash crop in Kentucky before it was made illegal and it continues to maintain a relatively high profile in the state. In June 1996, for example, papers across the state were consumed with the arrest in Beattyville of television and movie actor Woody Harrelson, who staged his own arrest by planting four hemp seeds, one less than the felony amount, before a parade of reporters and cameramen (Mead 1996). Harrelson claimed he wanted to challenge antimarijuana laws that are used in Kentucky to prohibit the growth of industrial hemp. For Harrelson and a growing number of activists, the two crops are not the same plant. Given hemp's association with left–wing celebrities, I was a bit surprised to find hemp making an appearance at a patriot meeting.

People were beginning to head into the makeshift auditorium, so Tom and I followed. As we made our way down the aisle, the lights went out in the makeshift auditorium, leaving the concession lights in the next room as the only source of light. "It's those damn black helicopters!" Tom cracked. I chuckled softly. My background research on the movement had mentioned black helicopters in some detail. Patriots believe black helicopters belong to the United Nations (UN). Their presence in the United States is viewed as ominous evidence of an impending UN takeover. I had also witnessed in person the seriousness with which patriots make such claims. In September 1996, I went to a "preparedness expo"[2] in Indianapolis, Indiana. There I stumbled upon a "book of evidence" at the Militia of Montana display. As John Trochmann told those of us gathered around the table for a look, his photos of black helicopters and UN tanks and troops—purportedly taken within U.S. borders—provided conclusive evidence that the UN was maneuvering for an imminent takeover.

As people fished out lighters, Tom and I made our way to some seats about midway down the room. A few more lighters came out, but it was still quite dark. No one seemed particularly bothered. People kept filing in and the men in the suits and ties were busy working on something behind the stage. After a few minutes, the power was restored and the tall, lanky man walked up to the podium, tapping it purposefully. Clearing his throat, he leaned down and toward the mike, "We're about ready to get this thing started, so if ya'll could please take your seats we'll get goin' in a minute."

With the lights restored, I took a look around the room, interested to see what the crowd that had assembled around me looked like. I immediately noticed I was not the only woman there. While the room was being lit by stray lighters, a few couples had entered the room and one had even brought their children. Young families were not the norm, however. Neither were single women. As I was to discover at subsequent meetings, women rarely came to these meetings unaccompanied by men. Moreover, by my rough estimates at that first meeting and those to follow, women made up only, at the most, 10 percent of any meeting group. The vast majority were men over forty. Many appeared to be over retirement age. A few were quite frail. One attendee that night was an elderly blind man. He wore large shaded glasses, walked with a cane, and had to be escorted to and from his seat.

While I did not notice it that night, I would come to notice at later meetings that most of these men carried guns in small holsters on their hips. For some reason, however, I never feared for my safety. I came to see the overt display of guns by attendees as a marker of a commitment to the cause rather than as threatening. I must admit to being disturbed one summer night, however, when my friend Tom pointed at the elderly blind man, a regular attendee, and whispered incredulously in my ear, "The blind guy's packing heat!"

In my perusal of the room, I also noted that of the hundred or so people in attendance all but one was white. He appeared to be African American and was carrying a television camera marked with the insignia of one of the local network affiliates. As I would soon discover, meetings were all-white affairs: invited speakers were white and so were the audiences that came to see them.

The baritone voice of the tall, lanky man suddenly interrupted my thoughts. "My name is Gatewood Galbraith," he said, "and I've been asked to moderate this meeting." I leaned over to Tom. "Is that the lawyer who was arrested two years ago for protesting the UN float in the Lexington Fourth of July parade?" I asked. Tom replied that he was. Gatewood Galbraith, as I would later learn, is an iconoclastic celebrity of sorts in Central Kentucky. He is a longtime advocate of the legalization of hemp and marijuana, he admits publicly to smoking marijuana, and at the time of the first CCK meeting he had made two unsuccessful bids for governor in the Democratic primaries. In his mid-fifties, Galbraith has cross-generational appeal. Readers' polls in *Ace Magazine,* Lexington's youth-oriented, alternative news weekly, have twice selected Galbraith as the winner of the "most beloved local celebrity" category. He also appears to have appeal among "lefties." In the magazine's 1999 "best of" poll Galbraith won in the cheekily, but affectionately, named category of the "best local example of a vast left–wing conspiracy." The more I learned about Galbraith in the weeks after the first CCK meeting, the more surprised I was that he had not only been present at the meeting, but that he had been chosen to moderate it and had accepted.

Galbraith began the meeting by asking everyone to rise and say the Pledge of Allegiance. Directly behind the stage was a large American flag. Everyone rose and put their hands to their hearts. I followed suit, feeling silly. I have always found overt displays of nationalism annoying. Given everyone's rote response, however, I decided to go along. I put my hand over my heart and mumbled along with the words seared into memory from my elementary school days. As people in the audience took their seats, Galbraith moved to the podium. "What about a prayer?" somebody called out, interrupting the flow. Looking slightly annoyed, Galbraith apologized and pointed to a man in the front row, who stood up, asked us to bow our heads, and delivered a prayer in a hushed tone.

Galbraith returned to the microphone. He began by explaining the purpose of that night's meeting and those that were to follow. "This is your meeting!" he told the audience. He explained that these meetings would be open forums where people could come together to discuss the declining situation in America today. "It may sound old-fashioned," he continued, "but solutions can be found in the Constitution and the Bill of Rights!" As I was to discover over time, Galbraith's public speaking mixes the rhetoric of a good, populist stump speech with the crescendo of a Southern Baptist preacher working up to the fever pitch of an altar call. Galbraith ended his speech that night in similar fashion. Pounding on the podium for emphasis, he queried the audience, "Communism is over, but do you feel any relief from the pressure?" A collective "No!" reverberated through the room.

After Galbraith's warm-up, a shorter fellow came to the podium. He was wearing a dark blue suit and a colorful tie. He introduced himself as Charlie Puckett, commander of the Central Kentucky Militia. Puckett lacked the presence of Galbraith. His speech was short and disorganized. Within a five-minute time frame he complained about a myriad of problems. He began with the first President Bush's designation of China as a most-favored nation. Puckett argued that Bush had "thrown human rights out the window." He then turned to the UN, calling it the anti-Christ. "They are coming to get our guns!" he said. "If we are not ready, they will take them all." He also complained about foreign aid, arguing that when the government gives money to foreigners it hurts Americans. He targeted Alan Greenspan as well, concluding that Greenspan held a lot of power for an unelected official. He ended his short speech by saying that political parties had nothing to do with his brand of politics. For Puckett, the real dividing line was between "the scumbags and the patriots." I would hear Puckett use this sound bite on several occasions, from the interview he did with the *Herald-Leader* advertising the meeting to my interview with him several months later.

While Puckett lacked the charisma of Galbraith, I would discover later that he was a key behind-the-scenes leader in the movement. Puckett's militia is one of the better-organized patriot groups in Central Kentucky. It has approximately six hundred members (Powell 1997) and under Puckett's command has extended its power base. In the fall of 1997, Puckett combined all of the state's militias into one statewide group, which he renamed the Kentucky State Militia (KSM). He continues as commander. Puckett's militia is active in the state on a number of fronts. Its members engage in frequent training sessions throughout the year. Usually held in remote areas of the state, these sessions emphasize survivalist training as well as practice for "offensive" maneuvers. A Vietnam veteran, Puckett has organized his militia along the lines of a standard military hierarchy and he has recruited actively among vets in the state. Puckett has also emphasized a political role for his militia. Several state representatives told me that Puckett and others in his militia are fixtures in the State House when the legislature is in session and that they immediately e-mail members and supporters when "bad" bills are introduced. Puckett would present yet another face for his militia when I interviewed him several months later. "KSM," he told me, "is dedicated to public service." When northern Kentucky experienced severe flooding that same spring, Puckett told me his members were asked to help with the sand-bagging efforts.

The next speaker was Norm "the Bear" Davis. Galbraith introduced Davis as a Second Amendment rights activist. Davis's speech, which like Puckett's was brief, focused on the formation of a biosphere reserve in the Land Between the Lakes Region of Kentucky (see figure 7.1). Davis, a resident near the area, began by telling the audience what biospheres were. "In case you don't know what they are," he explained, "I do—they want to put one in my backyard!" Davis took no time getting to the point. Biospheres were a UN plot to take over American land, a plot aided by the U.S. government. Davis concluded his short speech by telling those of us in the audience that the government does not have its priorities in the right place. "They're gonna take care of the bugs, but not you!" he exclaimed with disgust. There was little to write about Davis's speech, but I remember scribbling down this final comment, thinking to myself that it would make a good sound bite. The local paper must have as well. His closing comment was quoted in the *Lexington Herald-Leader* the next day in the article about the gathering (Edelen 1997).

Like Puckett before him, Davis lacked stage presence. He came across as a curmudgeon who had a message but resented having to actually tell it. As with Puckett, however, I would soon discover that he was a key behind-the-scenes activist in the movement. Kentuckians for the Right to Bear Arms (KRBA), the group Davis founded in 1993, is widely credited with organizing a successful grassroots campaign to lobby for concealed weapons legislation in the state legislature. Davis also served as the campaign manager for Gatewood Galbraith's 1999 bid for governor as a Reform Party candidate. Davis's connections across the state allowed Galbraith to garner significant numbers of votes in counties that the campaign, short on funds, was unable to visit.

When Davis left the stage, I looked at my watch and realized that the meeting had been going on for about an hour. I noticed several people had gotten up for a smoke. You could see the telltale wisps gliding by the cracked doorway they had snuck out of. I was getting fidgety, too. It was cold in the building. I doubted it had any insulation; it felt about fifty-five degrees inside. I wanted to get up and stretch, but Galbraith was introducing the next speaker. His name was Ed Parker, chairman of the Kentucky Taxpayers Party.

Parker said he would spend his allotted time providing a history of the new age movement and its "unruly child," the "biodiversity monster." Biodiversity, Parker argued, was based on taking away basic American freedoms. The problems began in the 1960s, Parker informed the audience, when groups began protesting energy development, such as nuclear power, off-shore drilling, and the Alaska pipeline. These protests, he argued, were predicated on the "ridiculous" assumption that human needs must be sacrificed for those of "obscure" animals. The 1970s were no better, Parker concluded. The "so-called" oil crisis, Parker said, was nothing but a farce put forward by "new agers."

Parker then asked the audience if they knew the extent of the new age movement. A few "No" responses peppered the attentive room. "Well, it's expansive," he responded. Parker named Bob Dole, Newt Gingrich, Al Gore, Bill and Hillary Clinton, Mitch McConnell (a Republican senator for Kentucky), and Ted Turner as especially egregious offenders. He concluded by warning the audience that the new age movement was full of nature worshipers, people who don't believe in Jesus Christ, "amoral" socialists and communists. As Parker walked from the stage, I could not help but wonder who was not in the new age movement.

Galbraith returned to the stage. He said he wanted to take a minute to recognize the elected officials in the audience. Three of these officials, Galbraith proudly proclaimed, were legislators who voted in support of Kentucky's concealed weapons law, House Bill 40, which passed in 1996. Galbraith first recognized Lonnie Naper, a Republican representative for the General Assembly in district 36, a three-county area just south of Lexington (figure 1.3). Naper stood up briefly, waved, and said he wanted to thank James Laughlin for providing the venue for the meeting. Galbraith then recognized Tom Buford, a Republican senator in the General Assembly whose Senate district 22 encompassed Lexington and several counties south of it (figure 1.4). Buford also thanked Laughlin and told the audience he was delighted to hear what his constituents thought about the issues at hand.

After Buford took his seat, Galbraith introduced Representative Robert Damron from Nicholasville (district 39), the only Democrat in the group (figure 1.3). Despite his political affiliation, Damron is vigorously pro–Second Amendment. He authored the concealed weapons legislation and is highly regarded in the movement. Later, when I interviewed Damron, I learned that he works closely with the movement. He openly admitted to me that he consulted with Norman Davis and Charlie Puckett when he formulated the bill and he marveled at patriots' elaborate e-mail "warning" systems, going so far as to tell me that their persistent lobbying across the state brought "wayward" legislators behind his bill. Unlike Naper or Buford, Damron came onto the makeshift stage that night to speak to the audience. He thanked his constituency for helping to get the legislation passed. "Your phone calls to those of us here were crucial," he told the audience. And because of their support, he informed the audience, twenty-two thousand Kentuckians would soon be or already were able to carry concealed weapons.

Galbraith concluded by introducing Barry Metcalf, a Republican senator from east of Lexington (district 34) and then a candidate in the Republican

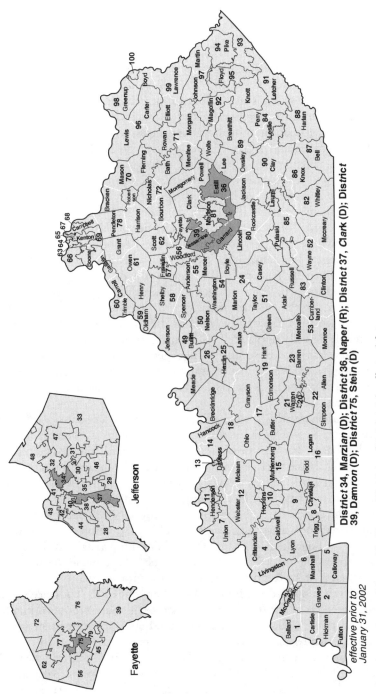

Figure 1.3   General Assembly House Districts of Patriot-Friendly Legislators

District 34, *Marzian* (D); District 36, *Naper* (R); District 37, *Clark* (D); District 39, *Damron* (D); District 75, *Stein* (D)

effective prior to January 31, 2002

primary race for the U.S. Senate in the 1998 elections (figure 1.4). Metcalf said he was a hard worker and that he hoped people would consider voting for him. He eventually lost his bid for the Republican nomination in the May primary to Jim Bunning. Bunning went on to win the general election and now serves in the U.S. Senate with Mitch McConnell.

After Metcalf took his seat, Galbraith introduced Wes Majors. Majors wore a denim shirt and a bright tie. He appeared to be in his early to middle twenties, somewhat of an anomaly in this crowd, dominated as it was by men in their forties and fifties. Majors is a Second Amendment activist in Lexington. He had prepared a speech and, unlike many of the other speakers, his style was polished. Majors must have recognized the age differential coming in because he had tailored his speech appropriately. He began by asking the audience members to recall the first time they had seen or held a gun. "It was probably with your father or granddad," he speculated. Majors said the image for him and his generation was different. "A lot of guys my age have never seen a gun," he lamented, adding that when his peers did think of weapons they usually pictured bad scenarios of kids taking guns to school. "But," Majors intoned, "these images are not reality." Majors concluded by saying he wants to change these negative connotations so his children's generation will see guns the way his father's did. Majors was a hit. As he sat down, people actually applauded. Galbraith returned to the podium, smiling. He said it was good to see the younger generation getting involved. Generation X, he lectured the audience, is not being taught the American Dream. "It's time," he argued, "to envision that dream as patriots move to take America back."

Galbraith then abruptly switched gears, turning to a discussion of hemp. He argued that Kentucky farmers should be able to grow hemp in conjunction with tobacco. Farmers need more options, he said, and providing these options can enable farmers to stay on the land. The cigarette market, Galbraith continued, will not go away if American politicians get rid of tobacco farmers. Rather, there will be a change in who produces the crop. Small tobacco farmers will be replaced by multinational corporations, the same companies that took away hemp and cannabis production from farmers in the first place. Pounding on the podium, Galbraith proclaimed disgustedly that growers in the third world would soon be able to grow the same crop for a pittance of what Kentucky farmers grow it for today.

Galbraith then opened the floor, asking if anyone in the audience wanted to speak. A man near the front raised his hand. Galbraith motioned him forward. As he stood, I noticed he had a stack of books under one arm. He was tall and very slender and he wore a serious expression. He leaned down to the microphone, which was several inches below him, and introduced himself as John Bales[3] from the Fully Informed Jury Association. Bales did not have a speech prepared and it was difficult to follow him. He was mumbling

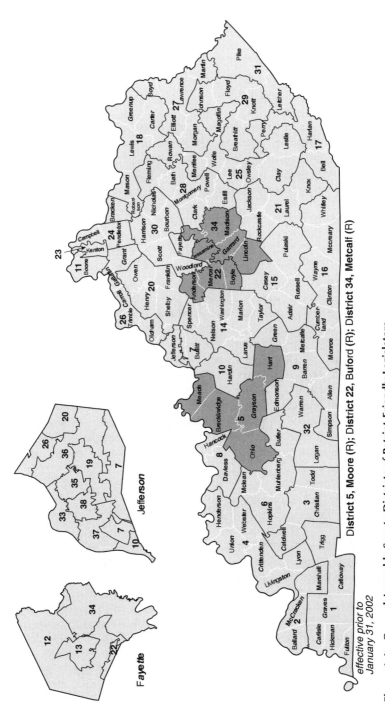

Figure 1.4 General Assembly Senate Districts of Patriot-Friendly Legislators

District 5, Moore (R); District 22, Buford (R); District 34, Metcalf (R)

effective prior to
January 31, 2002

into the microphone and it was difficult to hear him until Galbraith abruptly interrupted, telling him to speak up. Bales cleared his throat, looking more annoyed than embarrassed, and continued, louder this time. He said that he wanted to tell people about his organization. Most people, he argued, think an informed jury is one that does what the judge instructs them to do. In fact, Bales informed us, juries are not bound by judges' orders. Rather, they have more rights than they are presently told they have by judges and prosecutors. Bales then pulled open one of his books, *Black's Law Dictionary*, saying he was going to read a passage from it to prove his point. People in the audience were fidgeting and Galbraith was pacing behind Bales. When Bales finished with his lengthy recitation, Galbraith told him to "Get to the point."

Looking annoyed again, but saying nothing, Bales got to the point. He said that his organization, and others across the country, believe that jurors have not only the right to decide someone's guilt or innocence, but also the right to decide if the law under which someone is being prosecuted is constitutional. If jurors decide that a law is not constitutional, he told us, they have the right to throw the case out of court by delivering an innocent verdict. I was struck by Bales's argument because I had read a similar analysis by leftist rabble-rouser and longtime *Nation* contributor Alexander Cockburn. Cockburn has argued that jurors should apply these tactics in drug use and possession cases because such crimes are "victimless" and in no way merit the lengthy prison terms judges are now required to give to those convicted of them (Cockburn 1995a, 1995b).

Bales did not attend CCK meetings on a regular basis, although I noticed that he attended more frequently in the summer months. He was never an invited speaker, but he always raised his hand to speak at the end of meetings when the moderator opened the floor for comments and questions. Each time he did, the moderator (sometimes Galbraith, at others a preacher named Rick Tyler) would look slightly perturbed. At one meeting, Rick Tyler responded that Bales could speak, but only for seven minutes, even producing a small oven timer out of his pocket and setting it promptly on the podium. Initially, I was struck with how abrupt Galbraith had been with Bales at that first meeting, thinking it seemed unduly harsh. Bales's bellicose rhetoric at later meetings, however, indicates that Galbraith and Tyler may have known Bales had the potential for "over-the-top" behavior. With each meeting Bales attended, he became more self-assured speaking in public. He spoke more freely and relied less and less on quotes from books to make his point. His speeches were also more forceful and his rhetoric more inflammatory. In the open forum section of a late June meeting, for example, Bales asked to speak on the concealed weapons law. He strode to the podium and told those of us assembled that muggy night that he thought the law was invalid because it failed to adequately define the term "weapon." As such, if someone was cited for carrying a concealed weapon without a permit, Bales argued, that person should ask the officer or court official to define what constitutes a weapon. They would not, he concluded, be able to do it. He continued, adding that such laws were "redundant" anyway because, as he put it, "Carrying a gun is a God-given right." As Bales concluded harshly from the podium that night, "I should be able to carry a bazooka into Wal-Mart if I want to!"

The audience went deathly quiet. The moderator that night, Rick Tyler, returned to the podium, smiling nervously. He closed the meeting by saying that despite Bales's "brilliant" analysis, people should know that taking such actions could result in the use of force by the police and prosecution by the government. But then, turning an about-face almost as abruptly as Bales had ended his speech, Tyler hedged, adding "But, if God calls on you to carry a bazooka into Wal-Mart, or to tear up your driver's license, then you should follow the calling."

After Bales left the makeshift stage on that first night, Galbraith closed the meeting, which had been going for over two hours. He thanked everyone for attending and told the audience to be on the lookout for more meetings in the near future. Tom and I rose and headed for the foyer. There were a lot of people milling around and talking, but we decided to leave, as we both had to teach in the morning. As I was leaving, I noticed a suggestion box and a sign encouraging attendees to put their names on a mailing list. I found a scrap of paper in my pocket and dropped my address into the box.

This small act, which I thought little of at the time, proved to be an instrumental entry point into the movement. I soon started receiving regular mailings from CCK announcing meetings, invited speakers, and occasional commentary on local events. Eventually, I decided to do my research locally rather than moving to Montana. I found the movement in Kentucky more interesting. Many of the issues discussed that night, such as hemp, are not traditionally considered patriot issues. I was also interested in the group because it was obviously an umbrella group. The choice of speakers, all leaders of their own patriot groups, was clearly designed for individual patriots to advertise their individual groups. And the relative lack of extremist rhetoric (especially by white supremacists) meant that I would be able to see how patriot rhetoric framed the varied concerns of the white working-class men these various patriot leaders hoped to mobilize. Indeed, the more I read about the movement, the more convinced I became that such a study was necessary. While focusing on the extremist element within the movement is important, it tends to support the image that the entire movement is made up of bomb-making hate mongers. As the presence of politicians at this meeting indicated, and my interviews later confirmed, the Patriot Movement in Kentucky is as much a political force as it is a terrorist menace. Rather than trying to change things with threats, bombs, and assassinations, the patriots I interviewed chose instead to use the political system as a tool for achieving their goals. Their willingness to work through legal channels provides legitimacy to their cause and ultimately gives their message and their program for change a better chance for success. Indeed, as I will illustrate in greater detail later in this book, their efforts have resulted in legislation that favors their agenda, even as it often ignores the real issues confronting its constituent base.

Studying the above-ground portion of the movement also had its political appeal. As I sat in that cold, temporary structure that night and the many nights that followed, a simple thought kept recurring to me. It did not have to be this way. Many of these people felt left behind by the booming economy of the 1990s and felt alienated when they read news reports and saw television shows about how good things were. Indeed, despite the rosy forecasts, during the 1990s Kentuckians witnessed a net loss of factory jobs, an assault on their primary cash crop, the encroachment of dreaded chicken and hog farms into their state, and through it all, a government that seemed willing to do little about it. None of this is meant to imply that Kentuckians are blameless victims, working-class martyrs, or exceptionally virtuous people. Indeed, these events led, as they do in many places, to fingers pointed squarely at the blameless. Nonetheless, I came to see that the mobilization of such people as part of a radical right-wing movement was not a foregone conclusion. Rather, I realized that the progressive left could and should have something to say to these people, both in terms of their class-based anxieties, traditional terrain of the left, and their cultural anxieties, a more recent left-of-center concern. As a progressive, I wanted to highlight such potential, and to examine how the political right, in the absence of a concerted effort by the left, exploits this potential and, more importantly, to what effect.

THE NEW WORLD ORDER

As I left the meeting that night, I could not help but wonder what held these otherwise diverse interests and people together. Clearly, people were discontent with the status quo, but most seemed driven by specific issues, whether hemp, environmental legislation, guns, or juries. As I was to discover through the process of my research, however, despite its apparent lack of coherence, the movement is more organized than it first appears. As I note above, globalization provides a ready context for discontent. And patriot discourse provides the necessary glue to hold its resulting and varied anxieties together.

In particular, patriot positions on varied and diverse interests are given form through their theory of the new world order. In general patriots think the new world order is a conspiracy of actors and organizations whose goal is to eliminate national governments, replacing them with a one world government. Patriots often refer to this one world government as global communism. In its creation, patriots believe the United States will lose its sovereignty and its citizens the rights stemming from it. As the Militia of Montana posed the issue on its home page in 1999,

> We are slowly loosing [sic] our sovereignty and being consolidated under one rule, and that one rule will eventually do away with the Constitution and rule with an iron fist. There's no better time than now! Support your local Militia organization. One day soon your freedom will depend on it.

Although there are debates within the movement about who or what the new world order actually is, most patriots agree that the UN, the Federal Reserve Board, and the Trilateral Commission are its key architects. Added to the mix are individual actors within the U.S. government who patriots believe are helping these organizations to meet their goal. Not surprisingly, patriots often target former President George Bush, who first brought the phrase "new world order" into the common lexicon in a speech he gave shortly after the Gulf War (Bush 1998).[4] Patriots are also critical of President Clinton for pushing a globalizing "agenda," including support of the North American Free Trade Agreement (NAFTA) and fast-track legislation that would allow presidents to sign trade agreements without lengthy negotiations in Congress. Patriots regard Alan Greenspan, the chairman of the Federal Reserve, with similar disdain, frequently referring to him as Alan "Greenscam" and decrying the amount of power he has as an unelected official. In this regard, patriots stand outside of the traditional party dichotomy. They regard both Democrats and Republicans as tainted by their support of global economic integration.

Because patriots believe the new world order has infiltrated the U.S. government, they also regard domestic issues (which on the face of it seem to have little to do with global economic integration) as related to the one world government conspiracy. The events at Ruby Ridge, Idaho, and Waco, Texas, provide good examples. In both cases, the government engaged in a standoff with civilians charged with weapons violations. And in both cases civilians perished in the imbroglios that ensued. At Ruby Ridge, the unarmed wife of Randy Weaver, the fugitive wanted by the government, was shot and killed by sniper fire as she held the door open for her husband. Weaver's fourteen-year-old son, who was armed, was also killed by government fire during the standoff. At Waco, the government's forty-plus-day siege ended when the Branch Davidian compound the government had surrounded went up in flames, killing the seventy-four people inside. Citizens across the political spectrum were disturbed by government actions, which were deemed to be overly and needlessly aggressive (Cockburn 1993; Wieseltier 1993). Patriots, however, saw these events as the first step in the government's attempt to disarm the populace and pave the way for imminent takeover by the new world order. For this reason, patriots hold equal disdain for largely domestic actors such as Janet Reno, the attorney general at the time of the events in Waco, and Louis Freeh, then director of the Federal Bureau of Investigation (FBI). Both were regarded as "commanding" the national operations for the new world order.

Despite patriots' insistence that the new world order is thoroughly global in reach, patriots rely on well-worn, distinctly American narratives to explain it and the threat they believe it poses. Invoking long-established theories espoused at different times by Joseph McCarthy, the John Birch Society, and the Klan (among other groups), patriots believe the U.S. government has been "occupied" by an international cabal of Jewish bankers. This view gives rise to catchy slogans and terms within the movement such as ZOG, short for the Zionist Occupied Government. The continuity of such rhetoric has led many observers of the Patriot Movement to remark, as historian Catherine Stock (1996, 5) does, that the Patriot Movement is "hardly a new-fangled idea or a fly-by-the-night phenomenon. Instead, it follows an abundant, meaningful, and 'all-American' heritage especially common in rural America."

Despite its continuity over three hundred years, rural radicalism is a contradictory beast. Radicalism has sometimes been progressive, allowing farmers and others workers in rural America a chance to come together in an effort to protect their livelihood against social relations dominated by moneyed interests, such as robber barons, railroad companies, the dreaded furnishing merchants, and the government structures that supported them (Goodwyn 1976; Stock 1996). Just as often, however, rural radicals acted as vigilantes, targeting "others" in society: at various junctures, vagabonds, African Americans, Native Americans, Catholics, Jews, "uppity women," or some combination thereof. Like their more progressive brethren, these vigilantes also targeted the government, which in their minds had abandoned an America based on white privilege and power for one defined by so-called inferiors. More often than not, progressive and regressive strains of rural radicalism have gone hand in hand, leaving rural radicals to occupy an uneasy space in American society, where they are at once the defenders of a yeoman heritage based on the ideals of social equality and the champions of a social agenda steeped in notions of white supremacy.

The Patriot Movement is but the most recent example of this long-enduring, distinctly American trend. As chapter 5 in this book will detail, modern rural radicalism, called the Patriot Movement by those inside of it, emerged in the Midwest as the result of macroeconomic restructuring of the agriculture sector. Following the advice of government agents, bankers, and university extension agents, farmers took out loans in the 1970s to expand their acreage, only to find themselves with insurmountable debts and looming farm foreclosures a decade later. Like many farmers before them, these farmers cum patriots organized to protest government policies that hurt their livelihood and government inaction in protecting it once the chips were down. And they were successful in spreading their message to their disenchanted city brethren in places like Michigan, where many workers have yet to rebound from the deindustrialization that eliminated their well-paying factory jobs. Despite their concerns over livelihood, farmers cum patriots and their later converts have largely articulated their problems and solutions in cultural terms, condemning Jews, for example, for "occupying" the U.S. government on behalf of communists, socialists, and other so-called malfeasants rather than blaming neoliberal economic policy.

These contradictions are inherent to the movement's primary constituency and reflect their own conflicting social positions. Patriots are overwhelmingly white and male, a positionality that affords them a whole host of social privileges. Yet most patriots are also working class, which means they are exploited (or exploitable) by virtue of their position within the global division of labor. Even those who are farmers may be broadly classified as working class for, while they own their own "means of production," most are small producers largely dependent on the agribusinesses that control the buying and distribution of their crops. In short, patriots stand on an identity fault line. They have one foot planted firmly on the terra firma of privilege while the other rests more precariously on the quake-prone landscape common to the average worker. While such contradictions are nothing new for the white worker, globalization and the economic restructuring it has entailed have brought them into sharp relief, challenging both patriots' racial privileges and their livelihood.

The *focus* of this book is the patriot identity politics through which so many of these white workers have been mobilized. This patriot politics, both in terms of its critiques and solutions, is fundamentally geographic. Patriots argue that international actors have power over increasing amounts of geographic space, a power mandated by neither a popular vote nor the public will. To hear patriots tell it, one world government is just around the corner. In response to these fears, patriots call for a realignment of space and power. On the face of it, their invocations to patriotism may be read as standard nationalism. A closer inspection of patriot rhetoric, however, reveals support for an extreme version of federalism. Indeed, patriots believe that power should reside at the local level, usually with the county, and that state and federal governments must bow to the word and law issued locally. "Sovereignty" is a word used liberally at patriot gatherings, but when patriots use the term they mean local sovereignty as often as (if not more than) they mean national sovereignty.

The *purpose* of this book is to examine how this patriot identity politics addresses the dual positionality of its primary constituent base—white working-class males. Because white workers stand on an identity fault line, their mobilization may take differing forms. They may mobilize through progressive outlets by focusing on their class position within a global capitalist system and their linkages with workers in other parts of the world, or they may mobilize through regressive outlets, focusing on what they regard as assaults on their social dominance. This book argues that discourses of patriotism, when applied to specific issues, deflect a sustained analysis of class-based concerns while buttressing notions of cultural and racial superiority through "safe" nationalistic coding.

To illustrate this argument, I examine two issues around which Kentucky patriots mobilized during the late 1990s. One of these issues concerns rural livelihood in Central Kentucky. Patriots in Kentucky want to legalize industrial hemp and they have called for legislation to do so. They claim that hemp, which has a long history in the state, should be legalized so the state's tobacco farmers have other crop options. Patriots' plans for reintroducing hemp into the economy, however, do not address farmers' concerns and in some cases actually work against them. As I illustrate in the empirical portion of this book, this seeming paradox results from the way that patriot discourse frames how patriots view the problem and how they pose solutions to it.

At first glance, the second issue also seems related to livelihood. Patriots want to eliminate a new biosphere reserve in the state. Patriots claim the biosphere will seize private property from small landowners in the region. They also claim that the biosphere will be owned by the UN and will represent an infringement of sovereignty. Despite these claims, the UN owns no biospheres in the United States. The biospheres are held in common by the U.S. government, often in conjunction with private interests. In Kentucky, the biosphere is owned by the U.S. Forest Service and operated by the Tennessee Valley Authority (TVA). Moreover, no property owners in the region lost land in the biosphere's creation, nor will they lose any in the future. As I demonstrate in chapter 7, a close examination of patriot positions reveals that patriots oppose the biosphere, not because of livelihood concerns, but because they associate the biosphere with the UN, an organization they regard as representative of culturally "inferior" peoples. Indeed, the battle over the biosphere designation is largely a symbolic fight through which patriots can express their cultural anxieties and reassert their cultural dominance.

Through an analysis of these issues, this book illustrates how "culture" trumps the "economy" in patriot discourse and how it does so without "playing the race card." Indeed, this is why the movement is in many ways more potent than the white supremacist movement in this country. It claims to address class-based concerns yet provides no material avenues of recourse. At the same time, it addresses white workers' race-based anxieties through coded speech, giving patriots a more broadly acceptable language and wider public legitimacy. Thus not only are patriots shielded from confronting their racial and cultural biases, but they are also permitted to see themselves, their positions, and their actions as on behalf of the nation. This explains in large part why many patriots can steadfastly claim, and with the utmost sincerity, that they are *not* racists.

The conclusion from this analysis is all too clear. White workers join the Patriot Movement for a variety of reasons, some class based, some race based, but through discourses of patriotism these concerns are funneled into a regressive political form. That white workers have been mobilized through a thoroughly constructed patriot identity politics illustrates that social alterity is always open to intervention and discursive (re)organization. At the risk of belaboring the point of this book, while the right may be winning the battle for white workers, there is no reason why the left may not make its own interventions, and to better end. The violence that has emerged from the movement only makes the power of such a possibility more pressing.

Before moving to the plan of the book, it is important to add an important caveat about what readers should and should not expect in the pages that are to follow. As the reader may have gleaned from the above paragraphs, while this book is about a social movement, its focus is at the discursive level, where identity politics is crafted, rather than the organizational level of the movement. Therefore readers will not find standard social movement questions (How are people recruited?) or approaches (survey data or statistical analysis of membership patterns) in this book. While this lack may disappoint some readers, I hope they will accept the book on its own terms, recognizing that there are numerous ways to approach such a topic. Indeed, whether the reader agrees or disagrees with my arguments, I hope she or he will respect the fact that I have organized this book as I have precisely because I sincerely believe this organization best suits the political goals of this project.

PLAN OF THE BOOK

To make and illustrate these arguments, this book addresses a wide body of theoretical and empirical work. Given the contradictory nature of patriot positionality, this book necessarily deals with a broad swath of academic literature, from theoretical considerations of class and race to journalistic and watchdog accounts of the Patriot Movement.

Chapter 2 sets the stage for the book by examining identity politics. Such an exploration requires both theoretical and empirical consideration. The chapter begins by briefly defining globalization. Given the importance of globalization to the reemergence of the Patriot Movement specifically, and to the appearance of identity-based social movements more generally, establishing a specific definition for what is arguably an overused term is important. The chapter then reviews the key theoretical precepts in poststructural identity theory and analyzes its place within the larger political field of the progressive left. Particular attention is paid to debates within and outside of the academy between identity scholars and marxists. The personal rancor and heated debates notwithstanding, this book holds that the Patriot Movement provides an excellent empirical site where these two theoretical approaches might be fruitfully combined. As this chapter has noted, most patriots are working class and many of their concerns emanate from this positionality. Yet patriots articulate their concerns through discourses of patriotism and patriot identity, rather than through class-based categories. Thus identity theory provides an ideal analytic model for analyzing how and to what effect class-based concerns are submerged within patriot identity.

The second part of chapter 2 examines a small but growing body of literature that specifically theorizes the "place" of the Patriot Movement and other new social movements organized against the state. Key precepts of the literature are detailed and important debates within it are discussed. This literature is fruitful for this study because it spatializes the analysis of social reaction, unraveling how a group of people wedded to the idea of local sovereignty can employ national signifiers to define their cause. It does so by establishing the effects of neoliberalism on the state and illustrating how the state's consequent delegitimation has spurred social movements organized specifically against it. As this literature illustrates, concerted action against the state is not without its logic. The state has lost its ability to work on behalf of labor, but its control over the means of violence and surveillance have actually increased. This recognition of state abuses, when coupled with the right-wing "patriotism" that has emerged in reaction to them, has, however, led to a strange silence on how to best evaluate such groups. This book argues that evaluation is necessary and that it must proceed by examining how patriots' contradictory social positions (at once dominant and exploited) are addressed and funneled through the patriot category. We must examine both how the patriot category is constructed and how the mostly symbolic deployment of nation affects the ability of patriots to see their structural links with other scales, and with workers across scales of difference and place.

Chapter 3 analyzes the role of race in the Patriot Movement. In particular, this chapter examines a subset of identity theory literature that focuses on white identity. This chapter overviews this literature, paying close attention to how presumption of whiteness as the unspoken norm informs the construction of other signifiers in modern life. This analytic understanding of whiteness is important for this analysis because, like class, race played an integral part in the emergence of the Patriot Movement and continues to play a part in the movement today. Yet, as with class, the race-based concerns of patriots are not articulated through traditional racist rhetoric. Thus this chapter lays out a framework for understanding how and to what effect race is submerged within patriot understandings of nation and patriotism.

Chapter 4 provides a brief history of the Patriot Movement. This book situates the Patriot Movement in a long tradition of rural radicalism. As the most recent example of rural radicalism, the Patriot Movement emerges out of rural political economy established in the 1930s under Franklin Roosevelt's New Deal. Under Roosevelt's policies, farmers were given subsidies for limiting their production in exchange for stable prices. This system was called into question with the rural restructuring that began in the 1970s and culminated in the farm crisis of the 1980s, in which over 1 million small farmers lost their farms. As the farm crisis approached its zenith in the mid-1980s, white supremacists moved in to mobilize farmers. This chapter details the crisis and these mobilization campaigns, illustrating the blending of class-based concerns and race-based anxieties through nationalistic rhetoric. The chapter concludes by examining the spread of the Patriot Movement after the farm crisis. Of particular importance is the Oklahoma City bombing. After the bombing, the movement bifurcated. Some patriots chose to go underground. Others chose to stay above ground and try to bring their message to the mainstream. While the majority of scholarship has examined the below-ground portion of the movement, this book examines the above-ground portion. Above-ground patriots now run for public office and participate in political life. Their presence in the political field is influential because it brings many extremist or fringe ideas closer to the mainstream, where mainstream conservatives have adopted many of their positions.

Chapter 5 introduces readers to the Patriot Movement in Central Kentucky, the subject of the case study for this book. The chapter begins by describing the emergence of the movement in Central Kentucky. The movement emerged when people calling themselves patriots began lobbying state legislatures to pass a concealed weapons law in the state. The movement grew from there, as several patriot groups were formed, including a state militia, Second Amendment rights groups, and a fully informed jury group. Chapter 5 then introduces readers to the group this book focuses on, Citizens for a Constitutional Kentucky. This chapter also introduces readers to the patriots and other relevant parties interviewed for this book, thus providing basic background information for each as well as information on their roles in the movement in Central Kentucky.

Chapters 6 and 7 examine two issues around which patriots in Kentucky rallied during my time in the field—calls to legalize hemp and attempts to thwart the designation of a biosphere reserve in the state. Through a thorough analysis of how patriots construct their positions on these two issues, this book illustrates how patriot rhetoric deflects the class-based concerns of patriots while fostering their race-based anxieties through safe coding.

Chapter 8 examines the political aspirations of one of my research informants, Gatewood Galbraith. Galbraith ran for governor in 1999 in the state of Kentucky and for a congressional seat the following year. The purpose of this chapter is to highlight a trend in the Patriot Movement not normally considered—its attempt to co-opt parts of the mainstream to spread its message.

Chapter 9 summarizes the key theoretical arguments and empirical evidence posed in this book. This chapter examines what the arguments in this book can say to the progressive left as it considers those who, like patriots, find themselves on identity fault lines. These arguments are premised on the dual notion that not only are all people mobilizable by the progressive left, but also that social trajectories put in place by movements such as the Patriot Movement are not set in stone, but rather are subject to meaningful intervention. The book concludes with two special appendixes. The first is an epilogue and details significant events that occurred within the Kentucky Patriot Movement after the initial draft of this book was written. The second appendix concerns methodology. As I discovered during the process of my research, studying the Patriot Movement at various steps caused me to face complex dilemmas and ethical issues. My hope in this section is to identify these problems and address some potential solutions for them. This is, I think, particularly necessary for identity-based scholarship on the political right, because much of the literature on poststructuralist methodology assumes a certain level of political conformity between researcher and researched that did not exist in my case. By reflecting on my own mistakes in the field, I hope to provide some useful guidance for future scholarship on the political right.

NOTES

1. On September 7, 2000, Richard Butler and his organization Aryan Nations were found negligent and liable for actions by its bodyguards. The lawsuit was brought by a Victoria Keenan and her son Jason, who were assaulted by Aryan Nations security guards while the Keenans looked for a lost wallet in front of the group's compound. The jury awarded the Keenans $6.3 million in punitive damages. On October 27, First District judge Charles Hosack cleared the way for seizure of the property by the Keenans when he ruled that Butler's hate speech was not protected by the Constitution. While all appeals are exhausted, Butler plans to stay in the area and to continue running his organization on or off the compound.

2. Preparedness expos are traveling expositions in which vendors sell wares for survivalists, militias, and the generally curious. Visitors to these expos can purchase information on how to can vegetables, cure meat, deliver babies at home, build water-

storage facilities, and even build homemade guns and bombs. Some expos also feature speakers. For an extra fee, attendees may hear talks by patriot heroes such as Trochmann and J. J. Johnson.

3. This is a pseudonym. I approached Bales for an interview later in the summer. He reacted negatively, arguing that "You can't trust anyone!" Based on his reaction, I have chosen not to use his real name, in an effort to protect the anonymity he clearly wanted to guard.

4. For patriots, Bush's speech foreshadowed what was to come; noting the end of the cold war and the multinational force that defeated Saddam Hussein's offensive against Kuwait, Bush heralded a "new world order" in which the old divisions between nations no longer mattered.

2

What's Class Got to Do with It?

GLOBAL PRODUCTION AND
ITS SHIFTING TERRAIN

By now, the term "globalization" has many meanings in the academy, so in an effort to clarify how I understand the term, I begin this chapter with a brief detour from the topic of identity politics. My definition of "globalization" relies primarily on a regulation theory approach (Aglietta 1979; Lipietz 1992; Storper and Scott 1992). This approach is useful for this analysis because it links macroeconomic changes to political changes both broadly, in state/society relations, and more specifically, in the emergence of identity politics. This approach is also useful because it informs (though not without caveat) much of geography's approach to the study of global economic integration (see Harvey 1989; Pred and Watts 1992).

During the 1980s and early 1990s the United States and Western Europe experienced major restructurings of their economies. Economic strongholds such as Manchester, England; Pittsburgh, Pennsylvania; and Lyon, France, saw their industrial economies dismantled. The pace of change was swift. Within ten years, once-thriving cities like Flint, Michigan, and Baltimore, Maryland, were reduced to chaotic centers better defined by high unemployment rates, shrinking tax bases, and the associated social problems that come with them, including high crime, increased suicide, and an upturn in drug abuse and addiction (Harvey 2000; Moore 1997).

While some of these former industrial centers have been able to rebound economically by tapping into the burgeoning tech sector, few have made a full return to their glory days. Lipietz (1992) has characterized these former economies and the political pact that facilitated them as industrialization's "golden age." Based on the logic of Fordist production, these cities were generally organized around one or two key industries and the agglomeration industries that followed. Products were produced following Henry Ford's now famous assembly-line model. Workers performed repetitive tasks, delineated to achieve the highest rates of efficiency in the production process, and usually received benefits such as paid vacations and earned salaries high enough to own their own homes and to afford consumer goods such as cars, televisions, and appliances. The delicate balance between the needs of capital and labor within the context of productivity gains was achieved through a "grand compromise" between a regime of accumulation and a mode of regulation first articulated by Henry Ford in the 1920s. As Lipietz (1992, 5) notes,

> This grand compromise (sharing productivity gains) was at first accepted by only a small minority of employers—such as Henry Ford of Model T fame—and bankers and politicians, such as John Maynard Keynes. Ford and Keynes were aware that increased productivity gains from the Taylorist revolution would lead to a massive crisis of overproduction if there was no corresponding revolution on the demand side. And what could be a more powerful factor in the growth of demand for firms' goods than a steady growth in the real wages of the workers themselves?

While the broad contours of Lipietz's description above are correct, it is worth noting that Ford's motivation for increasing workers' wages initially had little to do with spurring consumption (Batchelor 1994; Alvarado and Alvarado 2001). Rather, labor problems precipitated Ford's decision to offer his workers the then unheard of rate of five dollars a day. Indeed, work at Ford's Highland Park plant was monotonous, tedious, and painful and, with other work available at comparable salaries, Ford had difficulty keeping a steady workforce. The average worker lasted only eighteen months in Ford's plant (Alvarado and Alvarado 2001) and by 1913 the situation was so dire that Ford found himself hiring 963 men for every 100 he needed (Batchelor 1994). Moreover, even after Ford initiated his five dollar a day wage, it came with strings attached. Workers were only guaranteed a base wage of thirty-four cents an hour ($2.72 a day). The remaining $2.28 was available only to workers who passed routine inspections by Ford's infamous sociology department (Batchelor 1994). Workers could and routinely did lose the remainder of their wages for offenses such as drinking, playing craps on the job, or having domestic strife (Batchelor 1994).

The "virtuous circle" set in place by Fordist production was broken in the early 1980s in both Europe and the United States, although the processes leading up to this development had begun a decade earlier. The compromise was fundamentally weakened by declining productivity, which led to declining profit margins, and by the new internationalization of markets, which limited the power of national modes of regulation. Evidence also suggests that technology played a role. In particular, the computer chip seems to have had a phenomenal impact (Greider 1997). Invented in the late 1950s and in semiwide use by the 1980s, the computer chip mimics the human brain in how it processes information. Its circuit-board design is able to handle huge data sets and when it first appeared it allowed companies to better predict demand, thus eliminating the need for huge supply-side inventories. Freed from the constraints of large inventories, many companies were able to move portions of their production overseas and "south of the border" in order to take advantage of cheap labor, low taxes, and lax environmental regulations.

The political ideology that developed in tandem with these processes helped speed along the change. While this ideology goes by various names—monetarist policy, neoliberalism, liberal-productivism—it always implies a dedication to the triad of deregulation, free trade, and technological innovation and asserts the triad's predominance as inevitable (Greider 1997; Harvey 2000; Lipietz 1992). Indeed, the proponents of this ideology view adherence to its ideals not only as necessary to increasing accumulation, but crucial for gaining competitive advantage in the world market. This model's most famous proponents have been without a doubt Ronald Reagan in the United States and Margaret Thatcher in Britain; Thatcher's now famous quip, "There is no alternative," set the rhetorical flavor for state-led neoliberalism (Harvey 1996, 2000; R. Williams 1989). Loved by some and reviled by others, Reagan and Thatcher gave shape and ideological flair to the neoliberal policies eventually seen as inevitable by even labor groups and socialist parties.

The regime of accumulation associated with this new development model was based on the ideal of the expanding profit margin. Indeed, profit, in and of itself, was no longer enough to secure good stock prices and favorable industry ratings. Companies and, increasingly, their stockholders, began to chart success by quarterly profit reports, assessing profit as satisfactory when it surpassed previous earnings or projections. William Greider has aptly called this the "manic logic of capitalism" (1997).

The production mechanisms associated with neoliberalism and the regulations that govern it are often termed "flexible specialization" or "just-in-time manufacturing" (Herod 2000; Piore and Sabel 1984). As the names imply, production under neoliberalism is more flexible and immediate than in the Fordist model. Production becomes "flexible" geographically because component parts can now be produced overseas or south of the border in order to take advantage of cheaper labor costs. Production is also more immediate because component parts are made to order, rather than warehoused on site. This international geography of production has given rise to a global assembly line.

Not surprisingly, workers are expected to be flexible as well. In first world contexts, workers are often hired as "full-time temporary workers"—a moniker that legally allows employers to avoid costly benefits packages while keeping their workforce full-time and otherwise at hand. Likewise, employers rely more frequently on women because they can be paid less. Deutsche (1991) has labeled this new mode of production "flexible sexism." As she and other feminist scholars (Christopherson 1989; McDowell 1991) note, while employers may argue that hiring women as temporary workers allows them needed flexibility for child care, such flexibility comes at the cost of lower wages, no benefits, and limited job security. In developing nations, workers are flexible by virtue of their "exploitability." Even though the labor laws are good in many developing countries, the competitive advantage that cheap labor can bring to developing countries in the short term means their governments are frequently unwilling to enforce them (Greider 1997).

Although flexible production regimes tend to disadvantage workers, there are also some inherent weaknesses in the production structure that may actually benefit workers. Indeed, Herod (2000) argues that just-in-time manufacturing's lack of inventory leaves plants in a production chain highly vulnerable to disruptions elsewhere in the system. When workers at a General Motors' metal-stamping plant in Flint, Michigan, went on strike in 1998, for example, the effects reverberated across the production system, with the closing of plants in Mexico, Singapore, and the United States. Moreover, the cost to GM, over $2 billion, made it, as Herod notes, "one of the most expensive strikes in U.S. history" (527).

While we are accustomed to considering globalization in terms of urban industrial manufacturing, the rural farmscape has also been touched by its logic. Indeed, the Keynesian-inspired compromise of Fordism is mirrored in farm policies of the same period, which were restructured by Fordism's breakup as well. During the Great Depression, Franklin Roosevelt embarked on an ambitious new plan to stabilize the rural economy. Roosevelt's Agricultural Adjustment Act of 1933 ensured stable commodity prices by limiting the amount of crops farmers grew and later sold to agricultural companies. Widespread farmer participation was guaranteed through government subsidy programs that paid farmers annual amounts to leave portions of their land fallow or to diversify their crops to limit the overproduction of any one crop. While many farmers resented what they perceived as the heavy hand of government regulators, they accepted the program for the relative stability it guaranteed them (Stock 1996).

Like their city brethren, however, farmers would find neoliberal logic seeping into their everyday lives by the early 1970s. In reaction to trade deficits and the increase in grain production overseas, the U.S. government, hoping to expand agricultural exports by taking advantage of economies of scale, embarked on an ambitious plan to modernize agriculture. New government policies encouraged farmers to expand their acreage and apply more-advanced technology to farming techniques and provided the capital necessary for farmers to do so. And lest any miss the message, Richard Nixon's secretary of agriculture, Earl Butz, issued the clarion call to farmers, bluntly warning them to "get big or get out" (Davidson 1996). These policies were phenomenally successful during the seventies. During a ten-year period, grain production in the United States increased by almost 20 percent (Davidson 1996).

While the neoliberal logic "modernized" agriculture and expanded production, small producers were often left behind as a result. After macroeconomic shifts related to inflation, the oil crisis, and rising interest rates, even those farmers "playing by the rules" would suffer from neoliberal logic. The farm crisis, discussed in more detail in chapter 4, rocked the rural Midwest during the 1980s. By the end of the decade, approximately 1 million small and medium-sized farms had been foreclosed. And the Reagan government, while feigning sympathy, did almost nothing to provide debt relief for its farmers, arguing that the logic of the market, while harsh, works best when unregulated (J. Dyer 1997). Most foreclosed farms were family affairs—the land often having been held by the same family for over one hundred years. After the crisis, land consolidation increased dramatically with often faceless corporations acting as rural America's new landlord class (Schlosser 1995).

GLOBALIZATION, NEW SOCIAL MOVEMENTS, AND THE POLITICS OF IDENTITY

While the changing nature of production may appear on the face of it to have little to do with identity-based social movements, the two are interrelated. Many of the new social movements of the 1960s and 1970s found their roots in the contradictions inherent to the "virtuous circle," particularly in terms of labor. While the Fordist mode of regulation embraced the idea that labor should share in greater portions of the profits, this compromise was predicated on the logic of creating and sustaining demand rather than worker satisfaction. Indeed, the compromise was also premised on continually improving worker productivity through the application of scientific methods in the workplace—methods that stretched workers to their limit without offering any concomitant dignity. Moreover, as the crisis came, labor was ultimately unable to effectively bargain on behalf of workers in a context where productivity was declining. Labor leaders found themselves fundamentally compromising the universal worker position in an effort to save at least some jobs. In such a context, trade unions, the traditional outlets for social unrest, lost legitimacy. As Lipietz (1992, 13) notes,

> It is no accident that, in May 1968, the massive youth and workers movement largely escaped the left's control and was often as hostile to it as the Gaullist regime. The May 1968 movement was the first mass revolt against the Fordist

paradigm. . . . All subsequent anti-Fordist social movements—ecologists, regionalists, feminists—had their beginnings outside the traditional left.

Social movement's theoreticians have argued that the changing mode of production paved the way for what is frequently termed "new social movements" (Lipietz 1992; Melucci 1989; Touraine 1985, 1995). Unlike their older counterparts, found in the trade unions and associations of the Fordist regime, these movements organized to address "social" problems. In the United States, black power, feminism, queer politics, and environmentalism are commonly cited as examples of new social movements. While each of these movements addresses class-based issues, class takes a secondary role in the articulation of their politics. Rather, these movements are defined by their recognition of oppression stemming from social positionality and by their decision to harness these social positions as categories of personal identity and action.

Several key literatures have evolved to study these new social movements. This book examines one of them, which may loosely be called poststructuralist identity theory (here, forward identity theory).[1] Identity theory has been particularly concerned to address the creation of identity out of otherwise unarticulated social positions. Indeed, while civil rights, feminism, and gay rights are relatively new phenomena, the social positions related to them have long existed. In studying the politics of these movements, identity theory seeks to analyze how these social positions are discursively articulated into "identity" and, once crafted, how they are maintained, policed, and at times, subverted.

Analytically, identity theory begins with the presumption that all identities, whether individual or group, are socially constructed. The constructed nature of identity means that no identity, even one presumed to be biological, is essential, predetermined, or permanent. As such, while a person may fit into any number of social "positions"—gay, African American, female— these positions are not automatically foregrounded in the individual's sense of herself and her place in the world. Nor is difference, once articulated, always maintained as an articulated moment.

In analyzing how social positionality is articulated into a person's individual identity (and how that person may act in concert with others espousing the same identity), identity theorists have also noted the importance of "othering" to the formation of any identity. Identity categories are given form and definition through opposition—a rhetorical move in which a "we" is defined in opposition to a "them." While such categories are constructed as diametrically opposed, they rely on one another for their construction. As such, all identities carry with them the trace of the other. As Derrida (1994), Mouffe (1995), and Natter and Jones (1997) note, the constitutive moment of identity formation is always the "outside," rendering any category "unstable" and only ever "fixed" temporarily.

While identity theory recognizes the necessity of an "other" or "others" to identity formation, most identity theorists recognize that social identities are not crafted on a frictionless plane. There are normative identities and those that gain meaning by being an other to them (Gilroy 1993; Hall 1991; hooks 1984; Morrison 1992; Rose 1993; Sedgwick 1993; Valentine 1993). In the West, social normativity is defined through the norms of white, heterosexual males. Those who are not white, male, and heterosexual are afforded lower social status and often suffer discrimination because of their position within this normative system. Because all social identities, even dominant ones, are inherently unstable, however, they are contingent and thus potentially collapsible (Butler 1990; Rose 1993).

Building on such work, geographers have introduced the concept of "space" to studies of identity politics (Anderson 1991; Gallaher 1997, 2000; Natter and Jones 1997; Pile and Thrift 1995; Radcliffe 1993; Sibley 1995). Geographers argue that the formation of any political identity relies on a spatial referent for its construction and maintenance. Through the construction of spaces of identity, identity may be reinforced by its material imprint on the ground. Like nonspatialized accounts of identity, spatialized accounts also recognize the role of exclusion in identity construction. As geographers note, an identity is maintained by the exclusion of others from inside "its" borders (Anderson 1991; Cresswell 1996; Natter and Jones 1997; Sibley 1995). In examining the spaces of identity, geographers have noted how space is crucial for oppressed groups who find "common places" not only useful for rejuvenation but also necessary for personal safety (Valentine 1993). Geographers have also noted how dominant space-identity configurations may be challenged when "others" transgress those spaces, creating visual and material cues to their construction and to the possibility of their reconfiguration (Radcliffe 1993).

The recognition that all identities are constructed, and thus contingent, is premised on a radical shift in the way scholars view the concept of hegemony. In short, poststructuralist identity theory turns the traditional definition of hegemony on its head. Traditional Marxist analysis holds that oppression results from the hegemony of capitalism and the extraction of surplus value from workers by capitalists. Within this framework, hegemony is usually examined through institutional analyses of the state, whose role it is to administer capitalism and conflicts within it.

In contrast, poststructuralists argue that hegemony is the ability, through discourse, to define categories of identity and to clearly delineate who does and does not belong to them (LaClau and Mouffe 1985; Mouffe 1995; Natter and Jones 1997). Indeed, some scholars view hegemony as "fully discursive." LaClau and Mouffe (1985), for example, argue that hegemony is the ability,

through discourse, to fix social alterity around a "nodal point" of identification. They argue that such a process can be done not only by dominant
groups, but also by marginal groups, as both have equal ability to define categories of meaning. The terms "queer" and "homosexual" may serve as
illustrations here. Dominant groups have long used these terms in a deroga-
tory fashion, to dismiss gays and lesbians. By the 1970s, however, the gay
community had embraced them, making such epithets their own. They
invoked them as sources of identity, proudly proclaiming, as one street flyer
from the Stonewall era did, "Do You Think Homosexuals Are Revolting?
You Bet Your Sweet Ass We Are!"(People with a History 2001). The ability
to harness such terms and imbue them with positive meaning led to a "queer
politics" in the streets and a whole body of social theory in the academy
designed to unpack "queerness" (Frye 1993; Geltmaker 1992; Sedgwick
1993; Phelan 1994; Shugar 1995; Turner 2000).

Identity theory's insistence on the necessity of an other to the construction of social identity has also radically changed the way the left views its
purpose and goals. As poststructuralists note, the us/them component of
identity is ever present (LaClau and Mouffe 1985; Mouffe 1995; Natter and
Jones 1997). Thus they oppose traditional liberal attempts to erase difference
as seen, for example, in liberal calls for a "color-blind" society. Rather, identity theory holds that progressives should busy themselves with identifying
and domesticating those identity categories in which the "them" is constructed antagonistically—as dangerous to "us" and thus in need of meta-
phorical and physical destruction. As Mouffe (1995, 263) succinctly puts it,
"what is at stake is how to establish this 'us-them' discrimination in a way
that is compatible with pluralist democracy."

This position bears immediate relevance for this study in two ways. First,
it impels us to reconsider how we respond to right-wing groups such as the
Patriot Movement. Traditionally, the liberal approach calls for the elimination of such movements through aggressive campaigns to jail law-breaking
members and delegitimize the rest. While the intended result of such a strategy is certainly desirable, it is based on faulty logic. We may be repulsed by
the movement's choice of gays, feminists, and environmentalists as others,
but as long as these categories exist, there are likely to be people who define
themselves against them. What is dangerous about the Patriot Movement is
not so much its choice of others as the antagonistic manner in which these
groups are constructed as others. Indeed, many groups espouse conservative
social values (not a few churches do), yet not all act out antagonistically
because of them, as the Patriot Movement does. Patriot actions against its
others have often been ferociously direct—some patriots have been arrested
for assassinating liberal targets (Stern 1996). They may also be indirect, yet
no less threatening—in Kentucky, a patriot legislator recently introduced a
bill to allow the legal use of deadly force against "deviate sexual inter-

course."[2] Such a bill illustrates not only disapproval of a gay lifestyle by patriots, but also raw antagonism; it is a thinly veiled attempt to legally justify violence against gays.

Secondly, this position impels us to question standard left-wing approaches to categories such as patriotism. Traditionally, the left has called for the eradication of nationalism and, in some cases, of the nation itself. As Mouffe (1995, 264) notes, however,

> It is very dangerous to ignore the strong libidinal investment that can be mobilized by the signifier "nation"; and it is futile to hope that all national identities could be replaced by so-called "post conventional" identities. The struggle against the exclusive type of ethnic nationalism can only be carried out by articulating another type of nationalism, a "civic" nationalism expressing allegiance to the value specific to the democratic tradition and the forms that are constitutive of it.

As LaClau and Mouffe (1985) note in their earlier and now seminal work, such a project requires that the left embrace the concept of citizenship and that it work to create a nonessentialist "chain of equivalence" between varied nodal points of identification under its rubric (see also Mouffe 1993). In their schema, difference is an accepted, even integral part of the ideal of nation. Yet because no difference may be considered essential, the category is fluid, open, and on guard against antagonisms rooted in traditionally essentialist conceptions of nation. This recognition is especially pertinent to the left's approach to the Patriot Movement. Rather than decry patriots for their nationalism, we should instead decry the form of their nationalism, which is undemocratic in its rigid, essentialist definition of who may or may not be a part of the nation.

IDENTITY THEORY AND LEFT POLITICS

Despite invocations to pluralism and talk of "reaching out," the left has had difficulty living up to its words. This problem is nowhere more apparent than within the left itself. The divide noted by Lipietz (1992) above, between "old" and "new" social movements, has remained a persistent one. Much of the tension stems from the disapproval and ill will many new activists felt from traditional left circles. In her new memoir, feminist Robin Morgan (2000) recounts how her concerns for the oppression of women were ridiculed and marginalized by the left of the 1960s. Her decision, for example, to protest the Miss America pageant in 1968 rather than attend the protest of the Democratic National Convention in Chicago drew jeers from her leftist male counterparts. Similar complaints have been lodged in the academy. During the late 1980s and early 1990s, many feminist and queer scholars

sought to position their work in direct opposition to Marxism. These scholars argued that, by insisting on the primacy of class as a category of social
action, Marxists ignore not only other sorts of oppression but also the
important forms of political action that evolve from them (Bondi 1990; Massey 1993; Phelan 1994). Phelan, for example, defines identity politics "as a
general name for social movements based on categories not adequately captured or valued in Marxist theory" (76). In assessing the emergence of feminism in the academy, Liz Bondi (1990, 160) notes that while Marxists "claim
that historical materialism can and should 'recuperate' issues of race and gender . . . no attempt is made to do so."

The couching of identity theory as a reaction and response to the limitations of traditional Marxism, not surprisingly, has led to countercritiques by
those situating themselves in Marxist camps. In particular, David Harvey
(1996) decries what he sees as the tendency of identity theorists to ignore the
fact that class positioning continues to bind peoples across identity categories and that focus on these forms of oppression need not be to the exclusion
of class. To illustrate his point, Harvey describes a fire that occurred in 1991
at a chicken processing plant in Hamlet, North Carolina. Of the twenty-five
who died, twelve were African American and eighteen were women. As Harvey notes, while the fire itself may have been unavoidable, the level of devastation it wrought clearly was not. In its eleven years of operation, the plant
had never been checked for safety violations; during the fire, key exit doors
were locked and the plant's sprinkler system failed. The conditions that led
to the death of twenty-five employees resulted from more than the shoddy
safety precautions of a particular corporation or plant. Places like rural
North Carolina have been doubly hit by the globalization of capital. As
farming has become increasingly mechanized to afford global competition,
and as the number of family farms have decreased, rural employment options
have dwindled. Simultaneously, as manufacturing has declined in the United
States, traditional forms of working-class power have also declined. In this
void, corporations are able to avoid areas with strong unions and good
wages, locating instead in places like Hamlet, where wages are low, labor is
unorganized, and the state touts its "right to work" legislation and "friendly
business climate." Lamenting these conditions, Harvey (1996, 338) observes
that "the commonality that cuts across race and gender lines in this instance
is quite obviously that of class and it is not hard to see the immediate impli-
cation that a simple, traditional form of class politics could have protected
the interests of women and minorities as well as those of white males.

Harvey's argument may be viewed as a wake-up call to the progressive
left. In particular, he wants to remind those on the left that all left-oriented
social struggles lose when class—a key locus around which gender, race, and
ethnicity are frequently organized—is ignored. Indeed, he asserts quite con-
troversially that in most of these new social movements class has not only

taken a "back seat," but has at times been regarded with open hostility. As he notes, again in reference to the Hamlet fire,

> I think it is instructive here to note that as far as I know, none of the institutions associated with such new social movements saw fit to engage politically with what happened in Hamlet, North Carolina. Women's organizations, for example, were heavily preoccupied with the question of sexual harassment and mobilizing against the Clarence Thomas appointment, even though it was mainly women who died in the North Carolina fire and women who continue to bear an enormous burden of exploitation in the "Broiler Belt." And apart from the Rainbow Coalition and Jesse Jackson, African-American (and Hispanic) organizations also remained strangely silent on the matter, while some ecologists (particularly the animal rights wing) exhibited more sympathy for the chickens than for the workers. (Harvey 1996, 341)

In the tense atmosphere surrounding debates between poststructuralists and Marxists, it is not surprising that Harvey's remarks would be controversial. Much of the criticism has been leveled at the general fuzziness of Harvey's theoretical position. Some critics are puzzled by what they see as an incongruous blending of structuralist and poststructuralist ideas and methodologies (see Eagleton 1997). Others were angry with Harvey for initiating what they perceived as a "blame game" that aggravated just the sort of divisions within the left that Harvey has long decried (Braun 1998).

While Harvey's insistence on class as the primary locus of social positionality invokes controversy, his analysis is important at three levels in regard to this study. First, Harvey's analysis points to a trend that has effected the formation of new social movements—militant particularism. Drawing on the work of Raymond Williams (1989), Harvey notes that in the absence of broad-based categories of social action, social actors are increasingly unable to see either their oppression or their resistance to it as crossing categories or scale. Thus groups resisting dominant structures, whether of patriarchy or classism, are unable to see the links between their struggles. The Patriot Movement is indicative of this sort of politics. Invoking local sovereignty, many patriots are even suspicious of national militias and of patriots claiming to speak on behalf of the movement as a whole.

Secondly, as my analysis in the next section will indicate, Harvey's call for a reinsertion of class into the fragmented terrain of the left is timely when we consider that, in the left's "absence," the revolutionary banner of class has been adopted by the right (Greider 1997). By invoking populist rhetoric, the right wing has successfully mobilized people through invocations to class anxiety while remaining true to none of its emancipatory logic. The right has also been adept at linking right-wing populist economic rhetoric with conservative social causes, including antichoice, antigay, and anti-immigration stances (see my earlier work on the religious right and the Republican

Party, 1997). Ironically, the right has done what LaClau and Mouffe (1985) have suggested for the left: they have created equivalencies between varied right-wing constituencies. Unlike those imagined for the left, however, this right-wing chain of equivalence is constructed in essentialist terms, construed as equal and grounded as such through invocations to biblical and constitutional mandates. This chain thus takes on the character of a metanarrative whose others (varied and often disjointed left-leaning causes) are antagonistically constructed as evil, dangerous, and worthy targets for an American holy war.

Third and finally, the decline of macrolevel class politics has been exacerbated by the concomitant decline of state intervention on behalf of labor. Under Fordism's so-called virtuous circle, the state worked to absorb a fair amount of class-based discontent by brokering and regulating an agreement between capital and labor to share productivity gains. As capital has been loosened from its national territorial confines, the "deal" has collapsed. The state is no longer able or willing to force the hand of capital on behalf of labor. This trend has had direct consequences for the formation of an even "newer" breed of new social movements—movements that target the government as the enemy, even as they do so in the name of the nation. Whether one labels these movements "anti-statist" (Kirby 1997; Steinberg 1997), "Buchananist" (Luke and O'Tuathail 1998), or as movements opposing the "new global order" (Castells 1997), the state is now regarded as the enemy of the nation. The Patriot Movement is the premier example of this new breed of movement in the United States. Its emergence illustrates the continued importance of political and economic restructuring to the constitution of social movements. And, as I will demonstrate in the next section, it also highlights a juncture at which the debate between poststructuralists and Marxism might be fruitfully addressed.

SOCIAL POSITIONALITY, CLASS, AND ANTI-STATISM

A wide variety of groups have been categorized as anti-statist, including the Zapatistas in Chiapas, Mexico, the Aum Shinryko in Japan, and of relevance to this book, the Patriot Movement in the United States (Castells 1997; Kirby 1997; Luke and O'Tuathail 1998; Sparke 1998; Steinberg 1997). Given the different cultural contexts in which these movements operate, there is neither a singular definition of anti-statist movements nor a singular framework established to analyze them. One can, however, identify basic trends that hold constant across these otherwise diverse movements, as well as certain agreed-upon analytic understandings of their commonalties.

First and foremost, these movements have emerged broadly out of the context of globalization and specifically out of its effects on the state. As noted in the previous section, the breakup of the "virtuous circle" left the state unwilling or unable to speak on behalf of labor. The role of the state in fostering multilateral trade agreements and promoting organizations to monitor them (e.g., the World Trade Organization) has further eroded the state's popular legitimacy as its ability to control traditional economic functions, such as setting the value of currency, protecting domestic products, and ensuring jobs, has devolved. Replacing the "virtuous circle" was the free-market model and its accompanying "there is no alternative" rhetoric. This has left a broad spectrum of people who see the state as increasingly weak in its ability to act on their behalf. This does not, however, mean that the state has lost power. Indeed, in many instances, even as states have abandoned their traditional roles, they have bolstered their control over the means of violence. This is especially the case in the United States, where during the past ten years the state has increased its domestically oriented surveillance technologies (Pickles 1995), fortified its international borders, and militarized domestically oriented federal agencies, such as the Drug Enforcement Administration and the BATF (Kirby 1997). Government strong-arming in both the Waco and Ruby Ridge incidents, for example, left people across the political spectrum fearful that in the absence of foreign enemies the state would focus its power and might internally (Cockburn 1993; Wieseltier 1993). The state's failure/inability to act on behalf of its citizens when coupled with its internal strong-arming has paved the way for the emergence of anti-statist movements. This fact was acknowledged in a recent issue of *Political Geography* dedicated to anti-statist movements, when lead author Andrew Kirby (1997) queried "Is the state our enemy?" and responded with a tentative "Yes."

Second, the seriousness with which anti-statist groups view the government as a threat has led individuals, groups, and communities to form private militaries and "protection units" for a potential showdown with the government. Episodes in a variety of places bear witness to this disturbing trend. In 1996, a group of tax protestors calling themselves the Montana Freemen declared their compound a sovereign entity separate from the United States. Government agents investigating the group alleged they had cashed over $1 million in bogus checks and that some of their members had engaged in serious tax fraud. Agents staking out the compound also documented the stockpiling of military-style weapons (Pankratz 1996). In a similar incident a year later, an armed group calling itself the Republic of Texas declared war against the United States, issuing their call from the tract house of an elderly couple they had taken hostage (Cooper 1997). Prior to the kidnapping, the group had attracted the attention of the state's deputy attorney general by filing $93 trillion worth of liens against state property (Zewe 1997).

Lest the reader think only "fringe" groups partake of this sort of behavior, it is relevant to note that in 1995 the county commission in Nye County, Nevada, passed a local control ordinance that proclaimed local jurisdiction over federal lands (Kenworthy 1995a). Counties and cities have also adopted paramilitary-style ordinances (Greene 2000). As early as 1982, for example, the city of Kennesaw, Georgia, adopted an ordinance requiring all heads of households to own and maintain a firearm. More recently, in June 2000, the tiny hamlet of Virgin, Utah, adopted a similar "must own" ordinance, sending, as Biele (2001) notes, "a message, in italics, to Washington: Stay out of our lives." Anti-statist patriots have also launched direct offensives against the government that range from threatening National Park Service employees to the infamous bombing of the Murrah Federal Building in Oklahoma City in 1995 (Kenworthy 1995b; Stern 1996).

Third, while anti-statist movements target the state for verbal and material attack, they do so in the name of nation and patriotism to it. Commentators on the Patriot Movement have long found this troubling, labeling patriots' invocations to nation ironic and those doing the invoking modern-day Benedict Arnolds. Scholars of anti-statist movements have analyzed this seeming paradox in a variety of ways. Steinberg (1997) argues that what is perhaps most radical about anti-statist movements is that they have called into question the presumption that "nation" and "state" are necessary bedfellows. This is no small feat, given that the nation-state/identity-territory nexus is as Giddens (1985) notes, the premier power container of the modern age.

Luke and O'Tuathail (1998) take a somewhat different approach from Steinberg (1997). Luke and O'Tuathail label the broad rhetoric employed by anti-statist groups "Buchananism" after right-wing populist pundit and three-time presidential contender Pat Buchanan. They argue that Buchananist claims are not grounded in a desire to fundamentally delink the nation from the state. Rather, they hold that anti-statist rhetoric has employed an updated version of cold war containment logic. Instead of attempting to keep communists at bay, however, new regimes of containment would protect American soil from global capitalism's frenetic flows—flows that bring Taiwanese T-shirts and Indonesian shoes to Wal-Mart and Mexican labor and Islamic prayer rituals to small towns in the Midwest. Indeed, Buchananist logic would replace state intervention on behalf of capital's free flow with state intervention on behalf of capital's containment within national territory. It is safe to conclude from Luke and O'Tuathail's analysis that the only objection to the state in Buchananist logic is the particular set of politicians currently governing it. In my earlier work, I have contributed to this debate by adding complexity to Luke and O'Tuathail's analysis, showing how patriots in Kentucky have taken "containerist" logic and reapplied it to the locality—in the process eschewing this logic's application at the federal or state levels (Gallaher 2000).

Whether one follows Steinberg's separation argument or Luke and O'Tuathail's and my more measured accounts, it is clear that anti-statist movements reside in a netherworld of space and identity. By employing the signifiers and sometimes the logic of the modern nation-state, patriots are considering along the way whether to reposition it, eradicate it, or replace it with a space/identity nexus of their own making. The importance of the scholarly work on anti-statism sketched above should not be underestimated. Such work has legitimated the study of groups once considered beyond the purvey of social science, while its scholars have shown how such groups, when taken "at face value" (Kirby 1997), can tell us much about the changing role of the state and the nature of political violence under new regimes of capital accumulation.

Perhaps of greatest importance, the focus on these movements works to highlight a key contradiction in neoliberal ideology. That is, while neoliberalism seeks to eradicate the regulatory mechanisms of the state on trade and the movement of capital, it also requires the state to regulate and enforce the conditions that maintain the weaknesses of boundaries and regulation. Recognizing contradictions and highlighting conditions where they come into sharp relief is important because it is here that alternatives might arise. As Harvey notes in *Spaces of Hope* (2000, 193), his most recent book, dedicated specifically to the consideration of alternatives, "If the seeds of revolutionary transformation must be found in the present and if no society can launch upon a task of radical reorganization for which it is not at least partially prepared, then those internal contradictions provide raw materials for growing an alternative." Harvey's concern with alternatives is clearly relevant to the case at hand. The Patriot Movement emerges from contradictions in neoliberalism, yet the alternatives it poses represent a regression to a blood-and-soil politics based on fear, hate, and exclusion (Dees 1996; J. Dyer 1997; Junas 1995; Mozzochi 1995).

Considering alternatives (or even responses) to the Patriot Movement seems even more prescient when we realize that such groups often court reaction. One of the gravest dangers confronting those who deal with these groups (whether through a research, law-enforcement, or watchdog capacity) is that their actions will feed the apocalyptic scenarios enshrined in these groups' belief systems, thereby leading to more, not less, violence. Richardson (1995, 164) details an extreme example of this potential in his analysis of the government's handling of the Waco incident:

> The drama seemed to imitate a Greek tragedy, moving inexorably toward its predictable climax, and we know that Greek tragedies always involved predetermined sacrifices. That tragic sense of the "meaning" of the Waco tragedy was borne out on April 19 [the day of the final raid] when authorities did what Koresh had been predicting all along to his followers.

The danger of another Waco clearly impels us to understand such belief systems (knowledge the government lacked or at least failed to apply at Waco; see Wright 1995) and to formulate responses to them that can be tailored to contexts ranging from the armed standoff to the discursive battle for hearts and minds.

Given the importance of internal contradictions to the construction of alternatives and the difficulty in dealing with such movements "from a distance," not to mention the stark reality of the regressive alternative posited by the Patriot Movement, it is interesting that most of the nascent anti-statist scholarship seems hesitant to articulate progressive alternatives for those who would become patriots. The failure to adequately respond to the Patriot Movement plays out in different ways and depends largely on the perspective of the author in question. Castells failure (1997) to respond to anti-statist movements, for example, comes from the constructivist analytic perspective he employs. This approach leads him not only to refuse evaluation of and between groups, but also to explicitly condemn such attempts as well. As Castells argues, "Since there is no sense of history other than the history we sense, from an analytical perspective there are no 'good' and 'bad,' progressive and regressive social movements. They are all symptoms of who we are, and avenues of our transformation, since transformation may equally lead to a whole range of heavens, hells, or heavenly hells" (3). Yet when Castells begins his analysis of anti-statist movements, he admits that he finds movements like the Zapatistas likable while he regards Aum Shinryko and the Patriots as unpalatable (70). In calling attention to the progressive or regressive tendencies of just a few of these movements, he draws attention to the pathways these movements envision for not just themselves, but for all of society. And, in calling attention to the avenues they propose to direct society toward, he necessarily raises the question of why we should not at least analyze the political aims associated with these projected pathways even as we recognize the ever possible changes to them that might occur.

Unlike Castells, however, most scholarship on anti-statism carries with it at least implicit evaluative criteria. Luke and O'Tuathail (1998), for example, are highly critical of the Buchananist logic that undergirds much of the Patriot Movement. Yet their analysis of the movement seems to echo Margaret Thatcher's now infamous phrase, "There is no alternative." As they note,

Shuttered up in populist autarchy policed by Buchananist plebiscites, the USA might well be able to keep some more workers working, a few foreign aid dollars at home, and a number of illegal migrants out. In becoming disencumbered from global flows, however, this hardened nationalized territorial space will undoubtedly be eclipsed technologically, financially and culturally. . . . Thus a farcical move to resurrect the never-never land of omnipotent Cold War America will culminate tragically in autarkic impotence not unlike the stagnation induced in Franco's Spain, Mao's China, or Stalin's Russia. (Luke and O'Tuathail 1998, 90)

While Luke and O'Tuathail's prediction may very well be accurate, there is no alternative posed for those hurt by neoliberalism and therefore most attracted to Buchananism, except, perhaps, to accept the "inevitable."

Steinberg (1997) is also critical of the "right-wing" anti-statism of the patriot position. He argues that patriots are defending dominant social positions of race, gender, and sexuality that are challenged by global flows and that these social positions drive patriot attempts to rearticulate the nation-state nexus. As Steinberg (1997, 15) explains, "One must treat their politics not as incidental but as lying deep within their members' social positions." While Steinberg is correct to point to the centrality of patriots' dominant social positions, his analysis all but ignores the role played by their class positioning. This is no mere analytic oversight. Indeed, if patriots' status anxiety has been dangerously exacerbated by global flows, it seems at least logical to ask why their class positions have not been mobilized, and to much better effect. In failing to note the role of class, even as an unarticulated moment in the movement's emergence, Steinberg unintentionally forecloses any progressive outlet for patriots themselves.

Sparke (1998) is also critical of right-wing varieties of anti-statism such as the Patriot Movement. Focusing his analysis on the Oklahoma City bombing, he argues that patriots like Timothy McVeigh have rescripted traditional understandings of what lies "outside" of patriotism, identifying its location as "inside" the United States and launching an armed insurrection to excise it. As Sparke reminds us, however, "McVeigh's own act of terrorism was itself ideologically underpinned by the very same inside/outside analytics" long espoused by the U.S. government against its citizenry (2). The lesson we can learn from unpacking such a horrific tragedy is, Sparke concludes, to remember "the secret truths of patriotism: that it is precarious, personal, shifting, exclusionary and always potentially violent" (28).

Although Sparke's discursive analysis is sound, it has the effect of dismissing two categories of action—nation and patriotism—in which, as Mouffe (1995, 264) notes, many have a strong "libidinal investment," and that she therefore rightly cautions us not to dismiss. In dismissing patriotism, Sparke can provide no discursive counterweight to patriots, nor to those who may fall prey to patriot discourse in the future. Such a counterweight is crucial because, while many white males are attracted to the Patriot Movement out of a desire to protect their social dominance, many are also attracted to it in hopes of addressing their class-based concerns. A democratically articulated alternative might not eliminate right-wing alternatives altogether, but it could certainly diminish their impact.

It is here, at the intersection of patriots' contradictory social positions and their attempts to rework the nation-state nexus, that identity theory and Harvey's critique of it may be fruitfully merged. Because the patriot position emerges from the social positionality of its adherents, identity theory is useful for understanding how these positions are fixed (if only temporarily) through patriot identity. As the next chapter will analyze in greater detail, an emerging body of identity theory has developed to analyze the politics of identity emerging from dominant social positions of race and gender—dominant positions held by the large majority of patriots. But patriots' class positions are also an important part of this analysis. And because these positions are not articulated through traditional class-based categories, identity theory may also analyze how class, as a social position, comes to be subsumed within non–class-based categories of social meaning. My use of identity theory to analyze the role of class in the movement follows the lead first established by Gibson-Graham (1996), who takes a similar approach to unpacking the concept of capitalism.

It is not enough, however, to simply recognize that class has been submerged within other categories of meaning. It is also important to understand how the submergence of class within patriot rhetoric leads to regressive politics. Indeed, the submergence of class within other categories of social action does not necessarily lead to regressive politics. Many streams of black intellectual thought, for example, foreground the role of white supremacy in their analyses of inequality and resistance to it, thereby positioning unequal class relations as a lesser or "secondary" source of oppression (Fanon 1963). Yet the politics that emerges from their analysis is not regressive. Thus it is important to examine how the patriot category leads to regressive solutions, when its rhetoric is applied to patriots' class-based concerns. I argue, and illustrate in the empirical portions of this book, that much of the answer to this question lies in the current form of the category of nation. In the next chapter, I will detail how the category of nation in the United States has historically been a "white" construct and how it remains one today.

When the category of nation is deployed around class-based issues, it is also important to examine why patriots deploy the category of nation and patriotism to it. As the empirical portion of this book illustrates, these appeals are mostly symbolic—for the purposes of legitimation. As such, while it is a stretch to compare the struggles of the American Revolution with those of today's patriots, it is this very incongruency that makes it so fitting for patriot politics. They can borrow from, and mix and match within, a whole host of generalized Revolutionary-era symbols invoking freedom, absence of tyranny, and the fight against oppression and apply them today without constraint of historical fact. And by invoking the Revolution, patriots are also able to position themselves and their cause within this sacred founding moment, thereby legitimizing their cause.

When patriots do stray from their Revolutionary-era grab bag of symbols, they usually turn to the cold war era. While the cold war context has more in common with the circumstances of today than those of the Revolutionary era, it too describes a world order that has vanished. The Soviet Union, which Ronald Reagan once called the "evil empire," no longer exists, and the Washington consensus of the early 1990s continues to have relatively free reign in setting domestic and international monetary and trade agendas. Invoking the cold war vision of the world, grounded as it was on the dualistic logic of good versus evil, freedom versus tyranny, capitalism versus communism, allows patriots to invoke an American hegemony that seemed to include them. It also allows them to target their enemies—free-trade agreements, American corporations, finance capitalists—without confronting the thoroughly American hegemony that created them. When the system fails patriots, as it did frequently throughout the 1980s and 1990s, cold war logic, dressed in patriot rhetoric, deflects a sustained analysis and critique of the Patriot Movement, because the enemy is always, first and foremost, un-American. It is in this way that a post–cold war government of the United States, now an unchecked superpower, the sole global hegemon, comes to be branded as "occupied" by forces who will "communize" the entire globe.

In this generalized discursive terrain, the combination of Revolutionary symbols and cold war logic creates a wished-for nation grounded in myth rather than reality. It also creates a politics in which the nation is only tenuously attached to the state. In this discursive terrain, the nation-state is no longer the "power container" to invoke or to defend. Rather, patriots see the locality, generally defined at the county level, as the space where power resides, trumping state and federal power. The nation, as a symbolic entity, legitimates local patriot struggles on the ground, but it no longer links them together in a structural way. This delegitimation of the state in patriot discourse forecloses either macro or cross-scalar vision: power and action become locked in the local, sealed off from anything but an empty symbolic link to other scales.

This foreclosure of macro/cross-scalar vision prohibits patriots from seeing how the state could protect their class-based interests. This is no small matter, because the state apparatus designed to protect workers has not been completely dismantled, and because its role is central to many patriot issues, particularly issues related to rural livelihood. As I describe in more detail in chapter 6, this state apparatus became an important topic for consideration in my case study area, where discussions about the state's role in agricultural subsidies were central to one of the issues that galvanized Kentucky patriots—their calls to legalize industrial hemp. Although hemp is currently illegal, patriots believe hemp would be a good supplemental crop for the region's embattled tobacco farmers. Tobacco is currently subsidized by the government, although its subsidies were almost eliminated by the 1997

McCain tobacco bill. Despite the importance of subsidies to tobacco farmers, even as they consider other crop alternatives, patriots in my case study found subsidies hard to accept. Indeed, whether they supported them as a necessary evil or shunned them as "socialist," patriots could see no good long-term benefit to their locality being yoked to a federal apparatus. Federal intervention, even on behalf of their economic interests, is regarded as flatly wrong. The power of the local in patriot rhetoric even limits patriots' ability to see patriot causes in other locales as solvable by the same means. When I asked the patriots in my study area if they would work on patriot causes in other areas of the country, for example, most expressed solidarity, but replied that these issues were "out of jurisdiction."

In sum, patriot rhetoric tends to mask class-based issues in two ways. First, it discursively links notions of patriotism with capitalism. So equated, patriots find it difficult to criticize the neoliberal logic through a frame built on the assumption of capitalism's might and right. Second, the insistence in patriot rhetoric that the state has been "co-opted" or "occupied" means that, while the nation plays an important symbolic role, any structural role for it is foreclosed. Using this construction, patriots are unable to see how the state may protect their class-based interests, even if for the short term.

Patriot rhetoric tends to muddle and distort solutions to class-based dilemmas. Its rhetoric is, however, powerful in other ways, and this power tends to funnel adherents' generalized discontent into issues better served by it. These issues tend to revolve around issues of race and culture—issues that are, as the next chapter will show, embedded within constructions of America. It is to these issues that I now turn.

NOTES

1. Perhaps the best-known literature to address these movements is the burgeoning subfield within sociology called new social movements. While this literature is clearly important, its key questions are not those of this book. New social movements literature is largely interested in categorizing the emergence of social movements, analyzing their mobilization strategies, and assessing their relative success or failure over the long term. The purpose of this book is to analyze how patriot leaders construct a patriot identity and how this identity politics addresses the contradictory social positions of its target audience. For this reason, this book uses identity theory to analyze the Patriot Movement and cites very little new social movement literature.

2. Representative Robert Damron (D-House District 39) filed the bill (House Bill 49) in the 2001 Kentucky General Assembly.

3

On the Fault Line: Whiteness and Class in the New World Order

Traditionally, identity theory has been concerned with the formation of identities that may be labeled broadly as resistance identities. In the United States, resistance identities emerged through social movements organized to challenge dominant identity norms, whether of race, gender, or sexuality, and to embrace "othered" social positions in their own right. Identity theory now includes distinct subfields of literature dedicated to the study of "othered" social positions and the unique resistance strategies they employ. Feminist theory, queer theory, and race theory are now well-developed fields of theoretical and empirical inquiry (Delgado 1995; Jackson and Jones 1998; Turner 2000). The strength of these subfields is further evidenced by the robust debates within them.

In the last ten years, however, scholars have also turned their attention to dominant identity construction and how dominant identity infuses political action, from social movements to government policy making. Today there are emerging and vibrant literatures on masculinity (Gibson 1994; Jeffords 1989, 1994), heterosexuality (Blum and Nast 1996), and whiteness (Fields 2002; Frakenberg 1993; Ignatiev 1995; Roediger 1994; Newitz and Wray 1997). The understandings derived from these literatures are relevant for analyzing the Patriot Movement, whose members are overwhelmingly white, male, and presumably heterosexual.[1] This chapter examines one of these literatures, that of whiteness studies.

In focusing my analysis on whiteness, I foreground patriots' dominant racial positions. The choice to focus on whiteness is based on the way patriots presented their cause to me. During my time in the field, the patriots I interviewed or engaged in casual conversation were always quick to disassociate their cause from white supremacist groups. Indeed, these pronouncements were usually unsolicited comments, spurred by patriots' desires to "set the record straight" at the beginning of a conversation or interview, and not in response to questions from me about race. One patriot I interviewed even stressed to me the diversity of the movement in Kentucky, telling me proudly that the Kentucky movement counted a native Hawaiian among its ranks.

In contrast, patriots never seemed particularly compelled to stress to me that the Patriot Movement was *not* sexist. This was especially interesting given that I am female and all of the patriots I interviewed were male. Moreover, when I asked patriots if women could be members of their respective groups, they all replied matter of factly, "Yes." They never seemed concerned, however, to use their coed memberships rolls to prove a point about a lack of sexism in the movement. Similarly, while patriots generally hold antigay sentiments, the patriots I interviewed never made a point of telling me they were *not* homophobic.

In short, while patriots possess dominant gender and sexual social positionality, these positions are less dominant in their politics than their race and class positions are. This is not to say, however, that masculinity and heterosexuality will not become dominant in the Kentucky Patriot Movement in the future. As I indicate in chapter 9, there is a growing body of evidence that suggests that homosexuality, in particular, is becoming an issue there. Nor is this to say that patriots have articulated an identity politics explicitly defined through class or race. Rather, both positions have been subsumed within the category of "patriot." As I illustrated in the last chapter in regard to class, such coding works to muddle progressive class-based analysis. And, as I will demonstrate in this chapter in regard to race, such coding tends to buttress notions of racial and cultural superiority by creating safe, palatable codes for their expression.

THE ROLE OF WHITENESS

Race is a thoroughly modern concept. It is, as a variety of scholars note, a direct product of the colonial era. As colonialism progressed, Europeans became increasingly obsessed with the differences they saw between themselves and those whom they colonized. This obsession led to the creation of race—a "scientifically" grounded way to define these differences in discrete, pat categories. Caught up in the social Darwinism of the day, and buttressed by the Cartesian logic that searched for universals, scholars looked to biology to "ground" the differences between themselves and their colonial subjects (Gregory 1994; Livingstone 1992). European colonizers were fastidious in their search for biological grounds for race. They set about measuring cranium size, nose width and length, and height to catalog the differences in measurable fashion (Gourevitch 1998). So crafted, the study of race came to mean the study of people who were "black," "brown," and "yellow," and thus *not* "white."

With the advent of decolonization struggles across the globe and civil rights struggles in the United States, scholars of race developed new, critical approaches to the study of race. They argued that race was not grounded in biological difference, but was a social construction created through and justifying unequal relations in power. While these studies were critical, and indispensable to progressive thought, race was nonetheless equated with categories that were not white. Such a perspective assumed that to be white was to lack "race." As whiteness scholars now argue, however, we must also recognize that whiteness is a "race" as well and go about unpacking the contents of whiteness in the same manner that we have with categories denoting other races.

Calls to study whiteness are not, however, merely additive. Rather, whiteness scholars define their calls for the study of "white" as crucial for unpacking key power relations in the United States and much of the world today. As Richard Dyer (1997, 1) notes in the introduction of his book *White*, studying whiteness "is not done merely to fill a gap in the analytic literature, but because there is something at stake in looking at, or continuing to ignore, white racial imagery. As long as race is something only applied to non-white peoples, as long as white people are not racially seen and named, they/we function as a human norm. Other people are raced, we are just people." In Dyer's justification lies a precept that is central to the study of whiteness—whiteness serves as a "norm," the standard against which others are deemed to have, or not to have, race. In short, whiteness is rendered invisible. Lacking no position, whiteness comes to represent the universal, the natural, and the human.

David Roediger (1994) has called this the "empty culture of whiteness." Whiteness is not an identity marker for a distinct cultural tradition possessing its own body of self-representational work, such as music, dance, and the written word. Rather, Roediger argues, whiteness "is the empty and therefore terrifying attempt to build an identity based on what one isn't and on whom one can hold back" (13). Skillful writers working across disciplinary divides illustrate empirically how the taken-for-granted nature of whiteness serves not only to oppress, but also to entrench people of color as substandard "others" to a white norm. Such examples are found in a variety of contexts, from the policy roundtables of Congress to the runways in Paris and Milan. The oppressive power of white normativity even rears its head in otherwise progressive political venues.

In the policy context, the debate surrounding welfare reform in the mid-1990s is particularly illustrative. While the average welfare recipient in the United States is a white woman, proponents of "reform" (cutbacks) on both sides of the aisle tapped into stereotypes of the "black welfare queen"—a black woman with a large brood of children borne solely for the boosted welfare check—to forward their legislative agendas. Using this stereotype in newspapers, documentaries, and television ads to gain public support for reform allowed welfare reform activists to portray the extant system as one that perpetrated unnatural and morally wrong behavior (Delgado 1996; A. Reed 1995). The irony, of course, is that white women, being the largest recipients of welfare (Loprest and Zedlewski 1999), bore the brunt of reform. Perhaps most telling, however, is that welfare reform, enacted largely by white men and damaging to significant numbers of white women, illustrates the void of whiteness as a signifier of a distinct community of people.

In the realm of popular culture, hooks (1992) illustrates the oppressiveness of white normativity in the fashion industry. Eschewing commentators who see a racial victory in the ascendance of black models such as Iman and Naomi Campbell in the lily-white world of fashion, hooks argues that black participation in its current form only reinforces notions of beauty as inherently white. hooks sees two overarching themes to fashion spreads employing black models. Both reinforce whiteness as the beauty standard. The first is the "whitened passer." Here, black models are used, but only if they meet certain standards of Caucasian beauty, including thin lips, long noses, fairer skin, and straightened hair. In such a configuration, black is beautiful, but only if it mimics otherwise "white" characteristics. The other standard depiction of black models is that of the exotic, sexually insatiable, animalistic woman. Here, black women wear revealing clothing, are photographed in exotic locales, and ooze "forbidden" sex. While the models in these shoots may add "color" to "vanilla" fashion spreads and even be paid top dollar for their work, their presence does not represent beauty but rather a dirty fantasy that could never be brought home to mother. Caught between images that are either physically impossible to mimic or limiting (at best) and dehumanizing (at worst), most black women find beauty out of their symbolic reach. hooks argues that representations of beauty based on white norms are fundamental to keeping blacks from desiring and loving blackness, encouraging their self-loathing instead.

Progressive politics has even found it difficult to escape the normativity of whiteness and its negative effects. Much of the early feminist and lesbian struggles provide fertile ground for illustration. Betty Friedan's now seminal book, *The Feminine Mystique* (1963), for example, outlines a vigorous critique of gender roles that chained women to home and children, locking them out of avenues in which they could explore their individuality separate from traditional roles as wives and mothers. It became the early bible of a feminist movement desperately in need of a passionately crafted treatise. Friedan's critique was written as a rallying cry for all women, a call to arms for the female "race." Yet, as black, Hispanic, and even white working-class women noted, the articulation of oppression depicted in Friedan's book was that of the white middle- and upper-class woman's experience. For many African American and Hispanic women work was not a luxury or a place for self-definition, but a necessity for survival. The presumptive whiteness of early feminist politics meant not only that it failed to resonate with women of color, but that women of color themselves refused to answer the call to a "universal" sisterhood that seemed almost as oppressive in its ignorance as the workplace was in its frank discrimination (hooks 1992; Hull et al. 1982).

Shugar (1995) notes a similar problem in early versions of lesbian politics. She documents how the lesbian understanding of oppression carried with it the assumptions of white lesbians and how these assumptions worked to ignore or silence recognition that lesbians of color experienced multiple and overlapping forms of oppression. Shugar illustrates this problem in her study of lesbian separatist communes formed during the 1970s. These communes were based on the theoretical assumption that the primary locus of women's and lesbians' oppression was patriarchy and that the only way to end oppression from it was to completely separate from it. Mimicking structural marxism's insistence on class as the primary locus of oppression, lesbian separatists argued that women who sought to redress other systems of oppression, such as race or class, were at best deluded and at worst traitors to the cause. As such, lesbian communes, while open to women of color, often had difficulty attracting and especially keeping them as members. As Shugar (1995, 48) notes, these communes

> could not convince them [women of color] that racism would or could be eradicated through the elimination of sexism. Further, separatist insistence on the answer that racism was a man-made distinction curable only through the demise of the patriarchy sounded suspiciously like the argument given to women by leftist men on the issue of sexism—an argument that, of course, separatists themselves were quick to denounce.

As these diverse examples attest, assumptions of whiteness as the norm infuse a broad array of contexts. These examples illustrate how the unquestioned assumption that white skin and white experiences are "normal" work to denigrate those who are not white, silencing their voices, belittling their perspectives, exploiting their appearances, and manipulating their images. The importance of early whiteness studies lies in a simple recognition that had long been known to people of color—whiteness does not have to be a white man dressed in a white hood to oppress. As terrifying as such an image may be, the power of whiteness just as often lies in its invisible presence.

This central precept provides the basis for a second analytic moment common in the scholarship on whiteness—whiteness infuses even "universal," supposedly value-free categories of meaning. In recognizing the invisible presence of whiteness, scholars set about to explore its terrain, mapping along the way its intersection with the primary categorical boundaries of the modern age, including nation, freedom, and property. In analyzing the construction of these concepts, scholars found that ideals of whiteness infused the construction of these categories and were further reinforced by their construction (Barrett and Roediger 1997; Bell 1995; Morrison 1992; Harris 1993; hooks 1992). In the construction of these "universal" categories, however, the visible presence of whiteness was subsequently displaced once these new discursive moments were firmly defined. This allows white norms to shape categories meant to govern divergent groups in society and permits the oppression of those not meeting the (unspoken) white norm, who find themselves "others" to supposedly universal categories as well. It also keeps whites from questioning their racial motivations, giving them instead "palatable" categories through which to protect their dominance.

Novelist and scholar Toni Morrison (1992) provided one of the first studies illustrating the infusion of white norms into the construction of universal categories. Morrison examines the concepts of nation and freedom and makes her argument through a thorough unpacking of the early American literary canon—a place, as she notes, where the young nation could come to grips with itself and establish a clear idea of what it meant to be "American." Morrison begins by asking the reader to ponder a seeming paradox in the early literature. America was a young and vibrant nation, yet its first writers were overwhelmingly preoccupied with the gothic—themes and story lines that were not only out of fashion in Europe at the time, but seemingly incommensurate with the youth and vitality of the new nation. Morrison argues that focusing on the gothic provided a medium through which literate whites could meditate on the meaning of freedom and their simultaneous terror of and longing for it. And the gothic figure upon which all of these fears and anxieties were projected? The African "other." It was, Morrison argues, only in relation to this confined, bound, and thoroughly unfree "other" that the concept of freedom and free men could be articulated.

One of the books Morrison uses to illustrate her argument is Mark Twain's *Huckleberry Finn*, in which a slave figures prominently in the novel's narrative. Although Jim provides the voice of reason and truth in the narrative, as compared to Huck's aunts, for example, Morrison contends that Twain's refusal to free Jim at the end of the novel was necessary for the articulation of freedom that Twain so wanted to explore in his book. As such, historical controversy over where to place *Huckleberry Finn* in debates about Mark Twain and slavery misses the point. To debate whether or not Twain should have freed Jim at the end of the novel assumes that freedom could be articulated without him in the first place. As Morrison (1992, 56) notes,

> To let Jim go free, to let him enter the mouth of the Ohio River and pass into free territory, would be to abandon the whole premise of the book. Neither

Huck nor Mark Twain can tolerate, in imaginative terms, Jim freed. That would blast the predilection from its mooring. Thus the fatal ending becomes the elaborate deferment of a necessary and necessarily unfree Africanist character's escape, because freedom has no meaning to Huck or to the text without the specter of enslavement, the anodyne to individualism, the yardstick of absolute power over the life of another, the signed, marked, informing, and mutating presence of a black slave.

hooks's analysis of freedom (1992) provides a contemporary companion to Morrison's. Examining both the civil rights movement and the black Muslim movement, hooks analyzes the discourses of liberation employed by both movements. She argues that while black liberation was presumably about freedom from the oppression of white dominance, it was actually predicated on freedom to access the means of dominance—material wealth and the power to exclude it from others. As hooks concludes, fighting for the ability to move from the position of victim to that of exploiter offers no significant break with white-centered notions of freedom as freedom to exploit.

Harris (1993) also illustrates the infusion of whiteness within broad, "universal" categories of meaning. Analyzing the emergence of property laws, Harris argues that our current understanding of property was constructed in relation to race, the construction of which occurred in the context of colonialism. As a wide body of scholarly literature now suggests, in the earliest years of colonial settlement the concept of race was still poorly defined (see also Marx 1998; Roediger 1991; Takaki 1990). Of course, colonials were aware of the idea of race, but as Harris (1993, 1716) notes, "Racial lines were neither consistently nor sharply delineated among or within all social groups." Indeed, lower-class whites and blacks often participated in social activities together and whites collaborated in some of the earliest slave riots in urban areas (see Roediger 1991). These lines became pronounced only later. As Harris (1993, 1716) argues, "In the early years of the country, it was not the concept of race alone that operated to oppress Blacks and Indians; rather, it was the interaction between conceptions of race and property that played a critical role in establishing and maintaining racial and economic subordination."

The context in which race and property evolved into their modern forms began with labor shortages in the new colonies. For the first one hundred years of colonial settlement, the landed classes relied on a mixture of white indentured servants and black slaves. As increasing numbers of white indentured laborers completed their servitude, the gentry found themselves with a labor shortage. They reacted by instituting legal statutes that fortified their access to the remaining labor force—largely slaves. These legal statutes rigidified distinctions between whites and blacks through the legal articulation of property and property rights.

In particular, state legislatures set about the task of codifying definitions of property to guarantee the status of slaves. The Maryland legislature, for example, enacted legislation in 1661 that codified the status of slaves as slaves for life. Similarly, the South Carolina legislature effectively foreclosed a means to freedom for blacks by declaring that slaves were prohibited from gaining their freedom by converting to Christianity. By the early eighteenth century, Virginia's legislature had declared slaves property, paving the way for them to be exchanged, bartered, inherited, and even posted as collateral like any other form of currency. These distinctions not only denigrated the already low status of slaves, however, they also boosted and solidified understandings of whiteness. Whites were whites because they were not property, and property was property because it was a mode of being that was not white.

Scholars examining the links between property and the construction of race have also noted how whiteness itself serves as a form of property. This recognition, conscious or not, was particularly important during the colonial period because plantation owners were well aware that not only did poor whites have more in common with blacks than with white elites, but also that such legal distinctions did nothing to change access to landownership for poor whites. Filling the property void was whiteness. It became the symbolic capital through which poor whites were able to differentiate themselves from the rest of the so-called rabble, occasionally reaping small material gains in the process. Bell (1995, 79) notes that

> the creation of a black subclass enabled poor whites to identify with and support the politics of the upper white class. And large landowners, with the safe economic advantage provided by their slaves, were willing to grant poor whites a larger role in the political process. Thus, paradoxically, slavery for blacks led to greater freedom for poor whites, at least when compared with the denial of freedom to African slaves. Slavery also provided mainly propertyless whites with a property in their whiteness.

So constructed, whiteness became a form of property to protect and, later, to secure entitlements from, while blackness, conversely, became the process of becoming property with the strictures that that entailed. These constructions are important not just in their historical context, however. Indeed, the establishment of whiteness as a form of symbolic currency during this time set the discursive stage upon which many of today's poor and working-class whites decide to align themselves with wealthy whites instead of workers of other races, with whom they have much more in common. It is not a stretch to say that these divisions have been central to labor's inability to form a concerted and strong movement in the United States. As Noel Ignatiev (1995, 183–84), one of the earliest scholars to systematically study whiteness, explains it, "My insistence on addressing problems of race as central to the formation (or nonformation) of an American working class stems from my view that there have been (and continue to be) moments when an anticapitalist course is a real possibility, and that the adherence of some workers to an alliance with capital on the basis of a shared 'whiteness' has been and is the greatest obstacle to the realization of those possibilities." It is to these relations that I turn in the next section, focusing on the myriad ways that "white currency" has undermined class unity in the industrial United States. Unpacking these relations is obviously relevant to this study, because patriots, who are overwhelmingly working class, have chosen to align themselves (subtly and otherwise) along racial rather than class lines. By examining the neoliberal context in which patriots find themselves, I also highlight changes that affect how such divisions play out today and that the left must necessarily address in its efforts to enact progressive change.

HOW RACE TRUMPS CLASS

As the previous section indicates, the power of whiteness lies in its invisibility. Whiteness, as the unquestioned norm, takes on the characteristics of the "universal." Those not meeting its characteristics are regarded as different and inferior. As identity theory reminds us, however, all categories are constructed out of alterity—the mass of unarticulated differences that make every human different in some way. Indeed, in the construction of categories of meaning, any number of differences are temporarily erased, downplayed, or ignored at the expense of categorical unity. In the case of whiteness, a key line of difference within it has been that of class. Unlike other lines of difference that run through the category, however, class differentiation has always bubbled just beneath the surface, threatening to disrupt the fragile unity of white identity. The ebbs and flows of capital markets, when combined with capital's search for what Harvey (1989) has called a "spatial fix," make class relations inherently unstable. This instability means that white unity is perpetually under strain as well.

In examining attempts to maintain "white" unity, scholars have developed several theoretical generalizations in a myriad of empirical studies. The first of these concerns the "location" of hegemonic practices designed to protect white unity. While it is reasonable to assume that efforts to protect white unity emerged out of the enclaves of the white elite (especially given that white and black worker allegiance threatens their economic interests), such efforts have just as often swelled from white working-class quarters. These findings are consistent with the theoretical understandings of hegemony described in chapter 2 (LaClau and Mouffe 1985). Categories are constructed and maintained from above, but just as often from below.

In the case at hand, there are a variety of explanations in the whiteness literature for white workers' leading role in defending their access to whiteness. One explanation is that white workers choose race over class for very practical reasons. White workers recognize that the symbolic capital of whiteness is guaranteed, while the material benefits accruing from class politics are unrealized and carry no guarantees for realization in the future. Similarly, in a diverse array of instances across time and space, white workers have purposefully chosen to block workers of other races from acquiring jobs because they perceived these new workers as wage depressers rather than as providing strength in numbers. Still others argue that white workers find it psychologically difficult to make alliances with workers of other races because they have been taught since childhood to see themselves as superior to them. Having to share the factory floor with those once thought inferior requires whites not only to confront the lies of their society, but to accept a social positionality that is, once stripped of its lies, lower than previously believed.

A second theoretical generalization involves the remarkable latitude white workers have shown in extending the contours of whiteness in order to preserve the category's base of power. Over time, the reach of whiteness has been extended rather than narrowed. As a variety of scholars note, only a small fraction of the ethnic and linguistic diversity considered white today would have "made the cut" in the mid-nineteenth century (Barrett and Roediger 1997; Ignatiev 1995; Roediger 1994). Ignatiev's study of Irish immigration in the late 1800s (1995), for example, illustrates that Americans initially viewed the Irish as belonging to another race that was, in its presumed inferiority, distinctly *not* white. Indeed, the Irish were depicted in much the same way as domestic blacks were. Political cartoons of the day portrayed both groups as apish, with long arms and extended faces. Similarly, philanthropic discussions on how to extend social services to the Irish bore a remarkable resemblance to those about black communities; in both cases, white do-gooders lamented the "instinctual" nature of their clients and recommended the infusion of white, Protestant values as the solution.

Of course, for the newly arrived immigrants, such distinctions made little sense initially. While the modern idea of race was developed in Europe through the colonial project, its application was generally applied between Europe and its colonies rather than between or within European countries themselves. Instead, most Europeans defined themselves by their village of origin and upon arriving in the United States simply added country of origin to their complex social mapping of subnational space. The meaningful boundaries in Boston's early Irish slums, for example, were just as often internal, between areas dominated by settlers from, say, County Cork and County Sligo, as external, between the Irish part of town and the Italian part.

Similar distinctions were found in the Chicago slums of the early 1900s that housed Eastern and Southern European migrants.

A third generalization is that these migrants became "white" by becoming "American." Racial differences between domestic whites and European migrants were collapsed within the category of "American" and defined over and against the domestic black population, which constituted yet another threatening migratory wave to the industrial centers of the North and Midwest. In short, labor unions made "racial" concessions to some non-whites, and not to others, for strategic advantage. The actions of labor unions constituted a discursive reorganization that erased some racial differentiation (and the power differential that went with it) in order to maintain the overall ability to differentiate from whiteness, thereby holding down those not "white" and maintaining the white advantage in the workplace. Moreover, immigrants were willing coconspirators; they recognized that becoming white bore them fruitful privileges vis-à-vis nonwhite workers. The process was by no means simple or pat. Rather, it constituted a discursive reorganization, the process of which was, not surprisingly, sloppy, full of internal contradictions, and confusing to all parties involved. While it is difficult to find order in the discursive chaos that reigned for much of the late nineteenth and early twentieth centuries, the rhetorical shift from white man's wages to American wages provides a discursive thread by which to trace the process.

Each new and successive wave of migrants that came to the U.S. industrial centers was decried by domestic workers for undermining the "white man's wage." With each new wave, however, it became clear to native-born workers that they could not possibly maintain their power on the factory floor or their leverage with management without bolstering their numbers. As Barrett and Roediger (1997, 200) note, in reference to the conundrum confronting the American Federation of Labor (AFL) at the time, "To restrict immigration, however desirable from [AFL leader Samuel] Gompers' point of view, did not answer what to do about the majority of the working class which was by 1910 already of immigrant origins." The need to address the realities of a majority nonwhite labor force meant that invocations to the white man's wage would not rhetorically work. The discursive, and often utilitarian, response was to replace calls for protecting the white man's wage with calls to protect American wages. This discursive shift had the effect of whitening not only nonwhite laborers but also the category of American itself. And this rhetorical device was soon followed by material practices designed to enforce the shifting rhetorical terrain of Americanness and its unspoken, yet understood whiteness. In 1902, for example, Samuel Gompers supported literacy tests for AFL membership, knowing that it would effectively foreclose participation by domestic blacks and the newly arriving Slavic peoples, while having no appreciable impacts on older immigrant groups the AFL was willing to define as "American" (Barrett and Roediger 1997).

As the above discussion illustrates, these theoretical generalizations are derived largely from historical analyses that focus on the formation of the labor movement in the United States. Today's context of neoliberalism, however, presents new questions for analysis in whiteness studies. Such questions are varied, but three stand out as particularly relevant to the study of the Patriot Movement. I shall discuss them in turn.

First, the geographic context in which different groups of workers encounter one another has fundamentally changed. Historically, industrial employment was grounded in place; cheap labor responded by moving to "where the work was." The in situ nature of work meant that divergently paid groups of laborers encountered one another face to face on the factory floor and, increasingly, in the inner cities they shared. These encounters certainly contained instances of hostility, moments of bloodshed, and undercurrents of tension. Yet they made it possible for groups pitted against one another by capital to band together spatially to confront the power of capital. Today, cheap labor continues to uproot in search of work, as is evidenced by the steady stream of illegal migrants crossing the U.S.-Mexican border every day, but these workers rarely vie for the same jobs as domestic workers. More importantly, in today's globalized economy, capital moves as frequently as labor does. Capital's mobility means that today's global assembly line affords little opportunity either to encounter those who would compete for jobs or to forge alliances with them.

In terms of the Patriot Movement, then, we must examine how the globalized context impacts the racial formation of "patriot" and its "other." As I illustrate in the empirical portion of this book, the other is not "white," but her nonwhiteness is complicated by her status as of and in the "third world." Employing standard development tropes in the articulation of categories such as the American worker or the patriot gives white workers double cover for their whiteness. By couching the other in standard development tropes of difference ("third world"), white workers buttress the stability of "American" as "white" while hiding behind yet another categorical layer of obfuscation.

Second, the political landscape in which working-class concerns may be articulated has changed, and for the worse. Over the past two decades unions, the traditional political outlet for white workers, have suffered severe losses (Edwards 1993; Harvey 1996). While unions were not without their problems, they at least provided institutional structures through which varied groups of workers could attempt to unify over and against capital. During the same time period, the political left became increasingly concerned with resistance movements such as feminism, black power, and lesbigay rights—all politics resisting white, male, heterosexual dominance in some way. In short, left-of-center outlets for white working-class males have steadily declined.

The political right has been particularly adept at exploiting this political void (Lipsitz 1998). As a variety of scholars note, however, after the civil rights movement, many whites felt uncomfortable expressing their biases in overtly racial terms (Daniels 1997; Kincheloe and Steinberg 1998). Savvy far-right activists took these sentiments to heart, establishing their racist positions through antigovernment rhetoric. Such rhetoric created a discursive big tent that allowed organizers to address the race-based anxieties of white workers in palatable terms. Given that antigovernment sentiments may arise from a variety of contexts and take any number of articulations across the political spectrum, we must examine the discourses that give form to traditional right-wing parochialism and suspicion of government. Not surprisingly, anticommunism (a well-oiled theme in the history of right-wing politics) is recovered and deployed in the movement. Indeed, it seems to matter little that the cold war has ended. In patriot rhetoric, the U.S. government is depicted as co-opted by global forces intent to communize the globe in order to take from Americans and give to "the rest." This framing allows patriots to paint their attempts to shore up white privilege as something larger—work on behalf of capitalism and the freedom it presumably portends. Such a framing not only buttresses notions of cultural and racial superiority in safe, acceptable coding, but it also positions class-based critiques on shaky "moral" ground, further obfuscating the role of class in the movement's identity politics.

It is important to note here that the specter of Vietnam is never far from the surface and that its context provides added resonance for these interpretations. Many of the patriots I interviewed were veterans of the Vietnam War and most felt abused by their experience there and were skeptical of the government dedication to winning the war. As one of my informants succinctly put it, "I smelled a rat!" Patriots who were veterans were also angry at what they perceived as a lost chance. Unlike their fathers, who fought in World War II, they were given no hero's welcome and had few battles or successes to point to in their time in Vietnam. Fighting "communism" at home, then, no matter how paradoxical it may seem, gives them a proverbial second chance.

Third, while much of the whiteness scholarship considers investment in whiteness as it affects working-class politics in traditional urban, factory settings, many of today's important class struggles occur in rural America. As Osha Davidson (1996) notes, the American farm crisis of the 1980s devastated much of rural America. Many of its small towns now display poverty, suicide, and infant mortality rates as high as those of any inner city, leading Davidson to label America's breadbasket a "broken heartland" and a "rural ghetto." The neoliberal policies that set the crisis in motion replaced a farming system dominated by small and medium-sized farms with one dominated by agribusiness. These changes and the politics that arise from them necessitate that we examine how investment in whiteness may divide the working class along lines of race in rural contexts and, specifically, around issues of land and access to the livelihood it affords.

The Patriot Movement provides an important case through which to examine the politics of land. The movement's base is largely rural and the issues around which patriots mobilize frequently concern land and livelihood (Abanes 1996; J. Dyer 1997). Patriots in the intermountain West, for example, have made unrestricted access to Bureau of Land Management lands a battle cry in ranching communities stretching from New Mexico to Montana and have vigorously fought new regulations while also obstructing the enforcement of existing ones (Kenworthy 1995a; Pankratz 1996). The importance of looking at land-based struggles is perhaps most striking, however, when we consider that the Patriot Movement gained significant momentum from the farm crisis of the 1980s. As the research suggests, farmers in danger of foreclosure were easily mobilized because of their dire economic situations, yet their "patriot"-inspired responses to the crisis proposed racist and anti-Semitic "solutions" rather than class-conscious ones (Diamond 1995; J. Dyer 1997). Indeed, patriots' racist solutions protected the boundaries of whiteness but not of their farms. Moreover, as the movement expanded beyond the material and metaphoric confines of the farm crisis, these racist solutions were applied to a host of other land-based issues, some of which had little to do with class-based grievances. As chapter 7 illustrates, this is the case in Kentucky, where patriots have mobilized against the creation of a biosphere reserve in the southern portion of the sate. The reserve was created on previously protected land and has implemented no restrictions on surrounding private property, yet patriots have used the issue to mobilize cultural anxiety about foreigners, telling locals that "outsiders" will seize their land.

WHAT TO DO ABOUT THE WHITE WORKER?

As the above discussion illustrates, patriots find themselves on an identity fault line. Patriots have one foot solidly grounded in privilege. Their dominant positions in terms of their race, gender, and sexuality afford patriots enormous social capital and privilege. Yet patriots also have a foot solidly placed in the working class. Their position as workers renders them powerless to the mandates of the corporate profit margin. In short, while white workers have long protected the privileges associated with their whiteness, their status as workers leaves open the opportunity for their mobilization along class lines.

The question, of course, is how to encourage white workers to abandon their attachments to white privilege and to unite with workers of other races. Not surprisingly, there are varied positions on this matter and a vigorous debate has arisen to address the question. The debate is largely cast between two sides—those who call on whites to "disidentify" with whiteness and those who calls for the reconstruction of whiteness. I begin my discussion with the disidentification side of the argument, also known as the abolitionist paradigm. As I describe below, this perspective was part and parcel of the early theoretical ideas developed in the whiteness literature. The reconstructionist perspective came later, arising largely as a response to the problems identified with disidentifcation.

Scholars who call for disidentification argue that whites must learn to become "race traitors." In short, whites must actively disidentify themselves as white. They should stop calling themselves and others white and they should protest their categorization as whites by others. By doing so, they disassociate themselves from a category that not only bears them unearned privileges, but also does so at the expense of others. This perspective is fundamentally based on the belief that whiteness is an empty category, that it does not signify cultural practices, linguistic similarity, or a common experience as other racial categories do. Rather, whiteness is given form by its normativity and the oppressive social relations that develop from it. Only when white workers abandon their attachment to race can they begin to see how racism oppresses minorities and how their attachment to whiteness masks their own, class-based oppression. As Roediger (1994, 13) notes,

> The rejection of racial oppression by white workers must arise not just out of common participation in class, or even antiracist, struggles alongside Blacks, but also out of a critique of the empty culture of whiteness itself. Rejection of whiteness is then part of a process that gives rise to both attacks on racism and to the very recovery of 'sense of oppression' among white workers.

Disidentification is now widely accepted in the whiteness literature as a necessary precursor for class politics that can extend beyond rare and isolated incidents of cooperation. This perspective has sufficient following to have formed its own journal, *Race Traitor*, which is coedited by one of the earliest and most important whiteness scholars, Noel Ignatiev (see Ignatiev and Garvey 1996, a compilation of selected articles from the journal).

The abolitionist paradigm is not, however, without problems. A growing body of scholarship has taken it to task, arguing that whites are unlikely to mobilize around disidentification if there is nothing "to rally around or to affirm" in its place (Kincheloe and Steinberg 1998, 21). Such scholarship argues that whiteness as an identity must be reconstructed in ways that allow all whites, whether working class or wealthy, to join antiracist struggles without abandoning their identity in the process. Inherent in this perspective is the idea that whiteness as a category is not empty—it contains cultural and historical characteristics, only some of which are oppressive in nature. As Newitz (1997, 148) notes,

> While whiteness is undeniably linked to a series of oppressive social practices, it is also an identity which can be negotiated on an individual level. It is a diversity of cultures, histories, and finally, an inescapable physical marker. Even if we understand whiteness to be something like "dominant culture" what can we say about white women, white homosexuals, white Jews, white low-status men, and the white poor? These groups have certainly not unanimously experienced whiteness as a ticket into the ruling classes. What then, are we asking a white person to do when we ask her to abolish her whiteness?

The answer to Newitz's rhetorical question is clear. White workers imbue their whiteness with meaning outside of its ability to oppress, and asking them to abandon these parts of their identity is both unfair and unrealistic. While whiteness scholars discussed here do not cite LaClau and Mouffe (1985), the reconstruction paradigm is consistent with their position that progressive politics should be articulated through rather than against the category. As Mouffe (1995) argues, the goal of the progressive left should not be based on the utopian idea that social differentiation, and the problems that stem from it, can be simply erased. Differentiation is crucial to the formation of all identities. The better project for the left, then, is to consider how to eradicate (or to use Mouffe's term, to agonize) antagonistic us/them identity formations. Indeed, it can be argued that one of the most ironic things about disidentification is that it most benefits those in positions of dominance. White elites are better able to disidentify from whiteness than are their poor counterparts. The status and power afforded white elites by their wealth leaves them plenty of meaning to fall back on. Of late, conservative white elites have even embraced their own form of disidentification. The right wing's largely successful campaign to depict affirmative action and hate crimes legislation as bestowing "special rights," for example, allows whites/heterosexuals to actively ignore targeted discrimination and violence through appeals to a "universality" disidentified from race or sexuality-based privileges (Diamond 1994; Nakagawa 1995; A. Reed 1995). Such invocations are especially insidious because they buttress class and racial privileges without referencing either.

In response to these critiques, some scholars have argued that the oppressiveness of whiteness might be better addressed by attempting to "reconstruct" its meaning. In keeping with the idea that poor whites are crucial to the implementation of a lasting cross-racial class politics, scholars have looked to them for answers. Unfortunately, attempts to reconstruct whiteness have been problematic. In general, while such attempts are mindful of LaClau and Mouffe's entreaty to work through the category, they fail to heed equally important entreaties against antagonism.

Jim Goad's *Redneck Manifesto* provides the starkest example. Goad (1997, 15) begins his tour de force by asking the reader to consider the standard caricature of poor whites, querying ironically,

> Don't you just hate 'em? Every gap-toothed, inbred, uncivilized, violent, and hopelessly DUMB one of 'em? Jesus, how can you not hate 'em? There's no class of people with less honor. Less dignity. No one more ignorant. More gullible. They're a primitive breed with prehistoric manners, unfit for anything beyond petty crime and random bloodletting. Their stunted, subhuman minds are mesmerized by cheap alcohol, Lotto fever, and the asinine superstitions of poor-folks' religion. . . . They breed anencephalic, mouth-breathing children. Vulgarians. All of them. Bottom feeders. They really bring down their race.

Goad starts his book on a satirical note to rustle the reader out of a state of complicity. He reminds the reader that such depictions would deliver scathing critiques if leveled at blacks or other minority groups, yet go unquestioned when used to describe poor whites.

Goad's central argument is that the redneck is today's cultural bogeyman. He is a straw man created by elite whites to obscure their white power and embraced by a white liberal establishment looking to assuage their white guilt in the easiest possible manner. Liberal arguments place the blame for racism on poor whites, displacing their own elite positions beyond the purview of questioning and making specious arguments that do more to obscure power relations than to clarify them. As Goad (1997, 23) sarcastically puts it,

> They simultaneously depict white trash to be as dumb as oak sap, yet able to pull off an intercontinental conspiracy that enslaved most of the melanin-rich world. They flimsily assert that people who can't afford indoor plumbing somehow have a chokehold on the pipelines of global wealth. Rednecks are portrayed as the embodiment of white power, when the only time they're likely to encounter a powerful white man is when the boss barks at them down at the factory.

The answer, for Goad, is to reconstruct the redneck, to embrace him in all his beer-guzzling, Elvis-loving, NASCAR-watching glory. His reconstruction of the redneck, however, is problematic when we examine the category's construction. Goad's redneck reborn is an antagonistic creation, pitted against white elites and liberals of any race or ethnicity and given meaning largely by his anger. For Goad, the redneck is "someone both conscious of and comfortable with his designated role of cultural jerk. While hillbillies and white trash may act like idiots because they can't help it, a redneck does it to spite you. . . . [T]he redneck has the troublesome capacity to make ironic sport of the greater public's repulsion/fascination with him" (84).

Unfortunately, the recovered redneck's anger gives rise to more than mere ironic sport. His anger drives the political solutions of the identity politics Goad constructs for him. For Goad, the redneck manifests the rural and rugged individualism that made the United States great, but that, as the pathway to postliberal society, seems to end in a cultural cul de sac rather than an open space where workers of different races may meet. Goad concludes his book on an optimistic, if sarcastic note, proclaiming that "the cultural grease drippings of the 1960s will no longer be applicable in the twenty-first century. But class politics will" (254). Yet he finishes with a plot line that makes such a cross-racial politics seem unlikely. Indeed, rather than have his redneck reach out across the cultural divide, even while maintaining his feet solidly on his side of it, he sends his redneck back to the hills: "Redneck rural individualism, once thought to be a sure sign of mental retardation, will seem wise in the face of seething overpopulation. There are a lot of first-class philosophers hiding in the hills, too smart ever to come down into the city. . . . Up, up, ye mighty trailer park. The hills are alive with the sound of muskets. . . . Montani Semper Liberi." (255). In short, while Goad's redneck may find personal liberation through some sort of self-actualization, it is unclear where, if anywhere, the cross-racial class politics might begin.

While Goad becomes an unwitting apologist (Brooks 1998), other attempts to reconstruct whiteness ultimately fetishize poor and working-class white culture, turning its material and embodied symbols into a site of consumer culture rather than a space for cross-racial class politics. Art student and part-time performance artist Jennifer Reeder's character, White Trash Girl, provides a useful example. Reeder fashioned White Trash Girl from the dregs of white-trash dystopia. She is the product of an incestuous relationship and a foray into sewer life that began when her mother abandoned her by flushing her down a toilet. And, lest anyone think White Trash Girl does not embody her context, Reeder has also imbued her with toxic bodily fluids. She is, as Reeder describes her, "an inbred biological disaster turned superhero" (Kipnis and Reeder 1997, 118).

Reeder developed White Trash Girl as a form of self-therapy: playing White Trash Girl allows her to performatively grapple with the class contradictions in her own life and how they have been literally written onto her body. Growing up in Ohio, Reeder was a middle-class kid, but never felt fully a part of her class: "I think we were kind of a trashy white family more than a white trash family" (Kipnis and Reeder 1997, 120). Like any middle-class family, Reeder's never went "without" but, as Reeder remembers it, they never quite acculturated the polite banality of their class's trappings: "There was this family fascination with, like farting, and . . . to this day, if our entire family is together, by the end of the night we'll be talking about puking episodes. It's inevitable" (120). By high school, Reeder was also a confirmed anorexic and a bulimic.

While anorexia is generally associated with the upper middle class, Reeder believes that the symptoms of anorexia can and do "speak" across the class spectrum. By starving herself, an anorexic may aspire to the thin bodies of the class elite or, as in the case of Reeder, rebel against them by (un)consciously embodying the grotesque that governs its lower rung.

According to Reeder, her developing ideas about the relation of class positionality and the body led her to create White Trash Girl. By creating an improper body as a character in her own rite, and performing her for the art world, Reeder wants to confront class biases and, by her presence, make the art world do the same. Mining white-trash culture provides a provocative opportunity—few want to talk about class, yet even fewer want to admit that such distinctions exist within white culture. As Reeder notes, "I've found people at my school who really are into it, but I've also found plenty of people who are offended that I'm even talking about white trash. It's like they don't even want to acknowledge that there's this aspect of white culture that exists" (Kipnis and Reeder 1997, 127). This is especially the case in the art world, where professors and aficionados alike are, in Reeder's words, "prissy" and "PC." Striking unease among this set is her ultimate goal, because it works to destabilize the apparent unity of whiteness and encourages whites, especially those who did not grow up wealthy, to embrace their class backgrounds rather than trying to erase them.

While Reeder's intentions are progressive, it is unclear how her character will inspire such self-reflection, let alone foster a cross-racial politics based in class. Indeed, Reeder's character seems more intent on creating havoc for havoc's sake than on "doing politics." Indeed, Reeder (1997, 118) describes White Trash Girl as an "anti-hero" and gives her little beyond her rage to work with:

> She's also kind of an anti-hero. She doesn't always fight for truth and justice, she might get into a fight with the fry guy at McDonald's who's been harassing the girl who runs the takeout window. Or she might get into a fight with some guy who shoves her on the bus, or she might get into a fight with other superheroes, like Postmodern Girl. You can't pigeonhole White Trash Girl—she's very unpredictable.

While White Trash Girl may be personally empowering for Reeder, like the redneck for Goad, the character she has resurrected is more boundless rage than channeled anger, more antipolitics than politics. Anger is a necessary step in the reclamation of class by whites, but alone it is not necessarily progressive. Reeder's character provides a pressure release, but it fails to fundamentally push it forward. And so constructed, it stands ready for consumption by mainstream whites who can "get a bit of the other" (Bondi 1990, 1993; hooks 1992) while also using such a depiction to reaffirm their notions of superiority and dominance. Finally, Reeder's failure to align White Trash Girl with any collective (even with other performative superheroes) seems to contrast the very politics she hopes to foster through her performance. Indeed, it is hard to understand how any collective politics could emerge from such an individualized celebration of "trashiness."

While I find neither Goad's nor Reeder's attempt to reconstruct whiteness successful, I believe that the reconstructive paradigm is both theoretically sound and politically practical—two characteristics I find missing in the abolitionist perspective. As the empirical portion of this book illustrates, white workers are looking for categories through which to act politically. Yet in the limited landscape of class politics and with the continued presence of white supremacist categories of action, they choose neither, reaching instead for more generalized categories, such as that of the patriot. The patriot category allows them to deal with their multiplicity as social actors. Through the patriot category, white workers are able to address their race-based anxieties, their disquiet over "declining" morality, their worry over their place in the economy, and their anger at a state they see as oppressive.

Perhaps the greatest irony of the Patriot Movement is that it represents a right-wing version of LaClau and Mouffe's calls (1985) for radical citizenship based on equivalences between various left positions. Unfortunately, while the various constituencies of the left have largely worked in separation from one another, the right has actively linked a wide variety of social positions and causes. Indeed, as the following chapter will illustrate in greater detail, there are institutional links between militias, fundamentalist churches, and mainstream Republican politicos and these links are increasingly entwined through discourses of patriotism.

Three things are particularly troubling about theses links, especially as they concern left politics generally and the role of white workers within it more specifically. First, and as noted in chapter 2, this right-wing chain of equivalence now includes class positioning within its ranks. That Pat Buchanan now talks about class politics as much as his Democratic counterparts do provides a sobering illustration. The articulation of class through the patriot category, however, tends to erase its liberatory potential. Second, by acting through broad categories like "patriot" and "constitutionalist," the link in the chain denoting whiteness is rendered invisible, yet unlike the effacement of class, that of whiteness affords the Patriot Movement power. Patriots acting on behalf of race-based concerns can see themselves as acting on behalf of nation and country. This discursive coding makes the defense of white privilege "palatable" in a post–civil rights era, where few whites are comfortable publicly claiming racial supremacy, although many are willing to legitimate the protection of white privilege by casting such actions as defense of nation. Finally, although differences are recognized between right-wing positions—between, say, the pro-lifers and the Second Amendment types—the chain itself is essentially cast, defined in opposition to a variety of left-wing causes, from gay rights to black power, environmentalism, and feminism. The essentialist casting of this macrocategory of patriot means that its various others are considered antagonistically, as threatening and worthy of destruction.

Given this configuration, I believe the true reconstructive work for the progressive left is not on the category of whiteness but rather the macrocategory of patriot, through which both whiteness and class are rendered invisible, to regressive effect. While such a politics may seem impossible, or nearly so, it is important to remember, as identity theory reminds us, that no category is fixed through time and space. All categories are open to meaningful intervention. The category of patriot is no exception. And, despite the bleak forecast, there are bright spots on the horizon, instances where such a politics is currently under construction. I will, however, ask the reader to wait until the final chapter to consider these alternatives.

NOTE

1. While it is difficult to determine patriots' sexuality with the same ease that one may surmise their race or gender, it is reasonable to assume that patriots define themselves as heterosexuals (even if some may partake in same-sex sexual practices). Indeed, many patriots are members of fundamentalist churches (or other similar sects) that believe homosexuality is a sin.

4

Out of the Rubble: A Brief History of the Patriot Movement

On April 19, 1995, Timothy McVeigh parked a rented Ryder truck in front of the Murrah Federal Building in downtown Oklahoma City. A few minutes later, the bomb McVeigh had placed inside exploded, destroying the building and killing 169 people inside it. Countless others were seriously wounded.

Seventy-eight minutes after the bombing and sixty-six miles north of Oklahoma City, state trooper Charlie Hanger pulled Timothy McVeigh over on a routine traffic stop—his car was missing the back license plate. Driving a vehicle without plates is a minor offense in Oklahoma. The driver is usually ticketed and allowed to continue on his or her way. While Hanger was talking to McVeigh, however, he noticed a bulge under his clothing that looked like a handgun. Hanger arrested McVeigh a few minutes later for carrying a concealed weapon, which Oklahoma state law prohibits (S. Reed 1995). While McVeigh was in lockup, officers also discovered that his 9 mm Glock was loaded with illegal "cop-killer" bullets. It would take more than a week, however, before the various federal agencies investigating the case would definitively link McVeigh to the bombing (Pertman and Howe 1995).

In fact, while McVeigh sat in prison, the Oklahoma State Highway Patrol, working off an all-points bulletin, was searching for a brown pickup truck with three "Middle Eastern suspects" last sited in Oklahoma City (Gorov 1995). On- and off-the-record sources in Washington also implied an "Arab connection." They cited the sophistication of the bomb as an Arab marker and they speculated that the location of militant Islamic groups in Oklahoma made the otherwise benign federal building there a target (Holmes 1995; Quinn-Judge 1995). The media did little to quell the rumors. In the immediate wake of the bombing, most journalists uncritically reported the speculations as fact (Gorov 1995). Within the hour, television pundits were debating which Arab group was the most likely perpetrator.

While the government and the media blamed "Arabs" in the bombing's immediate aftermath, it soon became clear that the perpetrator was home-grown. The chagrin of commentators (if they expressed any at all over the news) soon turned to astonishment. As Stock (1996, 1) notes,

> How simple it was in those first hours to presume that such an unthinkable atrocity was created by people from outside the United States. . . . but then came the reports that the alleged perpetrator of the bombing seemed to be as much a representative of America's heartland as the victims were. A small-town boy, a Gulf War veteran—white skinned, blue-eyed, cleancut, and well shaven even as he marched under heavy guard in orange prison clothes—he seemed as an old army buddy described him, "so gullible, so vulnerable, just kind of a nerd."

For some, however, despair over the bombing was not accompanied by surprise or shock. Rather, it was met with the sinking sensation that, some-how, what had happened had been inevitable. Morris Dees, cofounder and chief trial counsel of the Southern Poverty Law Center (SPLC) in Montgom-ery, Alabama, was one of them. In early 1994, after the center's researchers uncovered links between white supremacists and the emerging Patriot Move-ment, it established the Militia Task Force to track antigovernment militias. By October 1994, the center was sufficiently worried about the threat the movement posed that it sent then Attorney General Janet Reno a letter of warning, written by Morris Dees (1996, 105):

> On behalf of the Southern Poverty Law Center and its supporters, I urge you to alert all federal law enforcement authorities to the growing danger posed by the unauthorized militias that have recently sprung up in at least eighteen states. . . . we have substantial evidence that white supremacists are infiltrating the leadership of these organizations. In our view, this mixture of armed groups and those who hate is a recipe for disaster.

In this chapter, I detail the history of the Patriot Movement. For most Americans, the Patriot Movement seemed to emerge out of the rubble of the bombed-out federal building, but as Dees's letter indicates, the creation of a Timothy McVeigh does not happen overnight. The movement that spawned McVeigh had been fomenting for almost twenty years (Davidson 1996; J. Dyer 1997). Catherine Stock (1996) has even argued that violence against the government is a recurring trend in American politics, something that has been with us since the earliest days of settlement. I begin this chapter by placing the Patriot Movement in this larger historical context. I then turn to the specific events that led to its emergence and discuss the factors that contributed to its political form.

The history of this violent movement is by no means a clear-cut story. Indeed, the differing rationales for analyzing the movement (some politically motivated, others academically oriented), the varied questions asked by researchers, and the diversity of analytic perspectives employed by them create a messy picture. In this disparate literature, two common themes do stand out. First, the movement's emergence is directly related to the ongoing dismantling of the modern welfare state by neoliberal "reforms," especially in rural America. These reforms, when coupled with the expansion of state militarization efforts focused internally, create a ready context for rural anger at the government. Second, while a distinct political economy underlies the formation of the movement, its political form is due in large part to the mobilization efforts of far-right groups, who outnumbered their progressive counterparts. The importance of these early mobilizers to the movement's current form highlights the open nature of social action against globalization and the need for intervention on behalf of progressive activists.

A RECURRING TREND

Despite the collective amnesia of the American public on display after the bombing, political violence against the government is nothing new in the United States. This is especially the case in rural America. Despite the rural idyll's privileged position in the American psyche, political violence in rural America has long simmered beneath the surface and has periodically bubbled over as serious conflict. In the pre-Revolutionary era, for example, the Regulators, a vigilante army of farmers in upland South Carolina, wreaked havoc on Native Americans, vagabonds, "uppity women," and escaped slaves, all the while thumbing their noses at nervous colonial authorities stationed in the port cities (Stock 1996). In the 1790s, whiskey rebels, first in Pennsylvania and later in Kentucky, Ohio, and North Carolina, organized tax boycotts of the newly imposed whiskey tariff, kidnapping and terrorizing tax collectors to demonstrate their resolve (Slaughter 1986). During the early days of the Great Depression, farmers also resorted to violence as conditions rapidly deteriorated. In Le Mars, Iowa, farmers associated with the Farmers' Holiday Association kidnapped a judge, beat him severely, and threatened to kill him if he signed any more foreclosure orders. As Stock argues, "Modern rural radicalism is thus hardly a new-fangled idea or a fly-by-night phenomenon. Instead, it follows an abundant, meaningful, and 'all-American' heritage" (Stock 1996, 5).

What makes these acts of political violence analytically cohesive (across time and place) is the common resentment of the federal government that undergirds them. Scholars have posited a variety of reasons for such rancor. An enduring school of thought, known broadly as American exceptionalism, holds that conditions on the American frontier were unique and led settlers to develop a culture that worshipped individualism, self-sufficiency, and freedom and scorned governing structures that might inhibit them (see Billington 1966 for a good overview). Fredrick Jackson Turner's 1893 "Frontier Thesis" provides the most recognizable example of exceptionalist thought in American history. Turner hypothesized that the frontier served as a safety valve for the United States. Entrepreneurial spirits, he argued, could always set out for the Western frontier. The "empty" land and limited government presence they found there facilitated cultural innovations that were distinctly American. Today, exceptionalism is largely out of favor in the academy. Scholars argue, for example, that exceptionalism ignores how slavery and the genocide of native groups were crucial to the development of American culture and politics (Gregg 2000). They also argue that exceptionalism ignores the role that immigrants' experience in Old World trade unions played in nation building more broadly (Halpern and Morris 1997). Although exceptionalism is out of favor, one of its underlying ideas, that American culture is somehow distinct in its unyielding suspicion of government, continues to inform academic and popular explanations of rural radicalism (see J. Dyer 1997, for example).

Others scholars have focused on the government's own role in fostering its enduring unpopularity among rural communities. Indeed, in spite of important exceptions, largely reserved to the far edge of the frontier, the government was a real and influential presence in rural America by the late eighteenth century. And, as a variety of scholars have painstakingly documented, it usually favored moneyed interests over and against those of small producers (Goodwyn 1976; Stock 1996; Zinn 1980, 1990). Even intense debates between the founding fathers were moderated by a shared belief that government should protect the interests of the wealthy. As Zinn (1990, 52) notes,

> The founding fathers, whether liberal like James Madison or conservative like Alexander Hamilton, felt the same way about the relationship of government and the wealthy classes. Madison and Hamilton collaborated on a series of articles (The Federalist Papers) to persuade voters in New York to ratify the new Constitution. In one of these articles Madison urged ratification on the grounds that the new government would be able to control class conflict.

Of course, these founding moments do not mean that the government has never acted on behalf of producer constituencies, both urban and rural. American history is dotted with important overtures to its producer classes. The 1863 Homestead Act, for example, opened up thousands of acres to small producers, providing many with the first opportunity they had ever had to own their own land. Yet government actions on behalf of its producer classes have rarely come without ulterior motives or strings attached and, when set in the context of cultural attachments to ideals of self-sufficiency, have made accepting such overtures particularly difficult for rural producers.

Scholars of the Patriot Movement, today's rural radicals, have traced its emergence to similar tensions. In particular, they argue that the emergence of the Patriot Movement is a direct legacy of Roosevelt's New Deal—both in terms of the tenuous alliance it created between rural producers and the state and of the fallout that has ensued from the breakup of this alliance (Davidson 1996; J. Dyer 1997; Stock 1996). While academics have noted the importance of the New Deal to the movement's formation, it is worth noting that many patriots have as well. As I note in chapters 6 and 7, my informants routinely cited Roosevelt's New Deal as the genesis of America's current problems, and they did so with no prodding from me.

Of particular relevance to the case at hand is the Agricultural Adjustment Act (AAA). Roosevelt initiated the program in 1933 in response to the Great Depression. While the entire country suffered from its effects, farmers were particularly devastated by the depression. In the three years that followed the 1929 stock market crash, farmers saw their income drop by a whopping 60 percent (Stock 1996). In the plains states, the debilitating effects of the depression were compounded by the beginnings of a drought that at its height a few years later would be called the dust bowl for the devastation it would wreak on the soils there. The AAA was designed to pull the farm economy out of this downward spiral. Its terms were relatively simple. The government would pay participating farmers a subsidy for keeping portions of their land fallow. The goal was to limit production in order to increase crop prices, thereby bolstering farm incomes to sustainable levels. By limiting production, the government was also giving a nod to small farmers (albeit the largest of them), because, unlike large-scale producers, family farms relied on high, relatively stable prices for their survival.

While desperate farmers signed up for the plan in droves, it was not a magic elixir that would purge rural producers of antigovernment sentiment. Rather, the compact was, as Stock notes, "built on shaky ground" (Stock 1996, 17). Farmers were grateful for the aid, yet like many who accept help in dire circumstances, they resented the implications that came with being recipients of "charity." Accepting government handouts contradicted basic rural values that equated hard work with success and failure with personal weakness. Structurally, it was also chaffing. Farmers accustomed to making their own decisions soon found themselves beholden to government bureaucrats who decided what and how much they could grow. While such decisions were frequently made "in Washington," farmers were often culpable for any mistakes related to them.

Roosevelt's New Deal would govern agricultural policy in the United States for almost fifty years. It would collapse during the farm crisis of the 1980s. Although its breakdown would be hastened in part by events beyond the control of the government, once the crisis hit it was managed in a way that worked against the interests of small and medium-sized producers. Not surprisingly, the farm crisis would reignite the latent malevolence producers felt toward the government. And it would provide fertile ground for the emergence of the Patriot Movement (J. Dyer 1997; Stock 1996).

While rural radicalism usually emerges in response to threats to rural livelihood, the political form it takes has varied through history (Davidson 1996; Marable 1981; Stock 1996). Stock (1996) identifies two prevailing types— producer radicalism and vigilantism. For their part, producer radicals have tended to highlight economic structures that limit rural livelihood and have sought to proscribe structural reforms as solutions to them. During the Populist era, for example, the Grangers, a voluntary organization for farmers, called on the government to reform railroad monopolies over grain distribution and transportation. During the 1873 depression, the Grangers rallied the government to expand the amount of currency in circulation, arguing that shortages in money supply benefited bankers and hurt debtors. The Grangers also combined their economic proscriptions with social ones. Many Granges, for example, rallied for women's suffrage, arguing that women were integral to farm life and should be in political life as well. As the Grangers' example illustrates, violence is not usually a part of producer radicalism. Rather what makes producer radicals *radical* is their message. Producer radicals question the basic assumptions of capitalist economy in the United States and they call for the elimination of the structural advantages enjoyed by moneyed interests.

Vigilante radicals, however, have tended to reply to economic uncertainty with cultural proscriptions and violent tactics (Stock 1996). They have targeted traditional "others" in society, including ethnic minorities, vagabonds, Mormons, Catholics, and Jews, for society's ills. When vigilantes target the government, it is for either extending rights and influence to such groups or for failing to "keep them in line." Indeed, the vigilante's battle cry is to take the law into one's own hands—the implicit assumption being that the government has abandoned it. Vigilante action is not only identifiable by its problematic targeting of the innocent, but also by its alignment with bankers, capitalists, and large landowners, whose class-based interests are, ironically, counter to those of the people who fill the ranks of vigilante "armies." When former Populist leader Tom Watson helped reinvigorate the Georgia Klan, for example, he not only turned his back on his nonwhite Populist brethren, but he also embraced the interests of Georgia's landed and merchant elite.

As Watson's transformation indicates, more often than not rural radicalism has espoused elements of both producer and vigilante forms. Today's Patriot Movement is no exception. Indeed, while many key patriots are notorious for their activity in white supremacist circles, it is not difficult to find patriots rabble-rousing on behalf of traditionally left-oriented causes, such as support for industrial hemp and opposition to industrial hog and chicken farming. In short, while the threats to livelihood provided fertile ground for the emergence of the Patriot Movement, it did not guarantee its political trajectory. Changing political economies require a discursive rendering to give form to the reactions to it. Political response is neither predetermined nor set in stone once established. This is especially important as we consider the emergence of the Patriot Movement in the next two sections. There, I lay out, respectively, the effects of neoliberal reforms in the U.S. agricultural sector and the political mobilization of farmers hurt by them. As I will demonstrate, while farmers had good reason to mobilize along traditional class lines, their mobilization was instead organized along largely cultural grounds, with traditional others such as Jews becoming the targets of their anger. And, as I document, their mobilization through right-wing discourses, rather than progressive ones, is due in large part to the concentrated efforts of right-wing activists to mobilize them.

RURAL RESTRUCTURING

The "farm crisis" is a popular term for the collapse of the family farm in the United States during the 1980s. The term invokes the misery and agony felt by many in rural America during the period, although it is hard to do justice with words to the rawness of their emotions. Put into words and strung into sentences, they fall flat on the page, almost like the farmers' voices did when aired on the nightly news. How do you tell a television cameraman how you feel about losing the farm that's been in your family for five generations? The emotionless monotone that often came out belied the private surge of emotions suppressed for the most public of venues.

I graduated from high school in 1987, during the worst year of the farm crisis. I remember watching the news reports about the farm crisis on television during my junior and senior years. I was a suburban kid in a sleepy southern town. The events in places like Iowa, Oklahoma, and Texas seemed far away to me. What I remember most from those reports was the sense of inevitability the TV anchors conveyed when reporting on the crisis. It seemed as if no one knew exactly why the events were occurring and, once they were set in motion, no one seemed to have any ability to control them.

Although the farm crisis was often presented as inevitable—the result of intangible "market" forces and thus irreversible—the rural restructuring that eventually led to the crisis was planned quite meticulously. These policies, political and economic in nature, mark the beginning of neoliberal reforms in the U.S. agricultural sector. They were designed to slowly undo the liberal pact established between the state and growers during the Roosevelt administration. And, although no one had planned the crisis itself, once it arrived, the Reagan government made a conscious decision not to intervene. Indeed, the political fallout notwithstanding, the crisis eliminated most small and medium-sized producers and paved the way for Reagan's signature "market-driven" approach, applied in this case to the agriculture sector.

Although the crisis occurred under Reagan's tenure, it is important to note that the groundwork for the crisis was laid during the early seventies, when the Nixon administration decided to dramatically increase the volume of U.S. agricultural exports. The decision was made in response to several trends. Politically, Nixon hoped to secure the farm vote for the Republican Party in the 1976 election by helping farmers increase their income. Also, the OPEC (Organization of Petroleum Exporting Countries) oil embargo in 1973 was contributing to a growing trade deficit, which coupled with declining exports for U.S. manufactured goods made agriculture an attractive income generator (Davidson 1996). Substantial increases in productivity, however, meant that farmers would have to "modernize."

To encourage modernization, the Farm Home Administration (FmHA), a government lender, began actively encouraging farmers to take out loans to expand their acreage and use of technology. The driving logic was that larger farms would allow farmers to benefit from economies of scale and, when buttressed by increased technology, from computerized irrigation networks to crop monitoring systems, would dramatically increase output per acre. To encourage wary farmers, the government also established loose qualification guidelines for their loans, ensuring that most farmers were eligible. Also, interest rates were low at the time, providing further incentive to borrow. And, lest any farmers miss the message, Earl Butz, then secretary of agriculture, issued the blunt warning to farmers to "get big or get out" (Davidson 1996, 15).

Not surprisingly, large numbers of farmers applied for the loans. Pleased with the initial momentum, the government expanded its programs. It offered farmers second loans and loosened its qualification standards even further. Indeed, at the height of the boom time, it seemed to some farmers as if the government was throwing unsolicited money their way. Davidson (1996), for example, recounts the story of a farm family in Iowa whose first loan installment came in over the application amount. When the family called the bank to report the error, their loan officer blithely replied, "Don't be foolish, go ahead and use the extra money for whatever you want. You're good for it" (15). The influx of cash and its ready availability to farmers secured the desired effect. Between 1970 and 1981 U.S. grain production increased 20 percent (Davidson 1996).

While the seventies were a boon to farmers and the government alike, the specific policies and "best practices" that accompanied them put farmers in a fragile position. The expansion in grain production by the United States, when coupled with similar rises in Green Revolution countries, was leading to market saturation for grain, depressing its price on the world market. The response, to produce more grain to make up for the shortfall, only contributed further to the depression of prices.

The infusion of capital into the rural economy and the land grabs that resulted also worked to inflate land values artificially and create a bubble effect. In Iowa alone, the average cost for an acre of farmland quintupled during the seventies (Davidson 1996). These sharp spikes in land value increased the value of farmers' equity on paper, making them, in the eyes of lenders, ideal candidates for more loans. In short order, farmers became grossly overextended, and they did so on collateral that was overvalued. By 1985, U.S. farm debt had surpassed the combined debt of Latin America's three largest economies—Argentina, Mexico, and Brazil (Staten 1987). It was, as Staten (1987) notes, the most capital-intensive agricultural system the world had ever seen.

The crisis began in 1979, when the chairman of the Federal Reserve Board, Paul Volker, instituted the first of several sharp interest rate hikes to curb inflation. The effect on farmers was doubly incapacitating. Because FmHA loans carried floating interest rates, farmers saw their monthly payments skyrocket. The intensity of the rate hikes was also devastating. It was not uncommon for farmers to see their loan rates climb 6 percent in four years (Davidson 1996). As rising interest rates led to deflating land values, farmers also saw their principle equity, farmland, dry up. The price "adjustments" were harsh. Preston, Minnesota, for example, recorded the largest one-year drop in history when its farmland dropped in value by more than 13 percent (Staten 1987). In Iowa, the value of the state's farmland decreased by 63 percent in five years. From 1982 to 1985, U.S. farmland as a whole lost $146 billion in value (Davidson 1996).

As conditions deteriorated in farm country, farmers tried a variety of mechanisms to increase their cash flow. Farmers began by eliminating "fat" from their operating budgets. They laid off farmhands, scrapped landscaping and other nonessential expenses, and cut the use of farm vehicles to a minimum to save on gasoline costs. Farmers also cut the "fat" from the family budget, canceling vacations, eliminating eating out, and skipping shopping trips for new school clothes (J. Dyer 1997). As interest rates continued to rise and land values continued to plummet, farmers were forced to make larger cuts. Many found themselves skipping monthly payments on gas and electricity, hoping at least to cover the bank payment.

Not surprisingly, these cuts had ripple effects across the rural economy. The vibrancy of small towns in rural America is dependent on the health of the farms that surround them. When farms are in bad shape, rural towns follow suit. Between 1976 and 1986, for example, small towns in Iowa lost 41 percent of their gas stations, 37 percent of their variety stores, and 27 percent of their grocery stores (Davidson 1996). The farm crisis also depressed ancillary activities, such as grain processing and construction, that rely on healthy farms to survive. The resulting loss of jobs was significant because these activities provided well-paying employment options for non-farmers and secondary wage earners in farm families alike.

The centrality of farms to the surrounding economy also created the context for negative momentum to build once the crisis hit. As farmers cut their discretionary spending, shops and businesses in nearby towns reacted by laying off workers to adjust to declining sales. Yet, because many of these laid-off workers were from farm families, their income took on added significance during hard times. The loss of their income led to even more trimming in farm family budgets, which further depressed shop revenues and eventually led many stores to close their doors for good.

A downward spiral also built around land values. In general, the first farmer to default in an area set the stage for reassessing the land values on neighboring farms. Not surprisingly, the bids for the first farm in an area to go down were usually well under its assessed value before the crisis. And the sale of that first farm, at deflated values, depressed the value of farms surrounding it (Staten 1987). Rural banks watched these foreclosures with worry—at a rural bank most loans are backed by land-based collateral—and they usually responded by requiring neighboring farmers to produce more collateral to secure their existing loans. To keep their loans afloat, farmers had no choice but to "cough up" more land and machinery for collateral, yet as more and more farmers succumbed to default, land values continued to slide. Bankers, at this point worried about their own liquidity, reacted by putting on the squeeze, forcing even more collateral from farmers. Eventually, even a farmer who had made all his payments could run out of collateral, and bankers, hoping to avoid default, would declare the farmer's loan "insecure" and require him to turn over his farm (Staten 1987).

While producers for the global market will always be subject to its ebbs and flows, it is important to note that the majority of farmers' problems stemmed from government policy rather than the natural flux of the market. In fact, while lowering grain prices can produce a bad year for farmers, lower prices are not sufficient to lead to widespread farm failure. The overextension of farmers was, however, crucial to farm collapse, because it placed farmers in a precarious position vis-à-vis interest rate fluctuations. And, as I note above, the Department of Agriculture, government lenders, banks, and even university agricultural extension agents actively encouraged farmers' overextension, even going so far as to warn naysayers to get out of farming. Yet, when the crisis began, the government did little to stop it. The first significant aid package for farmers, the 1986 Farm Bill, appeared six years into the crisis. Moreover, the programs for debt relief within the bill, which would have helped farmers keep their farms, were so poorly advertised that most farmers never knew they existed (J. Dyer 1997). In some cases, the government even seemed to be working against farmers. During the height of the crisis, the Reagan administration cut funding for rural mental health care, even though rural suicide rates were on the rise and the need for care was self-evident (J. Dyer 1997).

By the end of the 1980s, approximately one million family farms had been lost to foreclosure (J. Dyer 1997). Many of the foreclosed farms were not, however, purchased by other small and medium-sized farmers. Rather, nonfarmers purchased almost half the available land, with two of the largest purchasers being insurance giants and farm-management companies (Davidson 1996). Indeed, while the personal crises associated with farming tended to make the news, the most significant result of the farm crisis was the underlying structural changes it enacted in U.S. agriculture. Today, approximately 75 percent of U.S. farmland is owned by the top 5 percent of landowners, while 78 percent of owners control, in total, only 3 percent of the available land (Davidson 1996). As Davidson notes, land consolidation in the United States today is worse that it was in Cuba "on the eve of the Revolution" (35).

While a marxist revolution is highly unlikely in the United States (especially considering the lack of a sustained class-based politics), a growing inequality exists in rural America, as these data show. When the winners and losers in this battle are considered in light of government inaction on behalf of small farmers, these data may also be read as an indication of the government's approval of the structural changes that were occurring.

Certainly, most farmers "read" the situation that way. While small farmers sneered at corporate farming, they held a special disdain for the government for giving corporate farms the advantage. And some chose to launch their own social movement against the government because of it. In the next section, I describe how this quite legitimate rural anger, especially among farming communities hit hard by the farm crisis, was mobilized into the Patriot Movement.

POLITICAL OPPORTUNISTS

To date, there has been little sustained analysis of the mobilization of the Patriot Movement—that is, the process by which a good number of otherwise law-abiding farmers became radical-minded patriots. This is not to imply that scholars have not written on the Patriot Movement (many have), but when compared with the volume of material written on other contemporary social movement mobilizations, from the gay rights movement to the religious right, what we have is at best a sketchy picture. The majority of mobilization accounts that do exist come from watchdog groups such as the Center for Democratic Renewal, Political Research Associates, and the Southern Poverty Law Center (see Dees 1996; Junas 1995; Levitas and Zeskind 1986; Mozzochi 1995; Zeskind 1985). Given the conventions of the watchdog trade, watchdog accounts are based on firsthand data, such as interviews with patriots and their potential recruits, observations of patriot meetings, and collection of their propaganda. The explanatory power of such work is limited, however, by the mission of these organizations. In the rush to expose, researchers often overlook important nuances. In his account of the militia movement, for example, Morris Dees (1996) spends a lot of time exposing the nefarious tactics of patriot mobilizers, yet comparatively little examining why people join patriot groups in the first place or how progressive options might be formulated for them.

Journalists have also contributed to our general knowledge about patriot mobilization. Perhaps the two best accounts are Joel Dyer's *Harvest of Rage* (1997) and Osha Davidson's *Broken Heartland* (1996). These studies are also based on in-depth interviews and participant observation. Their research, however, is limited by the narrow scope of their analyses within farming communities. While the movement began in farming communities, its meteoric rise during the early 1990s was accomplished largely by mobilization campaigns focused outside of farm communities.

Since the Oklahoma City bombing, academics have also shown an increased interest in the Patriot Movement and its mobilization. Unfortunately, most academic accounts of the movement's mobilization are highly generalized and rely on secondary sources (e.g., Castells 1997; Kirby 1997; Sparke 1998; Steinberg 1997). The only academic account of the Patriot Movement to rely on extensive fieldwork within patriot communities is James Aho's study (1990) of Idaho patriots, *The Politics of Righteousness.* Using social movements theory, Aho argues that the Patriot Movement is not a grievance-driven movement. Rather, he argues that its emergence and continued mobilization are the results of resource mobilization—a process by which potential converts make rational, often conscious, decisions about whether affiliation with a group will further their interests. Aho also finds that mobilization tends to work through existing social networks. In his sample of patriots in Idaho, he found that having a family member or close friend in the movement was the primary factor influencing people's decisions to affiliate with a patriot group. Friends and coworkers were the second- and third-most influential factors respectively. Aho also discovered that the social bond between recruiter and recruitee was a necessary precursor to an intellectual attachment to patriot ideas.

Unfortunately, Aho's study has not been reproduced and tested in other settings. Thus the literature on the movement, with the exception of Aho's study, does not address the movement's mobilization in the parlance of new social movements theory. In fact, most studies do not identify the Patriot Movement as either a grievance-based movement or the result of resource mobilization. Rather, most tend to blend these frameworks in their analyses without making reference to either. Many studies, for example, highlight the importance of the farm crisis to the (re)emergence of the far right, yet they also overwhelming attribute the farmer to patriot transition to sophisticated mobilization campaigns undertaken by savvy right-wing agitators who provided "answers" and "solutions" for farmers (Abanes 1996; Davidson 1996; Diamond 1995; J. Dyer 1997; Levitas and Zeskind 1986; Zeskind 1985).

Given this confused context, in this section I do not use social movement's terminology (grievance or resource mobilization) to describe accounts of patriot mobilization. To do so would be irresponsible (it would require placing a theoretical framework onto others' data sets) and presumptive (I do not have access to these studies' survey instruments, so I am unable to ascertain how or even whether certain theoretical questions may be answered from them). Instead, in this section I focus on what the majority of patriot studies focus on—the role of right-wing mobilization campaigns in the movement's emergence. And, in contrast to most watchdog accounts, I emphasize the lessons progressives can draw from them.

As a variety of researchers note, when the farm crisis began, a plethora of right-wing groups, including the Posse Comitatus, the Populist Party, the Liberty Lobby, and the Aryan Nations, descended upon rural America. They were accompanied by unaffiliated but well-known right-wing gadflies such as Lyndon LaRouche and David Duke. Scholars, activists, and watchdog groups generally agree that the right viewed the crisis opportunistically. "Mainline" groups such the Liberty Lobby saw the farm crisis as a way to bolster their membership rolls, which were in decline by the early 1980s. That farmers were largely middle class and law abiding made them an especially attractive catch. They could provide legitimacy that more traditional converts (such as the unemployed, loners, or petty criminals) could never give to the cause. More radical groups on the right were also interested in farmers. Many of these groups had formed during the seventies in response to what they saw as the mainline right's overreliance on "above board" tactics and its refusal to launch an all-out race war (Daniels 1997). To these new, more radical agitators, distressed farmers, with nothing left to lose, seemed like ideal recruits for battle.

While there are important differences between the tactics of traditional white supremacists and their more radical brethren, both segments of the right appear to have agreed that the supremacist cause required some repackaging. Rather than delivering their traditional message, right-wing agitators decided to package their racist message within an antigovernment framework. In the context of the farm crisis, this framework had obvious resonance. Farmers felt abandoned by a government that had cajoled them into mechanizing and expanding, and even warned them to "get big or get out," yet stood by and watched as expansion backfired.

Although a variety of right-wing agitators launched mobilizing campaigns in crisis-stricken areas, research indicates that the Posse Comitatus had the most success (Diamond 1995). The first Posse chapters were founded in the late 1960s by William Gale and Mike Beach on the West Coast (Zeskind 1985). The Posse has its roots in the racist religion of Christian Identity. Identity is an Americanized form of British Israelism, which holds that the lost tribes of Israel settled in Great Britain and other parts of Northern Europe. William Gale and the Aryan Nations' Richard Butler were both early followers of Wesley Swift, a Klansman who popularized British Israelism in the United States during the 1940s (Diamond 1995). In its American context, Identity followers argue that the settlement of North America by the lost tribes of Israel makes the United States a Jewish homeland and its white, Anglo-Saxon Americans the "true" Jews. The real Jews are viewed as frauds and impersonators and, along with other minority groups, are considered a subhuman species. Some identity groups even refer to those of African origin as mud people (Stern 1996). In the late sixties, Gale and Beach melded Identity with a political philosophy that views the county as the highest level of legitimate power, thus the name Posse Comitatus, Latin for "power of the county" (Diamond 1995).

Posse leaders were successful at mobilizing farmers for a variety of reasons. At a fundamental level, and in the context of the ensuing crisis, posse leaders offered farmers an "invitation to live" (J. Dyer 1997). These invitations to live stood in stark contrast to the "invitations to die" that otherwise engulfed farmers during the crisis. As rural psychologist Glen Wallace explains it,

> [T]he invitation to die [comes] from others in our lives. A spouse strikes out because of heavy stress, the equipment dealer repossesses the equipment, and the land bank forecloses on the land. The lenders announce publicly in the newspapers that you have failed. Embarrassed and humiliated, you withdraw from all community activities and go into hiding. Where can you go and what can you do? There doesn't seem to be at this point but one thing to do. Suicide. (Wallace, quoted in J. Dyer 1997, 45)

The invitation to live began simply, by acknowledging farmers' problems as problems, rather than as something to be culpable for, embarrassed by, or ashamed of. Posse leaders might plaster the bulletin boards of the local diner, the town hall, and even the local churches, offering sympathy for the plight of the farmer or bold proclamations that farmers were "getting a raw deal." These sympathetic overtures were soon followed by announcements inviting farmers and other concerned parties to a "town hall" meeting or "Constitutional gatherings" to discuss the problem and potential solutions. At these meetings, activists would build upon their "invitation to live" by proffering an explanation for *why* decent, hardworking men and women were losing their farms. These explanations were a crucial ingredient to the invitation to live. Hard work and self-sufficiency have always been idealized values in rural culture. Within this value system, failure is read as a personal shortcoming and those failing are expected to accept the consequences quietly. Yet, as engrained as this "truth" may be in rural culture, it was hard to reconcile with the larger context in which farmers, expanding their productivity to levels never before witnessed in the U.S. heartland, could still lose their farms. They were further perplexed by the lackadaisical reaction to the crisis by the government. Heeding its advice, farmers had done as they were asked, yet they were now "hung out to dry."

To explain these apparent paradoxes, Posse leaders assured farmers that they had worked hard. Their efforts were fruitless, however, because there were sinister forces at work against them. The government, they claimed, had been secretly hijacked by members of an internationally organized Jewish cabal, whose ultimate goal was to seize U.S. farmland, make slaves of its former occupants, and reap the benefits of free land and labor. Wisconsin Posse leader James Wickstrom's essay "The American Farmer: 20th Century Slave," which blamed the farm crisis on the Jews, was widely distributed throughout the farm belt (Diamond 1995; Zeskind 1985). Posse leaders also took their message to the airwaves, spreading their conspiracy ideas on talk radio programs (Cohen and Solomon 1995).

The Posse explanatory framework was further reinforced by concrete "solutions" farmers could take to save their farms and, while they were at it, erase the corrupting influence of the federal government from their lives. Arguing that the lending practices of "Jewish" banks were exploitative and unconstitutional, Posse leaders showed farmers how to file liens against the property of bankers, judges, and other officers of the state responsible for foreclosure proceedings. While most liens were illegal, they not only delayed the foreclosure process for many farmers, but they also cost those filed against thousands of dollars in court fees. State and county governments also incurred costs related to patriot liens. They had to hire or train employees to root out illegal liens from the system and they had to prosecute the farmers who filed them.

Posse leaders also taught farmers about common law courts. Because Posse ideology holds that the county is the highest order of power, state and federal courts are viewed as illegitimate. That courts were responsible for the legal proceedings related to foreclosures only cemented the suspicion with which they were regarded. Posse leaders instructed farmers to ignore injunctions and other orders from "illegitimate" courts. They also taught farmers how to establish their own common law courts and to use them to try those held responsible for the farm crisis. In common law courts dotting the rural landscapes, local bankers, judges, and deputies were given death sentences for creating or assisting in the administration of "treason" against the Constitution. While these rulings carried no judicial weight, they intimidated those charged and required them to act with extreme caution.

These instructions also created important martyrs in the emerging Patriot Movement. Acting on the general Posse theory about courts, many farmers refused to show up at foreclosure hearings or to recognize the authority of police responsible for initiating farm repossession. The result was a rash of highly publicized shootouts between farmers and police/federal agents. The deaths in quick succession of posse members Gordon Kahl (1983), a North Dakota farmer, and Arthur Kirk (1984), a Nebraska farmer, in gun battles related to foreclosure proceedings created two highly recognizable martyrs for farmers and also reinforced the belief that the government was out to get farmers (Davidson 1996; Dees 1996; J. Dyer 1997). After Arthur Kirk's death, his wife Deloris made the rounds of the informal patriot speaker circuit, retelling the story of what she termed her husband's "execution" (Davidson 1996; Levitas and Zeskind 1986). In the Ruritan clubs and American Legion halls across the Midwest where she told her story, it had obvious resonance (Davidson 1996).

Some right-wing agitators even infiltrated the American Agricultural Movement (AAM), an important lobbying group for farmers. The message of the agitators, that Jewish bankers were to blame for the farm crisis, and their proposed solution, that Jews should be removed from the country, created huge debates within the organization and eventually led to serious splintering within its ranks. After the infighting began, some patriot-inspired AAM factions began holding training sessions on guerilla warfare tactics. One faction even issued a call for recruits to a "farmers' liberation army" (Diamond 1995; Zeskind 1985). While this splintering undermined the unity of the AAM just when it was needed most, these renegade factions obviously gave powerless farmers a palpable sense of strength.

Finally, Posse activists told farmers how they could break all ties between themselves and the federal government (J. Dyer 1997). According to Posse leaders, the Zionist-occupied government had stripped farmers of their "natural citizenship" and the rights attendant to it, subjecting them instead to Fourteenth Amendment citizenship and its onerous obligations. In Posse ideology, anyone born in one of the fifty states is a natural citizen. Natural citizens bear no obligation to the federal government or the laws issued from it. Fourteenth citizens, by contrast, are people who live in the District of Columbia and U.S. territories. Patriots argue federal jurisdiction only applies to these areas. In some patriot circles, African Americans are also considered Fourteenth citizens because they are presumably "granted" citizenship by the Fourteenth Amendment (the Fourteenth Amendment was ratified after the Civil War to prohibit whites from denying freed slaves constitutional freedoms). Posse leaders told white farmers, however, that they had *become* Fourteenth Amendment citizens by accepting contractual arrangements with the federal government. So they could regain natural citizenship, Posse leaders instructed farmers to revoke all "contracts" with the government and told them to tear up their drivers' licenses, throw out their license plates, and stop using their social security numbers. Obviously, such measures offered no material gain for farmers. They did, however, provide farmers a sense of power otherwise missing in their lives. And the racial overtones in the natural citizenship message allowed status-anxious farmers to salve their social anxiety by allowing them to symbolically reelevate themselves over and against a traditional other—the African American.

It is important to note in ending this section, however, that although farmers' desperation was an important ingredient in their mobilization, they were not hapless victims of right-wing rhetoric. Indeed, Davidson (1996) decries what he sees as facile portraits of farmers as unwitting dupes unable to recognize or evaluate racism and anti-Semitism. Bigotry, he contends, runs deep in rural America:

> The Heartland has a dirty little secret. Beneath the warm smiles and blank platitudes about "simple folk" and "real values" lies the same racial and ethnic intolerance that blights American society elsewhere—and perhaps to an even greater extent. The far right didn't create bigotry in the Midwest; it didn't need to. It merely had to tap into the existing undercurrent of prejudice once this had been inflamed by widespread economic failure and social discontent. (Davidson 1996, 120)

While I think Davidson is right to note the role that latent racism among white farming communities played in the emergence of the Patriot Movement, I think it is problematic to imply that racism and anti-Semitism are somehow more endemic to rural contexts than urban ones. Unfortunately, these biases run deep within all strands of American culture. Suggesting that rural people might be more bigoted than their urban and suburban counterparts is also a dangerous road to tread politically. It can lead to essentialist portrayals of rural people as "backwards" and to crudely drawn stereotypes of them. Most importantly, in the context of progressive politics, it tends to foreclose considerations of rural places and people as mobilizable, depicting them instead as a "lost cause."[1]

Indeed, while racism has been a recurring feature of rural radicalism, so too have progressive streams of thought. While right-wing agitators tapped into the latent anti-Semitism of farming communities, there is no reason why progressive mobilizers could not tap into the equally durable history of producer radicalism that Stock identifies as progressive in scope. So understood, the eventual mobilization of farmers into a right-wing social movement is better understood as a mobilizing victory for the right over the left, rather than an inevitable result of a rural mind-set.

Progressives and other left-wing lobbies active during the farm crisis have admitted as much. The right was better funded and better organized. They were also, in many cases, on the ground several years before any concerted progressive movement countered their message in any systematic way. As Leonard Zeskind, who worked at the Center for Democratic Renewal during the farm crisis, notes, "You've got to remember that by 1986 these groups had been very active for seven years. And until 1985 they had been pretty much unchallenged" (Zeskind, quoted in Davidson 1996, 121). Indeed, while their efforts are to be applauded, progressive activists often found themselves on the defensive, trying first and foremost to minimize damages. A 1986 report from the Center for Democratic Renewal, for example, found the organization in the unenviable position of proposing a "catch-up" strategy for progressives. Specifically, the report suggested that:

> The most vigorous defense of democratic ideals and principles can be realized by adopting a dual strategy of containment and counteraction. Containment can be achieved by educating the public, and by visibly opposing the radical right. Counteraction can be achieved by building coalitions and grassroots organizing. Direct, nonviolent public protest and similar activities that motivate rural residents towards participation in the larger political effort can also be useful. (Levitas and Zeskind 1986, 20)

Given the relatively late start, however, progressive groups often found their gains negligible when compared with those of their counterparts on the right.

THE MOVEMENT EXPANDS

During the early 1990s, the Patriot Movement expanded beyond the farm belt. It experienced phenomenal growth and by 1995 had obtained a national presence. In a survey conducted after the 1995 bombing in Oklahoma City, the SPLC's Militia Task Force estimated that every state in the nation had at least one active patriot group. Some states, including California, Colorado, Florida, Michigan, Pennsylvania, and Texas, had over thirty. Twenty-one states, including Kentucky, also had paramilitary training sites.

Scholars generally agree that the explosion of the Patriot Movement onto the national scene was the result of intensive mobilizing campaigns by right-wing activists charged up from their success during the farm crisis and more than happy to exploit the momentum it had garnered them. Unfortunately, these activists were aided by a series of government mishaps during the early 1990s that in retrospect seem to have been almost tailor-made to illustrate the far right's accusations of a government gone out of control.

The first mishap occurred in the Idaho panhandle, on a remote mountain bluff called Ruby Ridge (see figure 1.2). The panhandle of Idaho has been a magnet for white supremacists and other far-right radicals since the early 1970s, when the Aryan Nations' founder, Richard Butler, established a compound at Hayden Lake. The government has long kept a watchful eye on Butler's compound. As Diamond (1995) notes, Butler has never made a secret of his desire for a "race war." In the late eighties, government agencies stepped up their activities after a string of armed robberies and assassinations were tentatively linked to the group. The BATF tried to infiltrate the group, sending in undercover agents when possible and paying internal informants in other cases. In 1989, one of these informants, Kenneth Fadeley, approached Randy Weaver, who sometimes visited the compound, asking for his help in obtaining several sawed-off shotguns. Weaver agreed to get the guns for $300. In October, when Weaver delivered the requested weapons, BATF agents arrested him. While he was in custody the agents offered Weaver a deal. If Weaver would inform on the activities at Butler's compound, the BATF would drop the charges against him. Weaver refused and in 1990 a grand jury indicted him on federal gunrunning charges.

In February of 1991, Weaver failed to appear for his court date. Rather than apprehend Weaver, the U.S. Marshals Service decided to wait for him to descend from his mountaintop home. Ron Evans, the chief deputy marshal for Idaho and the person in charge of apprehending Weaver, said he wanted to avoid a bloody showdown. As he explained to the press, Weaver was well armed and his children could get caught in the crossfire a forced capture would surely produce. He was also, as Dees (1996) notes, likely influenced by his experience in North Dakota nine years earlier. As a marshal in North Dakota, Evans had been present when the local sheriff's department, in conjunction with the Marshals Service, engaged Posse member Gordon Kahl in a fierce gun battle on his foreclosure day. At the end of that gun battle, two marshals were dead and three others were seriously wounded.

While the marshals waited for Weaver to descend from his remote cabin, they conducted routine surveillance of the property to keep abreast of his actions. In August 1992, the service decided to collect information on the immediate terrain surrounding Weaver's cabin in case it eventually would have to apprehend him by force. Wearing face paint and camouflage clothing, marshals crawled through the underbrush near the cabin, mapping out the potential "battleground." Unfortunately, their actions caught the attention of the Weavers' dog, which started barking. Weaver's son, Sammy, and a family friend named Kevin Harris, left the cabin to investigate. Hoping to avoid giving away their location, marshals shot the dog. By that time, however, the younger Weaver and Harris were already halfway to the dog and they returned fire. The gun battle that Evans had hoped to avoid had begun. When it was over, fourteen-year-old Sammy Weaver and U.S. Marshal William Degan were both dead.

After the deadly exchange, the government permitted an all-out siege on the property and sent the FBI in to orchestrate it. The FBI's first act was to make an exception to its standard rules of engagement: agents could now fire on any adult male who was armed, regardless of whether he showed intent to use his firearm. The revisions took effect immediately and the next day FBI sharpshooter Lon Horiuchi killed Vicki Weaver. When she was shot, Vicki Weaver was standing on her porch, holding her ten-month-old daughter and propping the door open for her husband and Harris, who were returning from the outbuilding where Sammy's body lay. Horiuchi later testified that he was aiming at Harris.

Eleven days later, Weaver surrendered. However, there was nothing pretty about the government's victory. An unarmed woman and a fourteen-year-old boy had been killed by government fire. Reports that emerged later about the government's tactics during the siege were also troubling. The day after Vicki Weaver was shot, agents used a bullhorn to bellow out their morning menu, taunting the family whose food supply agents knew was running low (Hull 2001). Agents later testified they were unaware at the time that Vicki was dead, but such tactics garnered little sympathy when considered in light of the siege's result. The revised rules of engagement also came under intense scrutiny, especially given the presence of several children. The report on Ruby Ridge by the Senate Judiciary Committee's Subcommittee on Terrorism, Technology, and Government Information found that agents in the U.S. Marshals, the BATF, and the FBI had abused their power: they made critical mistakes in intelligence gathering, failed to follow protocol for changing the rules of engagement, and were frequently uncooperative with investigators (U.S. Senate 1995b). Several FBI agents were suspended or demoted as a result.

The second government mishap occurred less than a year later, on April 19, 1993, when the government-led siege of the Branch Davidian Compound ended in a fiery mess on the Texas prairie. When it was over, four BATF agents and eighty Davidians had lost their lives. The standoff had begun simply enough in December 1992. Relying on claims of child abuse by former members, as well as evidence that the compound was stockpiling military-style weapons, the BATF set up a surveillance house near the compound to keep track of the group's activities (Gaffney 1995). Agents posed as college students and one of them, Special Agent Robert Rodriguez, established contact with the Davidians' leader, David Koresh, by attending Bible studies at the compound. By mid-February, Rodriguez had acquired sufficient information about possible illegal weapons caches to apply for a warrant.

The BATF decided to execute the warrant on February 28. Fearful of what Koresh might do, agents decided to initiate a "dynamic entry" method to execute the warrants and arrest Koresh (Gaffney 1995). The agency also decided to alert a few people in the local media. Unfortunately, one of those notified, a TV cameraman named Jim Peeler, inadvertently tipped off the Davidians when he asked David Jones (who turned out to be an occupant at the compound) for directions along the road. Jones called Koresh immediately to tell him of the impending arrest (Gaffney 1995).

Rodriguez, who was in the compound when Jones called Koresh, immediately alerted his supervisors. The BATF's tactical coordinator, however, chose to continue with the raid. When the BATF agents entered the compound from a second-floor window, they were met by armed Davidians. A ninety-minute gun battle ensued. Four BATF agents and six Davidians died.

After the raid, the FBI took command of the operation. Initially, the bureau tried to negotiate a surrender with Koresh and within the first few days was able to persuade several adults to leave and to bring some of the children with them. After their initial success, however, the FBI was unable to persuade others to leave or Koresh to surrender. In response, the FBI intensified its efforts. They cut phone lines to the compound (except the one they controlled) and they stopped electricity and water service. They also deployed psychological warfare tactics on the compound in an effort to induce surrender. The government blared loud music and beamed high-intensity lights into the compound at night to disrupt the inhabitants' sleep patterns. One night, they played Nancy Sinatra's "These Boots Are Made for Walking" over and over again. Still, no one came out. Finally, after fifty days of tense stalemate, Attorney General Janet Reno gave the go-ahead to the FBI to enter the compound forcibly to end the standoff.

On the morning of April 19, government tanks began ramming the compound's exterior to open a hole in its wall and provide easier access. It also launched canisters of CS tear gas into the building to force out its occupants. A few hours after the assault began, a fire erupted in a wing of the compound. Within minutes it had engulfed the entire compound, which was made mostly of wood. Only nine Davidians escaped. The remaining seventy-four occupants died in the building.

The aftermath of Waco proved an even greater public relations debacle for the government than Ruby Ridge had. The death toll was higher and included twenty-one children. There was also a public outcry about the overly aggressive tactics employed by the government. Many commentators asked why the BATF chose a dynamic entry method to deliver Koresh's warrant when they could just as easily have served it to him while he was in town on one of his frequent visits to purchase supplies.

In the immediate aftermath, commentators also speculated that the government started the fire. CS gas can be explosive when launched into small spaces and produces symptoms such as gagging, vomiting, and nausea in those coming in contact with it. In 1993, the Chemical Weapons Convention, which was signed by the United States, banned the use of CS gas in military engagements (Gaffney 1995). The FBI vigorously denied starting the fire and accused Koresh of orchestrating a mass suicide and then starting the fire to cover up the evidence. The coroner's report on the bodies, however, which showed that the majority of children died of smoke inhalation rather than gunshot wounds, undermined the FBI's theory (Stone 1993). An independent probe launched in 1999 and headed by former Republican senator John Danforth also found that the government had indeed used "pyrotechnic devices" in the raid and that government employees had misled the American public by not disclosing their use (Vise 2000).

Perhaps most disturbing were the testimonies of the survivors. They maintained that, during the final raid, government agents fired machine guns into the compound from a helicopter (Fifth Estate Production 1997; Thibodeau and Whiteson 1999). While the government has consistently denied doing this, survivors have refused to recant their version of the raid. And, unfairly or not, the confirmation in 1999 that the FBI concealed relevant facts about the use of incendiary devices does little to bolster its credibility.

As they did during the farm crisis, white supremacists and other far-right activists exploited these events and the uproar they created to mobilize potential converts to the "cause." In particular, activists used the U.S. government's handling of both events to further invigorate their claims, articulated during the farm crisis, that the government would use deadly force against its citizens. Right-wing agitators soon discovered that the gun issue would be a highly effective issue around which to mobilize people across the country. They argued that events like Ruby Ridge and Waco could happen anywhere, intoning that no citizen was safe from the government's "jack-booted thugs." They warned that gun control legislation like the Brady Bill was a pretext for disarming the citizenry and that harsher legislation would soon follow. Activists also invoked their theory about an international Jewish conspiracy, although they dropped explicit reference to the Jews. Instead, they warned of an international plot, led by the UN, to seize U.S. weapons and take control of the government. The plot could succeed, they exhorted, because international conspirators had infiltrated all levels of government (Junas 1995; Mozzochi 1995).

Unfortunately, the antigovernment rhetoric right-wing agitators used met a receptive audience. A variety of factors appear to have contributed to this reception. The recession of the early 1990s clearly played a large role. In rust belt states like Michigan, for example, laid-off factory workers were some of the most responsive recruits (Moore 1996). The anger over job loss was compounded by the fear that NAFTA would eliminate even more of them. The increasing frequency of antigovernment sentiment also played a role. By the early 1990s, antigovernment rhetoric was a common theme, not only on the talk radio shows of Rush Limbaugh and G. Gordon Liddy, but in the halls of Congress as well (Cohen and Solomon 1995; Dees 1996). Indeed, the Republican "revolution" of 1994 was premised on the idea that government was inherently bad—not only was it unable to truly help people, the argument went, but in many cases it could hurt them. This context, as Dees (1996, 5) chillingly notes, was

> not missed by the ideological thinkers behind this frightening movement. William Pierce, the author of *The Turner Diaries*, pointed out to his followers in 1994 that "most people aren't joiners, but millions of white Americans who five years ago felt so cowed by the government and [the Jewish-]controlled media that they were afraid to agree with us are becoming fed up, and their exasperation is giving them courage.

As the above quote indicates, the movement's push to the national scale was masterminded, at least ideologically, by people with well-established far-right credentials. Dees (1996) identifies Louis Beam as a prototypical example of the white supremacist turned patriot activist. Although Beam now calls himself a "patriot," he is no stranger to the far right. During the 1980s, Beam was Grand Dragon of the Texas Knights of the Ku Klux Klan and the head of the Texas Emergency Reserve, an armed subgroup within the Klan. Under the auspices of the reserve, Beam and his supporters actively harassed and intimidated Vietnamese fisherman in Galveston Bay, Texas, during the 1981 fishing season. In 1982, the SPLC took Beam to court for violating a Texas law prohibiting the formation of independent military groups in the state. The Texas court found Beam guilty and ordered him to disband his reserve. A few years later, Beam would again encounter the court system when he was charged with conspiracy to overthrow the government. After his trial, in which he was acquitted, Beam retreated to Idaho, largely disappearing from public view.

Nearly a decade later, he would "reappear," calling himself a patriot and peddling his now famous treatise, "Leaderless Resistance," in which he encourages would-be patriots to establish armed cells in preparation for an eventual battle with the government. The treatise is now widely regarded as the blueprint for the movement's spread across the nation. It was used to validate the formation of paramilitary groups and, when "packaged" (along with other materials) and distributed by the well-oiled machine of the Militia of Montana, served as a blueprint for the formation of militias across the country.

White supremacists turned patriots were also careful to legitimize their newly founded militias. Invoking the well-worn Second Amendment clause, "a well regulated Militia, being necessary to the security of a free State, the right of the people to keep and bear arms, shall not be infringed," they argued that citizens' militias were constitutionally mandated. To those who responded that the National Guard fulfills this role, militias countered that the federal government's control of the National Guard invalidates its ability to protect citizens. Indeed, most militia Web home pages carry essays addressing this point. One of the most widely reproduced is Kenneth Maue's essay, "What is the Militia?" As he explains it,

> If the militia is to protect the Citizens against tyranny in government, and if the National Guard was the Militia, the president, being the commander/senior officer of the National Guard, surely wouldn't order the overthrow of tyranny in the government in which he is a part of, no matter how much the people proclaimed tyranny. (Militia of Montana 1999)

In addition to militias, the Patriot Movement would grow to include issue-oriented groups, such as pro–Second Amendment organizations, the Fully Informed Jury Association, home-schooling coalitions, and pro-life alliances. Although these causes are advocated by groups on the mainstream right, patriots generally view them as "soft" on the issues or corrupted by their proximity to Washington. In general, patriot groups tend to support more radical measures than their "mainstream" counterparts. While right-wing judicial groups campaign against the election/appointment of liberal judges, for example, the patriot-inspired Fully Informed Jury Association supports jury nullification. It maintains lists of federal and state laws it considers unconstitutional and instructs potential jurors how to obstruct convictions for those accused of breaking them.

Holding these diverse groups together are usually larger umbrella groups. Umbrella groups tend to have innocuous sounding names, such as Nebraskans for Constitutional Government,[2] a group Davidson (1996) encountered in his research, or Citizens for a Constitutional Kentucky, whose first meeting is detailed in chapter 1 of this book. Most umbrella groups are organized along a town hall format. Citizens hear from patriot leaders and arrange guest speakers and there is usually time reserved at the end of the meeting for attendees to ask questions or offer commentary. The meetings are unfocused in their presentations of the issues. Speakers keep facts to a minimum and concentrate on painting the big picture, introducing meeting attendees to patriot conspiracies and how they play out in the local context. By focusing on the government rather than racial hatred, patriots are able to draw on a larger community of discontent. They are also able to win converts to more hard-core beliefs by introducing anti-Semitic and racist ideals gradually and within the context of a web of interwoven conspiracy theories. The Montana Human Rights Network's Ken Toole describes the process by which people become slowly indoctrinated with racist ideology as "funneling":

At the front end, it's picking up lots and lots of people by hitting on issues that have wide appeal, like gun control and environmental restrictions, which enrage many people here out West. Then you go a little bit further into the funnel, and it's about ideology, about the oppressiveness of the federal government. Then, further in, you get into the belief system. The Conspiracy. The Illuminati. The Freemasons. Then, it's about the anti-Semitic conspiracy. Finally, at the narrowest end of the funnel, you've drawn in the hard core, where you get someone like Tim McVeigh popping out. (Toole, quoted in Stern 1996, 107)

THE BOMBING AND ITS AFTERMATH

Fortunately, the majority of people who join the Patriot Movement do not pop out at the other end of the funnel described by Toole. Indeed, Aho (1990) found that in Idaho adherents to the movement were not guaranteed to move toward increasing radicalism as their tenure in the movement grew. But sometimes all it takes is one person who does to yield the worst-case scenario. On April 19, Timothy McVeigh became that person when he bombed the Murrah Federal Building and killed 168 people.

Although McVeigh was never a member of a patriot group, his links to the movement, and the actions they inspired, were easy to trace. When investigators went through McVeigh's car after his arrest, they found pages from the now infamous *Turner Diaries,* a novel written by white supremacist William Pierce. Pierce's protagonist is a white warrior commanding a guerilla war against the government, which has been overtaken by Jews. There are eerie similarities between McVeigh's bombing plot and the one designed and launched by Pierce's protagonist. Of course, McVeigh's choice of April 19 for the explosion is also highly significant within patriot circles: it was the third anniversary of the government's final raid on the Branch Davidian compound in Waco, Texas. Later court testimony from McVeigh's friends and accomplices also indicate that, while McVeigh never joined any particular groups, he was known to skirt the edges of the movement, attending gun shows, expositions, and the occasional militia meeting.

The bombing generated reams of negative press for the Patriot Movement. And it put its most recognizable leaders on the defensive. Norman Olson, cofounder of the most-organized militia at the time, the Michigan Militia, denied media reports that McVeigh had been a member of his militia and vigorously denounced the bombing as brutal and unnecessary. John Trochmann, cofounder of another influential militia, the Militia of Montana, also offered a public statement in which he condemned the bombing.

Two months later, several well-known militia figures, including Trochmann, Olson, Ken Adams, J. J. Johnson, and Robert Fletcher, testified on behalf of the movement at the "militia hearings" organized by the U.S. Senate (1995a) Judiciary Committee's Subcommittee on Terrorism, Technology, and Government Information. While patriot leaders again denounced McVeigh, they also launched an offensive. One by one, the patriots assembled for the hearings scolded congress for the government's abuses against its people. Some were polite, others were not, but few minced words. As John Trochmann told the panel,

> When government refuses to hold hearings on government-sanctioned abuses and white washes those hearings that are held, when government tampers with or destroys evidence needed to solve crime and now considers the very idea of infringing upon the people's right of freedom of speech, assembly and the right to redress after having destroyed the second and fourth articles, how can senators and representatives ever question the loyalty of concerned Americans without first cleaning their own house? (U.S. Senate 1995a)

Others even expressed indignation when individual senators implied that the Patriot Movement was a cover for white supremacists. They countered, saying the Patriot Movement was for all citizens. A testy exchange between Norman Olson and Republican senator Arlen Specter of Pennsylvania, the committee's chairman, is particularly illustrative:

> *Olson:* May I make a correction for the record, too? Senator Kohl raised a poster a moment ago showing Hitler with his hand raised in the air—so that's a copyrighted poster produced by Jews for the Preservation of Firearm Ownership. It is not the work of some militia organization. So, just to make that comment for the record.
>
> *Specter:* Well, we'll pick up your comment about copyrights and about Jews in a few minutes—
>
> *Olson:* No, sir. I believe you're trying to lay at the feet—you're trying to lay at the feet of the militia some culpability as a responsibility. You're trying to make us out to be something that we are not, much like the press has tried to do over this last year. We are not what you think we are. We are not what the press wants to feed to the American people. We are people who are opposed to racism and hatred. We are people who love our government and love the Constitution. There's been the design in the blueprint for governments around this word, and we're proud of the United States of America. But the thing we stand against is corruption. We stand against oppression and tyranny in government. And we, many of us, are coming to the conclusion that you best represent that corruption and tyranny. (U.S. Senate 1995a)

Despite the efforts of leaders like Trochmann and Olson to defend the militias, and to give its image a makeover, the bombing left an indelible imprint on the movement. In particular, it forced to the fore a variety of contradictions within the movement. The movement's earliest mobilizers were far-right radicals—they held white supremacist beliefs and many espoused violence as an acceptable response to their identified enemy. The "moderated" message espoused during their mobilization campaigns, however, was muted in an effort to draw from a larger pool of potential adherents. This was especially the case among those recruited during the early 1990s. As Junas (1995) observes, many of the people who joined militias and other patriot groups during this time were largely unaware of the white supremacist logic that underpinned the movement's ideology. In the wake of the bombing, these divisions became harder to ignore.

Since the bombing, the movement has witnessed a major bifurcation. Some patriots have chosen to go underground with their message. They plot bombing targets, plan assassinations, and stockpile weapons. Without the worries attendant to attracting more mainstream adherents, underground patriots' beliefs have become more hardened and their rhetoric more inflamed. According to the SPLC, while the Patriot Movement as a whole is getting smaller, violent acts from its underground wing are actually on the rise (SPLC 1998). Other patriots have chosen to remain above ground. These patriots have focused their energies in the political sphere. They have created sophisticated political action networks and are increasingly grooming patriot candidates for local and state offices.

According to the available data, this divide seems to play out in contradictory ways. On the one hand, umbrella groups now find it harder to bring patriot groups together. These groups experience fragmentation or they implode altogether. In 1997, the Theatre Command Militia, an umbrella militia organized to facilitate communication and organization between militias, held its annual meeting in Knob Creek, Kentucky. Before the meeting commenced, however, it erupted in a raucous round of accusations and counteraccusations. Radical elements accused the Theatre's commander of being an undercover agent and called for his expulsion. The commander's supporters countered that the radical elements were tainted by their sympathy to Christian Identity. The meeting concluded with forty hard-core patriots walking out, vowing to start their own organization (SPLC 1998). As I describe in more detail in the next chapter, a similar event occurred within CCK, leading to its dissolution for a period of several months.

On the other hand, the divide between below- and above-ground patriots has tactical merit. It allows patriots to fight for their causes on two distinct fronts—an underground front where anything goes and a political front where change may be accomplished from within government. Without the hindrance of the ideological differences and tactical approaches of the other side, each side is free to pursue its goals relatively unencumbered. Yet, because the magnitude of these differences is minimal to those on the outside of the movement, the movement is more efficient and its overall impact is more significant.

The majority of watchdog reports on the movement since the bombing have focused on the below-ground portion of the movement. This is under-standable given that patriots who go underground tend to become more, rather than less, violent (SPLC 1998). In this book, however, I focus on the above-ground portion of the movement. Above-ground elements continue to provide a mainstream outlet (relatively speaking, of course) for the move-ment's more radical wing. And now that many above-ground patriots are engaging in the political process, lobbying state and federal legislators and in some cases running for office themselves, this outlet takes on heightened significance. Indeed, while radical patriots accuse their "mainstream" coun-terparts of being sellouts and informants, above-ground patriots who engage in politics are quite effective at introducing patriot conspiracy theories to mainstream America and making these notions more palatable to the general public.

I now turn to the Patriot Movement in Kentucky, the empirical focus of this book. In the next chapter, I sketch a brief history of the movement's emergence in Central Kentucky. I then introduce the reader to the patriot umbrella group whose meeting I attended and to the patriots I met there and later interviewed for this project.

NOTES

1. In highlighting an essentialist moment in Davidson's analysis, I do not mean to imply that his entire analysis is essentialist. Indeed, Davidson also painstakingly documents progressive aid workers who acknowledge their relative disadvantage, in terms of financing, resources, and time on the ground. Rather, I see these particular comments as contradictory to the tenor of his work as a whole. I mention them here, however, because this kind of essentialism has often kept even left-wing progressives from actively engaging rural peoples, further increasing the likelihood that they will mobilize along right-wing lines.

2. It was at a Nebraskans for Constitutional Government meeting that Arthur Kirk first heard a guest speaker outline Posse strategies for getting out of debt.

5

Kentucky Patriots

THE RIGHT TO CARRY CONCEALED WEAPONS

Like most states outside of the Midwestern farm belt, in Kentucky the Patriot Movement emerged during the early nineties. Its development there appears to have been self-generated rather than the result of a concerted mobilization campaign by outside agitators. Of course, by the early nineties, far-right organizers had laid much of the necessary groundwork for the movement's low-maintenance expansion. By 1990, patriot agitators had become regulars on the AM talk radio circuit, introducing patriot conspiracies to audiences across the country and providing "evidence" to prove them. In February 1992, Louis Beam penned his now infamous essay "Leaderless Resistance" and within months it was in wide circulation, passed around at gun shows, posted on militia Internet bulletin boards, and debated in antigovernment chat rooms. Two years later, John Trochmann's Militia of Montana was selling inexpensive kits online and at patriot expos, explaining how to start a local militia.

In Kentucky, it appears that citizens there first applied patriot logic to the gun issue. In late 1994 or early 1995, several pro–Second Amendment groups from around the state formed an alliance to lobby for the introduction of a concealed weapons bill in the Kentucky General Assembly (Breed 1995). Some groups, like the Kentucky Coalition to Carry Concealed (KC3), Kentuckians for the Right to Bear Arms, and the Fayette County Second Amendment Preservation Association, were new. Others, like the League of Kentucky Sportsmen and the Kentucky Houndsmen's Association, had been around substantially longer.

While few of these activists at the time publicly defined themselves as patriots, several factors indicate that the drive to have a concealed weapons bill introduced in the General Assembly was inspired by patriot rhetoric.

My conversation with Norman Davis, the founder of Kentuckians for the Right to Bear Arms (KRBA) and now a leading patriot leader in the state, is particularly illustrative. When I asked Davis to sketch the beginnings of the Patriot Movement in Kentucky and his part in it, his responses mirrored many of the "patriot talking points" developed by patriot mobilizers during the early nineties. He told me, for example, that the congressional debates about the Brady Bill propelled him to start his group, adding that "we knew more gun control laws were gonna come." The patriot conspiracy about a UN plot to control the world seems to have infused the group's push to enact pro-gun legislation as well. When I asked Davis *why* people were suddenly concerned about carrying a concealed weapon, he explained, "We started finding out about the United Nations and their gun-control plans for the entire world. Well, what's the first thing you do to fight that crap? Well, of course, you lobby your congressmen, and your senator!"

To get a bill drafted, KRBA and its partner groups began lobbying representatives and senators trying to find a sympathetic ear for the next year's General Assembly (until 2001, the Kentucky General Assembly only met every other year). They found their ally in freshman Representative Robert Damron, a Democrat from Nicholasville (see figure 1.3). He agreed to draft a bill, and to introduce it in the 1996 legislative session.

Damron is a Democrat whose politics mirror those of many Southern Democrats who are sometimes referred to as "Dixiecrats" by their northeastern counterparts. Dixiecrats have never fully embraced the liberal social causes espoused by their party even though they are wary of Republican calls to "reduce big government." Indeed, like Damron, many of them hail from rural areas where residents have relatively conservative social values, yet also rely on government dollars to meet a wide variety of community needs, from Women, Infants, and Children (WIC) program dollars for helping poor mothers to subsidies for farmers. Damron told me when I interviewed him, "My grandfather was a Democrat, my father is a Democrat, my mother is a yellow dog Democrat,[1] and she's gotten worse over the years, but . . . does party mean everything to me? No. Issues mean something to me. If you look at my legislation, I have usually as many Republican cosponsors as I have Democrats." This fluidity among so-called Dixiecrats is especially evident around the issue of guns. Although the Democratic National Convention supports what it calls "common sense" gun control measures, Dixiecrats in state and federal elections have not always followed suit. Indeed, many Dixiecrats support gun rights and argue that these positions merely reflect their constituents' wishes.

Damron is no exception. In numerous interviews he has given about gun rights, Damron has always been careful to describe his support as "in line" with the views of his constituency. In early press interviews about the concealed weapons bill, for example, Damron routinely offered anecdotes about respectable citizens in his district who felt compelled to carry concealed weapons for safety—farmers in isolated areas, businessmen carrying deposits to the bank—even though it was illegal. In a 1996 New Year's Day story in the *Lexington Herald-Leader,* Damron related the story of a seventy-five-year-old woman who had called his office to say she even carried her pistol to church. As Damron explained, "We've got a lot of people out there who are concerned for their safety. They're carrying a handgun now [but] they're illegal" (Estep 1996a). In my interview with Damron several years later, he again presented the bill as reflective of his constituency, telling me, "It started as a grassroots initiative in early '95—people in my district and state-wide as well. They came to me and said, 'You know, this is something we think we need to do for Kentucky.'"

Representative Damron was also keen to highlight his collaboration with constituents as he drafted the bill. In a June 1995 article in the *Lexington Herald-Leader,* Damron told the paper that he was working with a coalition of Second Amendment groups in the state to craft a bill that met both citizens' needs for safety and their concerns for personal liberty (Breed 1995). When I interviewed him several years later, he cited KC3 and KRBA as groups he collaborated with most closely.

After several meetings with KC3 and KRBA, Damron filed a concealed weapons bill on the 1996 General Assembly docket, where it was processed as House Bill 40. The bill proposed to allow Kentuckians over the age of twenty-one to apply for a permit to carry their weapons concealed. Persons with felony convictions, however, were automatically ineligible for permits and those with misdemeanor convictions for the sale or possession of controlled substances, for making terroristic threats, or for fourth-degree assault were barred from obtaining a permit for three years after their arrest date. Applicants were also required to take a firearm education course with the Department of Fish and Wildlife, the Department of Criminal Justice Training, or the National Rifle Association. The bill also stipulated that permit holders were prohibited from carrying concealed weapons into courtrooms, jails, police stations, and local government buildings. An exception was granted to state lawmakers with permits, who were allowed to carry concealed in the House and Senate chambers of the General Assembly (Estep 1996a).

On March 29, 1996, House Bill 40 was signed into law by Governor Paul Patton. Despite opposition from many lawmakers, the State Police Chief's Association, and the general public, Damron's bill faced relatively little opposition and fewer setbacks. This is particularly striking, given that a poll conducted in February of 1996 revealed that a majority of respondents, fifty-two percent, opposed the bill. The poll also found stronger views within the opposition camp, where 42 percent strongly opposed the bill, than in the supporters' ranks, where only 29 percent strongly favored it (AP Wire 1996).

Some opposition did exist, of course. When the bill was reviewed in the House Judiciary Committee, opponents tacked a number of restrictive amendments onto it: persons subject to domestic violence orders would be disqualified, applicants would be required to take a conflict resolution course, and the background check would be extended from thirty to ninety days (Estep 1996b). When the bill reached the house floor, however, Damron and his supporters were able to repeal all of the committee's amendments (Estep 1996c).

In the Senate Licensing and Occupations Committee, where the bill went upon arriving in the Senate, lawmakers were able to add a few provisions, including raising the license fee from fifty to sixty dollars and creating a public record of license holders (Estep 1996d). When the revised bill went back for final approval in the House, it handily passed sixty-nine to twenty-six (Estep 1996e). Riding on his decisive victory, Damron warned his bruised opponents that if the media or other groups abused the public record's provision (which he had opposed) and harassed permit holders, he would introduce legislation in the 1998 General Assembly to repeal it (Estep 1996e).

In reviewing Kentucky patriot history, it is clear that the passage of House Bill 40 was a watershed event for the burgeoning Patriot Movement there. Coming off the success of House Bill 40, the movement's grassroots backers were energized and were no longer shy to invoke the patriot label. Indeed, several of the key leaders in the coalition formed new groups that were easily identifiable as patriot groups. Some, like Charlie Puckett, an independent concealed-carry advocate, did not even wait for the bill's official passage. In late 1995, after the groundwork for the bill's support had been largely laid, he formed the Central Kentucky Militia, likely consolidating several local militia cells to do so. A year later, Norman Davis merged his group KRBA with several other right-wing interest groups to form a political counterpart to the militia called Take Back Kentucky (TBK). Shortly after he formed TBK, Davis also began hosting biannual patriot gatherings on his farm. The April 2001 gathering hosted two hundred patriots (Lovan 2001). These meetings adeptly combine the political (Davis holds seminars on "unpatriotic" legislation coming down the pipeline) with the paramilitary (Charlie Puckett runs training sessions for his militia and its new recruits). These gatherings are also promoted as family friendly affairs. Patriots are encouraged to bring their families, set up camp on the farm, and even enroll their kids in the youth firearms classes offered there.

By 1997, there was a strong enough patriot presence in Central Kentucky for the patriot umbrella group CCK to form. The existence of an umbrella group is generally a good indicator of the movement vibrancy in an area. Established leaders of individual groups usually form them to enable wider recruitment opportunities. Indeed, CCK's organizers, Charlie Puckett and Jim Laughlin, made no bones about their "patriot" roots, telling Cheryl

Powell, the *Herald-Leader* staff writer covering the event, that they were issuing a call to "all good patriots" to attend the meeting. As Charlie Puckett explained it, "You've got the good guys, and you've got the scumbags, the traitors and the patriots. [This meeting's] about education. Be on the lookout for what's coming. If you don't, it's going to bite you" (Powell 1997).

The successes surrounding House Bill 40 also clearly influenced the form that Kentucky's Patriot Movement took as it emerged. While there are patriot underground cells in Kentucky, many people invoking patriot rhetoric there chose from the beginning to operate above ground and, contrary to the popular stereotype, have embraced working within government structures. Indeed, since the passage of House Bill 40, patriots have worked with legislators throughout the state to draft patriot friendly bills, while legislators across the ideological spectrum readily admit their influence in state politics. More recently, there have been patriot candidates in state elections. The most notable patriot election campaign, Gatewood Galbraith's run for governor in 1999, is detailed in chapter 8 of this book.

It is also worth noting that in Kentucky the decision by people invoking patriot rhetoric to operate above ground (rather than below) was clearly given a boost, if an indirect one, by the National Rifle Association (NRA). In his exposé of the group, Jack Anderson (1996) argues that, during the early nineties, the NRA made a conscious decision to establish rhetorical and organizational links with the burgeoning Patriot Movement. These links, it was reasoned, would further the gun rights agenda while simultaneously expanding the influence of both groups.

After Ruby Ridge and Waco, for example, the NRA began invoking patriot rhetoric about government tyranny and the need for an armed citizenry in response to it to sell its gun rights agenda. Perhaps the most recognizable example is an early 1995 fund-raising letter the NRA's executive vice president, Wayne LaPierre, sent the membership. In the letter, LaPierre refers to government agents as "jack-booted thugs" and warns members that "unless we take action today, the long slide down the slippery slope will only continue until there's no freedom left in America at all" (as quoted in Anderson 1996). The NRA also arranged meetings with patriot groups. Just two months before the Oklahoma City bombing Tanya Metaksa, then head of the NRA's Institute for Legislative Action, met with representatives from the Michigan Militia. According to Ken Adams, one the militia leaders present at the time, the NRA requested the meeting.

During the same period, it also appears that the NRA conferred with patriot groups in Kentucky. In June 1995, the *Lexington Herald-Leader* first reported on the coalition of Second Amendment groups working to get a concealed weapons bill introduced in the General Assembly. In the article the reporter, Allen Breed, remarked that the coalition might be successful because it had "called in the big guns—the National Rifle Association."

Breed also reported that Lauren Rowley, the NRA's Kentucky liaison, was "working with state Rep. Robert Damron" (Breed 1995). Rowley told Breed that the bill had a good chance to succeed and noted that "we're going to try to do away with some of the opposition before the next session."[2]

I have to admit that when I first interviewed patriots in early 1997 (when my background research was still in its infancy), I was suspicious of their claims about working closely with legislators. It was not that I had trouble believing legislators might be sympathetic to their cause. Having grown up in the South, I know just how conservative rural legislators can be. Yet I doubted few would risk the political fallout that being publicly linked to a patriot group (especially after the Oklahoma City bombing) could produce. In my interview with Damron, however, his frank discussion about the tensions encountered in the drafting process indicate he was aware that many of the groups he worked with viewed gun control as a part of a larger government conspiracy. And while such views might not have been considered as "patriot" or "militia" inspired before the bombing, afterward such a connection would be difficult to miss.[3]

Indeed, Damron acknowledged in our interview that there were strong disagreements over how the bill should be worded. Some groups, he told me, had unreasonable demands. "Some of the initial advocates," he said, "wanted [it to be so] if you've got a driver's license you get a permit." Damron told me, however, that he felt a bill with no restrictions would never leave committee, let alone survive a vote on the House floor. He also cited Norman Davis's group, KRBA, as one of the primary culprits making unreasonable demands on the bill's form:

> Norman worked very hard for its passage and he was in some of the initial meetings as we drafted the bill. [But] Norman has a tendency every so often to go a little further than what you can get done. KC3 was probably a little more realistic in what we could and couldn't do. We had a meeting in Owensboro, I think it was. Well, I drove down there one night and before the session started it was basically a "put out the fires" meeting, because some in Norman's organization, and I don't know if Norman had driven it, but somebody down there was driving the fact that it was gonna be a $500 fee and you know, it was gonna be big government and they were gonna really limit their rights.

Norman Davis's recollection of those meetings in our interview corroborates Damron's account. Davis recalled, for example, that in one meeting he threatened to pull out his group's support for the bill if the permit fee was too high: "I told 'em, we'll go back and tell all of our people to tell them [General Assembly Representatives] No! No bill! No concealed carry! We'll all start carrying open!" Eventually Damron was able to consolidate support behind a more passable bill. Given the amount of participation by local grassroots activists from the Second Amendment coalition, however, it required active politicking on his part to win their trust and maintain their support. It is, therefore, highly likely that the NRA, whose Kentucky liaison began working with the Second Amendment coalition and Representative Damron nine months before the bill's passage, encountered not only these debates but the patriot context (such as Davis's theory about UN gun grabs) in which they were proffered. The NRA was apparently undisturbed, however, by either the patriot leanings of these groups or Representative Damron's collaboration with them. Not only did the NRA's Kentucky liaison talk with these groups, but the organization also contributed $438 to Damron's reelection bid in the fall of that same year.[4]

These donations, and the context in which they were made, are significant for a number of reasons. First, the NRA's conferral with these budding patriot groups and the state legislator that worked with them came *after* the Oklahoma City bombing. They indicate, as Anderson's research does, that despite the NRA's attempts to rhetorically distance itself from the Patriot Movement after the bombing, real links continued to be fostered. Indeed, the NRA contributed almost twice as much money to Damron's 2000 reelection campaign—donating 750 dollars to his primary bid and 300 to his general election fund.[5]

The NRA's willingness to work with patriot groups and legislators sympathetic to them, even in an advisory capacity, also lends legitimacy to the patriot cause, providing incentives for them to stay "above ground." Indeed, one of the great ironies in Kentucky is that while no one wants patriots there to go underground (a move that usually leads to violence), their links with the NRA are equally disturbing because they allow patriots to influence mainstream politics, pushing the so-called political center even further to the right. That the NRA can now speak openly to the media, and largely without ridicule, about public schools providing gun safety classes to children speaks volumes about the shifting center of the "gun debate" in the United States (see Scherer's 1999 story on the NRA's Eddie Eagle Program for kids).

Finally, while the NRA's contributions to Damron's campaigns are, relatively speaking, small donations (in the 2000 election Tennessee Senator Bill Frist received 7,950 dollars in contributions from the NRA),[6] these figures are meaningful when considered in their local context. When Representative Kathy Stein (D-Lexington), one of Kentucky's most vocal gun control advocates and an informal tracker of its Patriot Movement ran for reelection in 2000 she received no PAC money from gun control lobbies. As she explained it to me, "They don't care much about the state legislatures as best I can tell. It really is problematic because, you know, I would appreciate their money. . . . I'm the point man against the NRA, and you know, my name is reviled among them!"

CITIZENS FOR A CONSTITUTIONAL KENTUCKY

As Representative Stein's comments indicate, the Patriot Movement has
become a *political* force to be reckoned with in Kentucky. Its attempts to
mobilize the citizenry around a variety of political issues provide an excellent venue for analyzing how the identity politics created by them addresses
patriot anxieties (class and culturally based) about globalization. To analyze
this phenomenon, especially in the highly politicized environment of the
Kentucky Patriot Movement, I chose CCK, a patriot umbrella group, as my
point of entry into the movement's politics. CCK proved to be an excellent
point of entry for a variety of reasons.

Because umbrella groups are designed to help patriot leaders spread their
message to a wider public and recruit new members, these meetings are a
good place to identify patriot leaders. CCK was no different. While I did not
know it that first meeting night in Garrard County, most of the patriot leaders I would interview (or try to interview) were present that night. The meetings were also good places to observe how patriot leaders were framing their
movement politics and policing its boundaries once established. Indeed,
despite the folksy atmosphere patriot leaders tried to evoke at meetings and
the town hall format they employed, CCK meetings were highly orches-
trated affairs. Leaders were particularly careful to rein in patriots who
strayed from the norm the leaders had established. The manner in which
patriot leaders treated John Bales, who spoke about the Fully Informed Jury
Association at the first CCK meeting, is particularly indicative. As I noted
in chapter 1, although Bales headed his own patriot group, he was never an
invited speaker at CCK meetings. Rather, he had to resort to the question-
and-answer period to make his points and the moderator, whether Gatewood Galbraith or Rick Tyler, was always abrupt with him, telling him, as
Galbraith did at CCK's first meeting, to "get to the point" or producing an
oven timer to limit Bales's speaking time, as Tyler did at a meeting later in
the summer.

Because patriot leaders used CCK meetings to introduce political messages to members and potential recruits alike, it was also a good place to
identify the issues patriot leaders considered most important. When Charlie
Puckett and James Laughlin advertised their meeting in the local papers, they
cast their net broadly, telling reporters that they were going to focus on "an
erosion of citizen's constitutional rights" (Powell 1997). And while the first
meeting, as I note in chapter 1, presented a hodgepodge of ideas and theories,
as time passed CCK's message became more streamlined. Two issues in particular began to take up more energy—a push for the legalization of industrial hemp and the drive to stop the designation of a biosphere reserve in the
state. I discuss these issues respectively in chapters 6 and 7.

The open-to-all format of CCK meetings also made them an excellent venue to observe how patriot leaders tried to "mainstream" their cause and give it legitimacy and respectability, not only for the locals who sat on those hard wooden benches week after week, but also for the wider public. One of the tactics leaders employed in their mainstreaming efforts was to host special guest speakers at their bimonthly meetings. While the topics speakers addressed ranged the gamut, from the government's role in the Oklahoma City bombing to UN plans to seize American land, they all had several characteristics in common. All of the arranged guest speakers, for example, were essentially professional patriots. Each had made a name for himself in the larger movement by traveling the patriot circuit, producing patriot literature, or writing patriot books. Pat Shannon, for example, who was the guest speaker at the August 14, 1997, CCK meeting, wrote *The Gangster*, a book detailing patriot theories about the Federal Reserve. A two-time guest speaker, Henry Lamb is well-known in patriot circles for founding the Environmental Conservation Organization, a patriot group that lobbies against environmental restrictions and believes that biospheres are a UN plot to take over land in the United States. Harry BeCraft, who spoke at the July 24, 1997, meeting, was touted on CCK's promotional fliers as the "foremost Constitutional attorney in the nation and a longtime veteran of the battle against federal tyranny in the courtrooms of America."

Being a professional patriot also entailed "looking the part." While I cannot definitively assess whether most guest speakers made decent livings from their activities (as a CEO of a construction company, Lamb is likely well off), they certainly exhibited the trappings of success. They wore suits and ties, which stood in stark contrast to the blue jeans and khakis worn by the majority of audience members, and many of them were "pedigreed" and would pepper their talks with references to their degrees and professional experience. By and large, CCK guests also had well-honed public speaking skills. They were able to capture audience attention in a way that many of CCK's leaders (Gatewood Galbraith excepted) were unable to.

Over time, CCK leaders became adept at generating publicity through their guests. When CCK invited Henry Lamb to speak at their June 12, 1997, meeting, for example, it sent a press release to local papers advertising the meeting and highlighting Lamb's recent testimony before the General Assembly's House Committee on Resources in support of a resolution opposing biosphere reserves in Kentucky. The release resulted in a cover story (rather than a blurb on the public events page) in the local section of the *Lexington Herald-Leader* (Becker 1997). The article's matter-of-fact coverage of Lamb's theories and Kentucky patriots' adaptation of them not only gave CCK publicity, but also did so in a legitimate news source. Indeed, while the staff writer on the story quoted detractors, one of whom likened Lamb's theory to science fiction ("I like the *X-Files*, but it's strictly entertainment," he quipped), the title of the article, "Group Claims UN Is Quietly Seizing Land in US," proffered no skepticism.

Finally, as I would discover during my research, the intermingling of people and ideas an umbrella group facilitates also provides an excellent place from which to observe how internal contradictions between hard-core ideologues and aboveboard contingents played out in one corner of the patriot universe. While Kentucky's patriot leaders were, as I have noted, intent to keep their movement above ground and to cloak it in the trappings of legitimacy, they too would be forced to grapple with the divisions within the movement that the bombing brought into sharp relief.

In CCK, these divisions would largely play out over the role of Christian Identity in the movement, and their battleground would be the moderator's platform and proprietorship over it. As I noted in chapter 1, the first CCK meeting was moderated by Gatewood Galbraith. Galbraith tended to run CCK meetings like a tree-stumping populist priming for his next election. He rarely mentioned God or organized religion and, although he acquiesced every time an audience member piped in with a request for an opening prayer, he somehow never remembered to begin any meeting with a prayer without prompting and often looked visibly perturbed by the request.

At the third meeting, Galbraith was replaced as moderator by Rick Tyler, a pastor from Georgia and radio host of an AM show called *The Voice of Liberty*. Tyler's style differed significantly from that of Galbraith. Tyler spoke with the intonation of a Southern Baptist preacher, while his meeting introductions were longer than Galbraith's and liberally peppered with biblical references. As Tyler's tenure as moderator lengthened, he began to increasingly link patriot causes with a biblical mandate. His introductions became minisermons in which he identified the patriot cause as a Christian one and patriots as "God's people." At one late August meeting, Tyler's beginning prayer invoked God to "divide the enemy" and admonished the *Christians* in the crowd for failing to be activists for the cause. He reiterated the point later in the meeting when he noted, "The biblical principle is definitely to pray with your hand on the plow."

While Tyler's style varied substantially from Galbraith's, the religious context of Central Kentucky meant the leap was not a difficult one for most to make. More than 43 percent of Kentuckians are Southern Baptists and the percentages are even higher in Garrard County, where CCK meetings were held. There, over 60 percent of the population is Southern Baptist (Raitz and Schein 1998). Moreover, the historical links between Protestant fundamentalism and the far right mean that patriot "others" and fundamentalist "others" overlap significantly and require little to no interpretation across context.[7] In the rhetoric of both the Patriot Movement and the religious right, liberals, feminists, Jews, and gay people are viewed with suspicion and contempt (Diamond 1995, 1996).

Indeed, while few of my informants foregrounded religion in their definitions of the patriot cause and most admitted to at best sporadic church attendance, when pressed many drew on their Protestant roots to differentiate themselves as patriots. This became clear when I asked my informants if there were restrictions on who could and could not be a "patriot." One of my informants, Dan Wooten, told me that while the movement would not prohibit those of other religions, such as Islam, from joining the movement, any Muslim who wanted to join would have to recognize the superiority of Christianity over Islam. Another informant, who requested anonymity, made a similar argument. He contended that, even though the movement did not prohibit people of other religious backgrounds (understood in this context as non-Protestant), patriot beliefs are based in Christianity. Interestingly, it is worth noting that this same informant also confessed to me that he believed in reincarnation, the existence of missing books from the Bible, and extraterrestrial beings he called Luciferians.[8] Steve Kelly, a commander in the Kentucky State Militia, did not highlight non-Christians in his response to my question, but he did tell me that he became a patriot because, as he put it, "I didn't want to tell my God that I had copped out when he needed me."

Given the religious context of Central Kentucky, it is not surprising that Tyler's religious appeals initially generated little notice at CCK meetings. As patriot leaders were to discover, however, Tyler's religious views were more extreme than his first presentation of them indicated.[9] And the events that eventually revealed them seriously disrupted the group's activities. On September 17, 1997, CCK leaders sent the following brief and vague note to its mailing list:

Dear Friend of CCK:
This letter is to inform you that, due to unexpected events and concerns in the organization of Citizens for a Constitutional Kentucky, meetings are being put on hold for a few weeks. CCK in its first year, is still trying to fine tune its informational delivery. You will be notified as soon as this fine tuning is achieved.

It would be six months, however, before CCK had fine-tuned its delivery system and held its next meeting. And, despite the six-month gap, when CCK meetings started up again, no formal explanation was provided for the lapse. Indeed, I only discovered why the meetings were put on hold through one of my informants, Dan Wooten, who was a second-tier leader in the group.

When Tyler began moderating CCK meetings, he was still living in Georgia, where he broadcast his weekly *Voice of Liberty* radio show. He traveled to Kentucky for CCK's Thursday meetings and would sometimes stay over the weekend. As the summer progressed, he slowly relocated his family from Georgia to Kentucky and moved onto the property where CCK meetings were held. Given his location, literally in the center of things, his lifestyle inevitably came under close scrutiny, not only by CCK cofounder and meeting-place owner James Laughlin, but also by other leaders in the movement.

In particular, CCK leaders began to question the family's unorthodox living arrangements. Several patriots were concerned that Tyler's children did not attend school and they questioned the rigor of the children's home-schooling, since the children rarely seemed to be studying. Patriot leaders were also curious to know the role of a single young woman who lived with the Tylers, always came to meetings with the family, and was referred to as a "friend of the family." She and Tyler's wife worked the vending table at CCK meetings, selling items such as videocassettes detailing patriot conspiracies, inspirational books, patriot bumper stickers, and copies of the *Spotlight,* a right-wing news magazine published by the Liberty Lobby. According to Wooten, people liked her. "She was real sweet," he told me. While these living arrangements were viewed as unusual, it was only after the young woman appeared at meetings noticeably pregnant that CCK leaders began to seriously question the family's arrangement.

According to Wooten, CCK leaders held a special (unpublicized) meeting in which they confronted Tyler, demanding to know if he was a practicing polygamist.[10] Initially, Tyler denied it. As CCK leaders pressed him to explain how his family "friend" had become pregnant (especially since no one had ever seen her with a boyfriend or heard her mention any men in her life), he tacitly acknowledged his polygamy, arguing that he was practicing "God's law" rather than "man's law." Tyler also attempted to divert attention from his unusual practices by labeling some of his accusers as "traitors" to the patriot cause. In particular, he singled out Dan Wooten, calling him a "sodomist" for managing the campaign of a gay man in a then upcoming local election. He also accused Wooten of being a drug user.

In my time in the field, I was never able to persuade Tyler to grant me an interview. He never refused my request, but he continually put me off, telling me on one occasion, for example, that he needed to think about it and on another that he might have some time in a few months. Therefore I do not know for certain why Tyler singled Wooten out as a traitor. It is possible they had personal differences.

The contextual information I absorbed during my time in the field, however, indicates that Wooten was likely a tactical target for Tyler's attack. Of CCK's leaders Wooten was, by far, the youngest. When I interviewed him in 1997, he was in his early thirties. The average age of my other informants was in the middle to late forties and several were in their fifties and sixties. As the youngest patriot leader in CCK ranks, Wooten was obviously an easy target.

Wooten's ties to Gatewood Galbraith, whom Tyler had replaced, probably played an even greater role. Wooten was a campaign manager for Galbraith's 1991 gubernatorial bid in the Democratic primary and in our interviews it was clear that he was fond of his former boss. Indeed, it was Galbraith who suggested I interview Wooten and gave me his telephone number, instructing me to "tell him Gatewood sent you!" While Tyler was careful to avoid criticizing Galbraith publicly, there were clear tensions between them. Not only were their styles and foci different (Tyler's favored the "Christian" element of patriotism, while Galbraith's embraced the more secular concerns of personal liberty), Tyler seemed threatened by Galbraith's charisma and likability. On the first occasion I attempted to secure an interview with Tyler, for example, he asked me with whom I had spoken. When I mentioned Galbraith's name, he cautioned me, "Well, we don't all agree with Gatewood," even though he refused to arrange a specific interview time and date so as to "set the record straight." Tyler probably realized as well that Galbraith's longtime support for legalizing marijuana created some uneasiness among CCK's more socially conservative constituency. By focusing on Wooten, who was associated with Galbraith, Tyler probably hoped to divide the group along those lines.

In spite of Tyler's tactics, CCK leaders stood by Wooten and expelled Tyler from their group. Tyler, however, not only refused to abandon the group, but also declined to leave the property where CCK held its meetings. According to Wooten, James Laughlin, who owned the flea market where CCK meetings were held, had to sell the structure and the surrounding land in order to evict Tyler from it. The process took several months and in the interim CCK meetings were put on hold.

When I asked Wooten why CCK's leaders ejected Tyler, he informed me that they felt his polygamy served as a liability for the movement. CCK leaders did not, he told me, want to be associated with lawbreakers and other extremists. Indeed, in my interview with Charlie Puckett, he informed me that he requires his militia members to obtain (and maintain) a concealed carry permit, because the background check it mandates helps him weed out convicted felons and other undesirables.

On April 9, 1998, CCK resumed its bimonthly meetings and Gatewood Galbraith was once again its moderator. As before, the meeting began with a prayer, but this time Charlie Puckett prefaced the prayer by telling audience members that people with no religious beliefs were free to remain seated, adding that "no infringement [of rights] is intended." In the spirit of the more secular tone Puckett set for the meeting, Galbraith chose this event to make his first public announcement that he was running for governor in 1999, telling the audience he hoped all good patriots would support him.

Despite CCK's revival as an aboveboard patriot group, the tensions between above- and below-ground patriots that Rick Tyler's ejection from

CCK highlighted continue to exist in the Kentucky Patriot Movement. As I noted in chapter 4, an SPLC report in 1998 found that questions about the place of Christian Identity (and by association racism) in the movement led to an ideological split in the Theatre Command Militia, which is loosely based in Kentucky.[11] Moreover, while none of my informants defined themselves as Christian Identity adherents, at least two expressed an interest in its theories. My anonymous informant, whose belief in aliens I detail above, told me he was not an identity follower, but he then spent the next forty-five minutes in one of our interviews giving me a detailed rendition of how the lost tribes of Israel had migrated to the United States. Similarly, another informant named Joe Burton told me that he was not a follower of Christian Identity, but he did say he thought they had a right to believe what they did and that as a good patriot it was his duty to defend them: "I was raised a Baptist, so I don't agree with them totally religiously, but I believe in their right to practice their religion. See what I'm saying? And that's the thing, we have to take care of each other's rights. We have to protect each other's rights. That's what America was built on." And, while he responded "yes" to my query as to whether he would do the same for the Nation of Islam were it under assault, his efforts were clearly focused on defending Identity believers. In our interview, for example, Burton told me he was conducting research on the government manhunt of Eric Rudolph, who is a suspect in several bombings, including those of an abortion clinic in Alabama and Centennial Olympic Park in Atlanta. My informant contends that Rudolph has been unfairly targeted (and perhaps wrongly accused) by the FBI because of his Identity beliefs: "My personal opinion is he's probably as guilty as, in the Olympic bombing, Richard Jewel was."[12]

The most recent illustration of the coexistence of extremist and more moderate factions in the Kentucky movement came in April 2001, during Norman Davis's biannual patriot gathering on his farm. In early 2001, Davis invited two legislators from the state General Assembly, Democratic representative Perry Clark of Louisville and Republican senator Virgil Moore of Leitchfield, to speak at his gathering (see figures 1.3 and 1.4). They were asked to lead an all-day class to teach patriots how to effectively lobby the General Assembly. Both legislators agreed. When their scheduled appearance was made public the week before the gathering, however, a variety of religious organizations and several lawmakers delivered stinging criticisms of their decisions to attend (Wolfson 2001).

Critics claimed that the meeting's organizers espoused extremist positions and argued that attendance at the meeting by elected legislators would legitimate them. As evidence, they cited the inclusion at the event of a communications seminar by Steve Anderson, a self-professed follower of Christian Identity (Wolfson 2001).[13] Critics were also disturbed by a death threat against Representative Kathy Stein, the only Jewish member of the General

Assembly, which appeared on a web page affiliated with the Kentucky State Militia. On it, members were urged to "track down" Representative Stein and to "bring plenty of ammo" (Wolfson 2001).

In response to the criticism, KSM had the threat removed from the web page. Charlie Puckett told reporters that the threat was a "parody" and he extended Stein an invitation to speak at the gathering, saying that he respected her (Wolfson 2001). Stein did not accept the invitation. She also lodged a complaint with the State Police's legislative security office, which reviewed the case but declined to define the incident as a terroristic threat. In an apparent nod to the Kentucky State Militia, the deputy commissioner also reported that his office had no record of complaints against the militia for illegal activities and indicated the group had never been cited for connection to any crimes. Puckett also told reporters that his group opposes terrorism, adding that if he had known about the Oklahoma City bombing plot he would have "ripped Timothy McVeigh's head off" to stop it (Wolfson 2001).

While Puckett was careful in interviews with the local media to present a moderate face for his militia, there are several indications that extremist elements have made a reappearance in the operations of a group he heads. And in contrast to Puckett's resolve to oust Tyler from CCK in 1997, it appears that by 2001 he was more tolerant of extremist participation.

While Puckett claims his militia does not discriminate "on the basis of color, age, religion, gender, ancestry or ethnic origin" (Wolfson 2001), writings posted on web sites affiliated with KSM paint a different picture. The web site "Free Kentucky"[14] is particularly illustrative. The site is organized and run by Barry Bright, a major in the Kentucky State Militia. On his web page, Bright is up front about his association with Kentucky's most established patriot groups. The site has hyperlinks to Take Back Kentucky's web page[15] and an FAQ page about the Kentucky State Militia. Bright also has an archive of his political columns. In one of them, entitled "Race, Cards, or Dice" (Bright 2001), Bright lays out a racialized agenda that few would mistake for anything but white supremacy. Indeed, while Bright claims he bears no ill will toward people of color and is adamant that he is not racist, he believes, as he explains it, that "A simple examination of the western civilization that most of the rest of the world seeks to emulate shows that for some reason the 'white' race, and I include peoples some others would not, have somehow ended up on the top of the human food chain." And, like many white supremacists before him, Bright spends much, if not most, of his time targeting liberal whites for ignoring race and, by extension, hurting the entire race:

> What I do find funny is that the "liberals" who are always so concerned about not offending someone of another race, mostly because they depend on their

votes and money to maintain political power, are also so adamantly defensive of the "theory of evolution." Evolution in general is survival of the fittest. Yet the "liberal" freaks want to tell us to change the world to make it "fair" to everyone. Life cannot be "fair." This world is not that way, whether by design or accident or designed as an accident. To look at what is happening to whites in countries where they are minorities, particularly in Africa, is to see what happens when one is a minority in one's own country. The whites in Africa are descended from those who conquered and colonized the "dark continent." Now they are paying the price of not maintaining their dominance. Welcome to the food chain. If we, the descendants of those who conquered this continent do not maintain our dominance we are doomed to the same outcome.

Perhaps most disturbing is an acknowledgment Bright makes in the FAQ section of his web site devoted specifically to the Kentucky State Militia. In an e-mail sent to the FAQ page, a writer tells Bright that recently he met several people who claimed to be a part of KSM. As he became better acquainted with them, the writer tells Bright, he discovered that most had a "strong disdain for black folks in particular and all manner of minority groups" (Bright 2000). The writer ends his letter by asking Bright to clarify KSM's viewpoint on racism. In his response, Bright (2000) acknowledges that former Klansmen are members of the Kentucky State Militia, but he rationalizes their presence by adding this weak disclaimer: "We have members who are former Klansman [*sic*]. To my knowledge, they do not advocate lynching people based on their race."

Despite Bright's well-publicized beliefs, Puckett continues to maintain that his militia, in which Bright figures prominently as a major, is not racist. In light of Bright's comments, however, it is reasonable to assume that Puckett either has limited executive control of his militia, with extremist elements having growing influence, or is fully aware of their beliefs and tacitly permits them. It is likely that both are partly true.

Although Puckett is the founder and current commander of the Kentucky State Militia, he is by no means an autocratic figure. Recall from chapter 1 that when Puckett started his militia in 1995 it was called the Central Kentucky Militia and represented, roughly speaking, the Bluegrass region of the state. Less than two years later, Puckett consolidated the various militia and militia-like outfits across the state into a statewide militia. The emphasis on local control in patriot rhetoric, however, means not only that the Kentucky State Militia is organized into geographically defined divisions, which are further subdivided into brigades, battalions, and companies, but also that these subdivisions have a substantial amount of autonomy.

The internal autonomy within KSM is perhaps best illustrated by its web presence. Currently, the Kentucky State Militia does not have its own web site. Some of the divisions within KSM, however, do have a web presence. And while they present themselves as being parts of the Kentucky State Militia, they also assert their independence within the organization. On the official web site of the Kentucky State Militia 911 (9th Battalion, 1st Brigade, 1st Kentucky Division), for example, web master Patrick Perry posts this disclaimer:

> This site represents *only* the 9th Battalion, 1st Brigade, 1st Kentucky Division, of the Kentucky State Militia. The KSM911 comprises all of Western Kentucky, and nothing more. Since this site is only a representation of the KSM911, in some instances it may not reflect all of the views of those in our battalion. . . . There are thousands of people in the Kentucky State Militia scattered throughout the State of Kentucky, and even in surrounding states. These individuals are our husbands and our wives, our sons and daughters, our grandparents, and even our widows. They are our doctors, lawyers, representatives, repairmen, grocers, seamstresses, and executives. To reiterate, this website does not represent nor pretend to represent the entire views of these many units and individuals within the Kentucky State Militia. (KSM911 2001)

Internal autonomy is also illustrated by the recruiting tactics KSM employs. While Puckett claims that KSM recruits go through a vetting process (they must, he told me, be able to obtain and maintain a concealed weapons permit), recruitment appears to be more open-ended. The KSM911 web site supplies easy-to-print recruiting posters, with separate versions for different areas within the KSM911 geographic area (see figure 5.1). While sanctioned leaders within KSM911 may well use these posters, their appearance on the web in an easy-to-reproduce format *with* accompanying instructions for downloading and *without* any listed membership restrictions or criteria also indicates that KSM911's leaders support individual initiatives vis-à-vis recruiting.

These structural arrangements are important because they facilitate cooptation of existing structures by extremist elements, whose ends may be at odds with the movement's more mainstream factions. The internal autonomy built into KSM's structure, so organized, may function as a cover for racists and other extremist elements, while also allowing Charlie Puckett to claim his state militia does not discriminate (a claim he made in our interview in 1997 and one he recently reiterated in the media).

It is important to note here, however, that the growing influence of supremacists within the movement appears to have met little resistance. Indeed, despite the horizontal organization of Puckett's militia, Puckett is neither a figurehead nor unaware of the sentiments expressed by white supremacists within his militia's ranks. Rather, the evidence suggests that he is aware of the extremist elements within his militia and allows them to exist. Buried within the FAQ section on Bright's web page are cues to just this sort of arrangement. At the beginning of the FAQ e-mail described above, for example, Bright (2000) prefaces his response by saying, "I do not have the

WOULD YOU LIKE
TO DO SOMETHING
TO PRESERVE
OUR RIGHTS?

KENTUCKY
STATE MILITIA
(Western Kentucky Area)
www.militia.clarksriver.com
270.759.8998

The links below are for 8 1/2 x 11 inch printable renditions of this page for different locations in Western Kentucky.
(These should print properly by using the latest version of the Microsoft Internet Explorer web browser. You may need to adjust "Page Setup" under the "File" menu heading in Internet Explorer for correct printing. Always use the "Print Preview" command under the "File" menu heading, especially when making changes to the "Page Setup". Although "previewing before printing" takes a couple of seconds longer than clicking on the "print button", it will be a process which will undoubtedly save you reams of paper and ink in the long run if you do much internet printing at all.)

Murray, Kentucky, Printable Recruiting Poster	Paducah, Kentucky, Printable Recruiting Poster
Murray/Almo, Kentucky, Printable Recruiting Poster	Henderson, Kentucky, Printable Recruiting Poster

Figure 5.1   Kentucky State Militia Recruiting Poster

Source: This image appears courtesy of A. F. Branco and KeepAndBearArms.com.

authority to "speak for" the KSM. However I will attempt to answer your questions. Any further questions . . . may be answered by KSM Commander Charlie Puckett. I will forward your questions and my responses to him." Several days later, however, Bright (2000) added a postscript to the FAQ that says, "I was later informed by KSM Commander Charlie Puckett that I do have the 'authority' to speak for KSM." But, even Bright seems to recognize the benefit accrued to KSM by keeping more extremist elements only loosely connected to official KSM "policy." Directly after the statement listed above, Bright (2000) writes, "I wish to clarify my statement on this matter. I am only one among millions of possible 'able bodied' militia members with whom I might disagree strongly on various issues. It is in this spirit that I wish to welcome all 'reasonable' additions to our efforts."

As the above comments indicate, the internal autonomy built into Puckett's militia allows the Patriot Movement in Kentucky to create a largely seamless chain of equivalence between far-right and more mainstream right positions. The lower level organizational autonomy, when coupled with invocations to individual freedom of opinion, allows white supremacist beliefs to be equated with the ideal of nation, and protection of it, that patriots have made the cornerstone of their politics (which, as I note in chapter 4, makes them attractive to a wider audience). As I demonstrate in the next two chapters, this chain of equivalence has important implications for *how* a patriot politics addresses the anxieties its target audience has with globalization. In short, this system thwarts patriots' abilities to see their class-based concerns (which are couched in the changing global economy) as class-based, while it salves their cultural anxieties (also rooted in the vertigo of global flows) through patriotic platitudes that (thinly) disguise overtures to white supremacy. Before turning to an examination of two issues around which this process played out during my time in the field, however, I take the reader on a brief detour in order to introduce the patriots whose voices infuse the following chapters.

KENTUCKY PATRIOTS

As I embarked on my study of the Kentucky Patriot Movement, it became apparent to me that a scholar could employ a variety of methods and sources to acquire information about the movement. One could interview rank-and-file patriots, such as the audience members who faithfully came to CCK meetings, or members of a particular patriot group like KSM. One could also interview the patriot leaders who organized the meetings and made decisions about who would speak, about what, and for how long. For this study, I chose to interview patriot leaders. I did so because I was interested in examining how the patriot identity politics was articulated in Kentucky and because the extant literature indicates that leaders play a vital role, at least during mobilizing efforts, in determining how patriot rhetoric will be defined and deployed.

As I noted earlier in this chapter, identifying leaders was a fairly easy thing to do at CCK meetings. I began by creating a list of the local people who spoke at CCK meetings. As I note previously, most of these individuals headed their own patriot organizations and references to their groups, by the speakers themselves or by others who took to the podium, created a readily identifiable group of leaders. I then expanded my list of leaders by including Kentucky patriots who were in positions to frame issues through patriot discourses, including patriots who ran for office, produced patriot propaganda, or made the rounds of the patriot speaker circuit on behalf of Kentucky.

I also employed a tactic known as "snowballing" to expand my informant pool. Snowballing is usually used to reinforce an existing informant pool. It is not, however, without its problems. As Aho (1990), who used a similar method to expand his data pool, notes, there is obvious room for bias in the sample. A sample that relies in whole, or even in part (as this study does), on snowballing will not produce a random sample. Informants will tend to pass on the names of people with whom they agree or work closely. The obvious danger in the case at hand is that my sample represents the views of a clique of patriots to the exclusion of other equally important patriot leaders.

I believe, however, that while my interview pool probably represents a patriot clique within the state, my study is not adversely affected by the close connections between my informants. Because I am interested in examining how a Kentucky patriot politics evolved, my hope was to interview patriots intricately involved in the process. In 1997, it was difficult for me to assess who at CCK meetings would become influential in this process. And it is certainly true that a few of the patriots I identified as leaders seem to have largely ceased their activism in the movement. Yet, on the whole, as I indicate below, my pool of key informants includes patriots who went on to become the key movers and shakers of the Patriot Movement in Kentucky. Thus, clique or not, it is their perspectives that have driven the Kentucky movement to date and that must be analyzed to understand its current form.

The first patriot I interviewed for this book was Gatewood Galbraith. As I was to discover, Galbraith would become a key patriot leader in Kentucky, and his significance there would compel me to interview him on three more occasions during the next several years. His two most recent patriot-inspired campaigns represented a major step for Kentucky patriots whose vision has been to mainstream its movement by working through rather than against the political system in the state. And, while he did not win, the public access that each campaign afforded allowed him to introduce patriot rhetoric, ideas, and solutions to a wider audience than traditional means of communication within the movement ever would.

Of course, when I first interviewed Galbraith, his place in the movement seemed to be much less certain. Although Galbraith moderated the first CCK meeting, at the time most people in Kentucky associated him with left- rather than right-wing politics. Galbraith has been a long-standing advocate of the legalization of hemp and marijuana. And his previous attempts to seek public office were organized through the Democratic Party. By 1995, how- ever, some of Galbraith's actions began to take on a decidedly patriot flavor. As I noted briefly in chapter 1, Galbraith was arrested at the Lexington July 4th parade in 1995 for protesting a UN float commemorating its fiftieth anniversary. Moments before his arrest on the Fayette County courthouse steps that day, he shouted this patriot invective to the crowd assembled around him: "This misuse of Independence Day is yet another attack on US pride and sovereignty promoted by globalists and internationalists who apparently believe that the concepts of national sovereignty and state inde- pendence are obsolete" (Wagar 1995).

My second interview was with Dan Wooten, who as I note above, worked on Galbraith's 1991 campaign for governor and was referred to me by Gal- braith. When I met Wooten, he was in the process of starting a patriot orga- nization called the American Academy of Patriotism. The academy's purpose, as Wooten envisioned it, was to teach people their rights. In partic- ular, Wooten told me he hoped to hold large seminars to show people how to legally avoid paying federal taxes, which he claims the government has no legal right to collect. When I first interviewed Wooten, however, he sup- ported himself by working in the kitchen of a local restaurant. He told me proudly that, despite the fun his coworkers made of him, he had instructed his employers not to take federal income taxes from his check. As he told me, "They don't take federal taxes out of my paycheck. . . . Of course, some of my coworkers joke about it. Like today, I came in to get my check and they said, 'Hey, the ATF was just here to see you.' And I just joke back. [I said to them] 'Well I don't understand why they're coming here without the IRS.'"

Although Dan's academy would never get off the ground, he proved to be an excellent informant. In particular, as I note above in this chapter, it was Wooten who explained to me why CCK meetings were abruptly halted in September, roughly six months after they had first begun. Although it is dif- ficult to quantify such a trait, Wooten also seemed one of the most forthcom- ing of my informants. After our first interview, Wooten called me periodically to tell me how he was doing and to keep me abreast of happen- ings in the patriot world beyond the formal structures where I encountered it. He also granted me a second interview in which he graciously answered many of my questions about the movement, which at that early stage in my research were fairly simplistic. Perhaps because of our similarity in age (relative to other patriots), Wooten was also willing to discuss the strategy behind the moves other patriot leaders made.

Dan's frankness about his personal background also gave me insight into some of the personal motivations that drive people to become patriots. In our first interview, Wooten confessed to me that he had been illiterate until his early twenties. Like many illiterate adults, Dan told me he had learned to hide his inability to read, so few people around him knew his secret. When he finally decided to do something about his illiteracy, he told me, his whole life changed. In particular, he recounted to me how taking that first step toward learning to read empowered him and led him to fundamentally rethink the idea of personal responsibility. The government and the schools, he told me, had failed him and the lesson he said he had learned was to never depend on the government for your needs in the first place.

The third person I interviewed requested full anonymity. He is referred to from here forward as Richard Lee, the pseudonym he chose. I identified Lee as a potential leader at CCK meetings. Because he was very concerned about keeping his anonymity, however, I do not divulge any more personal information about him. As he and I well knew, the informal and formal leaders of the Patriot Movement in Central Kentucky in 1997, when I interviewed him, included a relatively small number of people. Very little personal information about him could, therefore, reveal his identity. While I grant Lee anonymity, I want to make clear that his anonymity is in no way extended to protect illegal activity on his part. While it is possible he was engaged in illegal activity aimed at overthrowing the government, nothing in my interview with him indicated that he was.

I spoke with Lee on two occasions. The first time we spoke, I called him, intending only to request an interview and to set up a time and place to meet if he agreed. My first conversation with Lee, however, lasted over two hours and turned into an interview in its own right. Our conversation opened a window for me into the paranoia and conspiracy that infuses parts of the movement's base. When I called Lee and explained who I was and what my project was about, for example, he abruptly asked me, "How did you get my number?" "From the phonebook," I meekly replied. In retrospect, I realized that using the phone to contact patriots was probably not the best method, even for a relatively mainstream group like CCK. While Galbraith had expressed no visible anxiety from my cold phone call (the perpetual politician in waiting, Galbraith is likely accustomed to cold calls from people he does not know), most patriots are not used to strangers calling them on the telephone. When coupled with the general suspicion of "outsiders," a cold call, as I discovered, required *post facto* damage control.

In particular, my anonymous informant was suspicious of my motives. From his initial comments, it appeared he thought I was a government operative. When I told him I was doing a research project on the Kentucky Patriot

Movement, for example, he snorted, "I know they can come into your computer from your modem and destroy your hard drive." And, when I told him that I usually interviewed patriots for an hour or two he sneered, "If that's all the time you've got, I won't waste my time. This movement takes longer than an hour to explain!" After I informed him that I would interview him for as many hours as he felt necessary, however, he seemed to relax a bit. And when I assured him that I was not working for or funded by any government agency his suspicion abated further.

I still felt, however, that I was skating on thin ice. Afraid I might lose the interview because of my poorly thought-out tactic for contacting him, I tried to engage Lee on some of the subjects he had spoken about at CCK meetings. On his own turf topically, Lee finally opened up. And the opinions and thoughts he expressed confirmed for me that, despite the moderate face CCK and many of its leaders tried to present, more hard-core patriot beliefs and theories were informing the movement as well. Lee was, for example, the first patriot to describe for me in detail the theory of Fourteenth Amendment citizenship discussed in chapter 4. As Joel Dyer notes in his book *Harvest of Rage,* right-wing agitators developed the theory in an attempt to rhetorically (and materially) separate themselves from the government during the farm crisis. Lee's rendition of the theory in our phone conversation provided me with the first clear evidence that patriot rhetoric developed during the farm crisis informed its more mainstream variants in the mid-nineties.

At the end of my phone conversation with Lee, we arranged to meet for a formal interview. In person, Lee was quite different from his phone persona. While he was still intense and his speech was sometimes frenzied, he was also very forthcoming about his personal place in the movement. It was during our second interview, for example, that he confessed to me he believed in aliens. He told me that he knew his beliefs put him at odds with the majority of patriots, so he kept quiet about them. As he put it, "If I did [tell them], I'd soon find myself on the outside looking in." His frank admissions provided me with my first taste of the substantial diversity that existed within the Kentucky movement and how it was discursively policed.

My fourth interviewee was Charlie Puckett, who is an auto mechanic in Nicholasville and, as noted previously, is the commander of the Kentucky State Militia. Unlike my other interviews, which I conducted in local restaurants, informants' homes, or in my office, my interview with Puckett was carried out on a local patriot television show. Dan Wooten called me in early October and asked me if I would be willing to interview Puckett on a show he was producing. The ethical and methodological issues I considered as I debated whether or not to conduct an interview "on patriot turf" are discussed in detail in the final section of the book, entitled "A Note on Method."

As I was to discover later, my interview with Puckett was vital for understanding the Kentucky Patriot Movement. In the wake of the Oklahoma City bombing, when other militias, such as the Michigan Militia, waned or underwent factional splitting, the Kentucky State Militia grew stronger. Indeed, the Anti-Defamation League (ADL) named KSM as "the strongest active militia in the US" (ADL 2001). According to reports on the ADL's web site, Puckett's militia also engages in regular paramilitary training. Pictures from KSM's August 2000 training session displayed on the "Free Kentucky" web site corroborate the ADL report.

While Puckett was an important interview for this study, he was not one of my most forthcoming informants. As I state in "A Note on Method," this may be partly explained by the format in which our interview occurred. However, after I left the field and began checking the facts of what patriots told me during my interviews with them, I realized that Puckett, in particular, told me things that were at worst untrue and at best economical with the truth. When I first spoke to Charlie Puckett on the phone before our interview, for example, he told me he was happy that I had chosen a "nonracist" militia to investigate. As I have monitored the movement since then, however, it is clear that even if Puckett does not personally subscribe to white supremacist ideals, he now allows his members to publicly and openly espouse them.

When I interviewed Puckett, he also told me that his militia did not engage in paramilitary training. Again, however, my fact checking, as noted above, indicated otherwise. It is possible that, when I interviewed Puckett in 1997, KSM was not engaged in training exercises. However, his discussion with the Associated Press at Norman Davis's patriot gathering in April 2001 indicates that he frequently relies on rhetorical technicalities rather than hard facts to answer questions about his militia's involvement in training. In April 2001 at Davis's farm, Puckett told Associated Press reporter Dylan Lovan that his group does not break the state's laws prohibiting paramilitary activity. As Lovan (2001) noted, however, a web site related to KSM's participation in the event listed "evening military training and combat seminars" on its itinerary, while many of the people Lovan saw at the meeting were "dressed in full camouflage and toting semiautomatic weapons." Because patriots believe unorganized (i.e., non–National Guard) militias are sanctioned by the U.S. Constitution, however, Puckett does not acknowledge KSM's training exercises as paramilitary (i.e., training by an unsanctioned military unit).

My fifth interviewee was Steve Kelly. Kelly is a deputy commander in KSM and Puckett gave me his name when I asked him if he had any suggestions of people I should interview for my research. When I interviewed Kelly, he lived in a trailer park in a small town outside of Lexington (he asked me not to identify the name of the town). Although Kelly was not a leader in the way that my previous informants were, he proved to be a valuable informant because he was very forthcoming about his personal and political background and how he saw it shaping his decision to join the militia.

Like many people in the Patriot Movement, Kelly is a Vietnam veteran. And, like many vets, he appears to be struggling financially. When I interviewed him, Kelly told me he was "self-employed," although my queries about his employment indicate he was probably unemployed or at best occasionally employed in the construction industry. He said his wife helped them meet ends by working in the local Pizza Hut.

When I interviewed Kelly, he seemed intent to stress to me his "leftist" past. He told me, for example, that when he returned from the war all he wanted to do was party and forget the war. He also described himself as a "hippie" and an "ultraliberal." "I supported McGovern," he confessed to me. And like most of my informants he stressed in our interview, and with no prompting from me, that KSM was not a white supremacist organization. As he explained it (although I have no way of verifying this contention), "I could never be racist. I was raised in a black foster family."

When I asked him why he had changed his political position so radically, he replied that he had received a calling from God. While I do not entirely discount Kelly's self-narrative, his own comments about religion contradict his narrative. In particular, he told me that he rarely went to church, even though his wife frequently asked him to go with her. He was, as he told me, no fan of organized religion. What did become clear to me as I interviewed Kelly, however, was his class position. He was not only not rich, but he appeared to be just scraping by. Whether or not Kelly views his socioeconomic status as relevant (he largely downplayed it in our interview), it is clearly a rich subtext for considering how he might have been, or might be in the future, mobilized to different ends.

The sixth person I interviewed was Wasley Krogdahl. Unlike with my other informants until then, I neither met Krogdahl at a CCK meeting nor learned about him directly from a previous informant. Rather, I identified Krogdahl as a potential informant through an e-mail I received in the spring of 1998. During my fieldwork in 1997, I gave my e-mail address to several patriots during the process of arranging interviews with them. At some point, my address ended up on what appears to have been a patriot e-mail list. Although I received few e-mails from the list, I always read the ones I did receive with interest. The "action alerts" and other notifications on the list helped me keep abreast of current happenings in the movement. One of these e-mails was a message announcing that Wasley Krogdahl had been nominated as the Kentucky Taxpayers Party's candidate for the 6th district congressional race (see figure 5.2). The following day, I e-mailed Krogdahl and requested an interview with him. Krogdahl agreed to my request and brought along his campaign manager, Robert Lind, who participated in our interview as well.

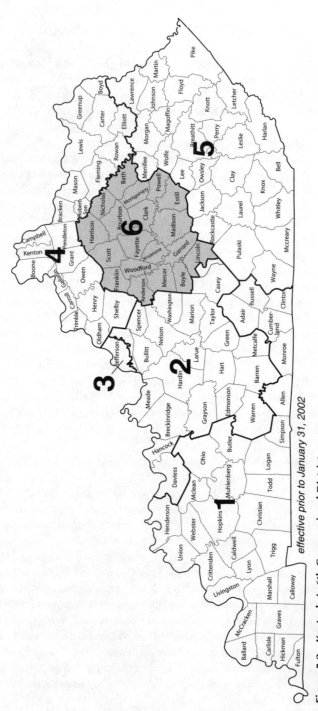

Figure 5.2   Kentucky's 6th Congressional District

effective prior to January 31, 2002

While Krogdahl never spoke at CCK meetings, I discovered in our interview that he had attended several of the early meetings. Moreover, as I note in chapter 1, the Kentucky Taxpayers Party was represented at CCK meetings on a semiregular basis by Ed Parker, who was then and is now the party's chairman. The U.S. Taxpayer's Party was consolidated in 1992 by Howard Phillips, a longtime right-wing ideologue (see Diamond 1995). In the late nineties, Phillips renamed the party the Constitution Party. However, the fundamental plank in its platform, that the scope and influence of the federal government should be sharply reduced, remained the same. The party holds, for example, that federal agencies such as the departments of Education and Health and Human Services are not constitutional and should be eliminated. Its platform also advocates conservative social legislation, including bills that would ban abortion.

While the national Constitution Party has not been formally linked to the Patriot Movement, in Kentucky there are several indications that formal connections are currently being forged. Not only did Ed Parker, as I note above, speak on occasion at CCK meetings, but the Constitution Party of Kentucky advertises Take Back Kentucky meetings on its e-mail list. In addition, the party sponsors regular seminars in which patriot leaders participate. A July 28, 2001, "Liberty Seminar," for example, featured national party chairman Howard Phillips as a keynote speaker and both Norman Davis and Gatewood Galbraith as state guest speakers (CPK 2001). Moreover, when I met with Krogdahl and Lind to discuss their platform for the upcoming race, both mentioned issues raised at CCK meetings, and in a patriot frame. As I describe in chapter 7, for example, Krogdahl's view of the biosphere reserve in the southern part of the state, and his proscriptions for it, mirrored the patriot positions espoused at CCK.

Krogdahl proved to be an interesting informant for a variety of reasons. First, as a retired professor at the University of Kentucky, Krogdahl was more educated than my average informant. His knowledge of the issues also appeared to be more in-depth, although it is possible that he was simply better equipped to articulate his positions than the average informant. As I note in the following chapter, Krogdahl was my only informant who seemed able to discuss the issues of tobacco subsidies and the way they relate to the potential reintroduction of hemp into the Kentucky economy.

Secondly, although Krogdahl was more subtle in showing it, he was also suspicious of my motives. When I arrived at his campaign headquarters for our interview, for example, he informed me that he would be taping our interview so that he could correct any potential misrepresentation I might make. I became acutely aware at that moment that I had become an object of study among my own objects of study.

Finally, even though Krogdahl seemed to have a good grasp on the issues and was a polished speaker, I nonetheless found him an unlikely political candidate. Simply put, he lacked charisma and presence, and I was not surprised when his candidacy garnered minimal attention in the local press. His candidacy, especially when contrasted with Galbraith's two bids for office, indicates the trial-and-error process associated with patriots' forays into electoral politics.

Doug Fiedor was the seventh patriot I interviewed. I identified Fiedor as a patriot because he writes a weekly patriot column entitled "Head's Up! From the Foothills of Appalachia." When I first encountered the column, it was hyperlinked to the Michigan Militia's home page (the page no longer exists, in the wake of the Michigan Militia's various factional splits). Some of his columns discussed issues in Kentucky, however, so I e-mailed him to find out if he was based there. Through my e-mail discussion with Fiedor, I discovered that he not only lived in northern Kentucky, but that he worked with many of the leaders in the Kentucky movement as well.

As I would discover during our interview, Fiedor was the second patriot I encountered who had a Ph.D. and, like Krogdahl, he was a former university professor, in this case in Michigan. I realized after interviewing Fiedor that, while the majority of patriot rank and file are working class, its ideological leaders are not only well educated, but also are situated relatively high on the socioeconomic ladder. On the whole it is the thinkers like Fiedor and Krogdahl who construct the discursive framework through which patriots view their context. In Krogdahl's case, he sets a discursive framework through running a campaign for the Taxpayers Party. Fiedor does this by writing a column in which he analyzes current events through a patriot frame, thereby continually defining and reinforcing the patriot category.

Fiedor was also an interesting informant because he refused to be labeled as "militia." As he put it in an early e-mail correspondence to me, "I do not belong to any group more ominous than the Republican Party." He told me that instead of "militia" or even "patriot" he preferred the term "Constitutionalist." He thought the term was more specific and, as he explained it to me in that same e-mail, "I can still remember when that was actually said to be a good thing. Part of my writing is to attempt to understand how and why that changed." Yet while Fiedor shuns the term "militia," his column, as noted above, was hyperlinked on the Michigan Militia home page. And when I asked him what Kentucky patriots thought about this or that issue he was at ease summarizing their thoughts. Indeed, Fiedor's self-distancing from the term "militia" is better read as a maneuver common to many opinion setters on the right, who provide the framework in which conspiracies and rumors can emerge yet claim no responsibility for such adaptations. Indeed, were Fiedor seriously concerned about militia groups invoking his work, it seems reasonable to assume that he would not have allowed his column to appear on a militia home page. Moreover, Fiedor, like most of my informants, was able to supply me with a variety of names of potential patriot interviewees. Indeed, most notable among the group of names and accompanying e-mails Fiedor gave me was the contact information for J. J. Johnson, a well-known African American patriot who testified along with John Trochmann and Norman Olson in the 1995 Subcommittee on Terrorism, Technology, and Government Information's militia hearings (U.S. Senate 1995a).

The eighth person I interviewed was Joe Burton. Burton was one of the local patriots Fiedor suggested I interview. Unlike my other informants, Burton did not live in Kentucky. Rather, he was a full-time resident of Tennessee, but lived near the Kentucky border, adjacent to the Land Between the Lakes region, where Kentucky patriots have protested the designation of a biosphere reserve. And, as I would discover in the process of our interview, he had been involved with several Kentucky patriots in protesting the biosphere.

Like my anonymous informant, Richard Lee, Burton spoke at length about Christian Identity, even though he claimed not to follow the "religion" and, like all of my informants, denied the Patriot Movement was racist. As he explained it, "Louie Free and them are demonizing, and Janet Reno, are demonizing Christian Identity, OK? Because a lot of Christian Identity people are very aware of what's been going on with the government for a long time. Long before us in the Patriot Movement!" His comments, when considered along with Lee's views, verified for me that hard-core patriot ideology continues to inform even more mainstream patriot groups.

When I interviewed Burton, we arranged to meet one another in the Kmart parking lot in Bluefield, West Virginia, which was near his childhood home. After we introduced ourselves, Burton suggested we walk about a block down the street to a nearby Southern Baptist church, where we sat on the shaded front stoop for our interview. As I discovered during our two hours together, Burton seemed to have made a second career out of being a patriot. He was retired and he and his wife traveled across the Southeast in their RV to patriot hot spots, such as Eric Rudolph's hometown, from where they had just returned. Burton also showed me a plethora of documents he had collected over the years to substantiate a variety of patriot conspiracies, including documents that he claimed proved UN troops were operating on U.S. military bases and paperwork proving a second bomb theory in Oklahoma City. Burton did not give me copies of his documents, so I was unable to verify his evidence. What is significant about his document collection, however, is what it says about the larger movement, especially its more mainstream varieties. Indeed, patriots provide these documents in order to give their claims legitimacy, not only among the faithful, but also among a wider target audience. That such "evidence" is often inconclusive and frequently forged is irrelevant to the mobilization context, because patriots have learned how to package it appropriately.

The ninth patriot I interviewed, Norman Davis, is perhaps the Kentucky movement's most important patriot, especially in terms of its successes in the political realm. When I initially created my list of important patriot leaders after my first several CCK meetings, however, I did not have Norman Davis at the top of my list. Indeed, although he spoke occasionally at CCK meetings, he did not live in Central Kentucky and as such seemed less relevant to my research, which at the time was focused regionally within the state. As I would discover throughout my time in the field, however, all roads eventually led back to Norman Davis. When I reinterviewed Gatewood Galbraith in the summer of 1999 about his gubernatorial campaign, for example, I learned that Davis was Galbraith's campaign manager. Similarly, whenever I spoke to patriots about the Land Between the Lakes biosphere controversy, Davis was always mentioned as a crucial person to interview.

I first tried to interview Davis after I discovered that he was running Galbraith's 1999 gubernatorial campaign. He agreed to the interview, although he and I were unable to coordinate our schedules (by that time, I was living in Washington, D.C.). I kept tabs on his organization, however, and realized that even in the wake of Galbraith's defeat Davis and his organization, Take Back Kentucky, seemed to be gaining rather than losing momentum. Indeed, Davis is regarded as a central figure by those within the movement as well as by those outside of and largely opposed to it. Representative Damron, who worked with Davis's group, KRBA, told me Norman Davis's lobbying efforts were highly successful. Perry Clark, a Democrat representative in the General Assembly from Louisville, who has also worked with Davis's group on legislation and who received criticism for attending Davis's patriot meeting in April 2001, described Davis to the media as "respected" in Frankfort (Wolfson 2001). Representative Stein, who recently found herself the target of a death threat on the "Free Kentucky" web site, also named him in our interview as a key patriot leader in Kentucky.

Davis's group has also attracted the attention of the national media, although his group's political (rather than underground) tactics, as I note below, have confounded the media, who are not yet accustomed to the more politicized wing of the movement. At the end of my interview with Davis, for example, he told me that MSNBC had been considering doing a story on his group. Davis suggested I contact one of the filmmakers on the project, Emily Fisher. She was a "good girl," he told me, adding that when she brought her footage back to her producers, they fired her for telling the truth about the movement. "She really loved what we had going here. She said people need to know about this, what you all are really doing, and they won't let 'em do it up there. They won't let her put out the truth."

When I contacted Fisher, she explained to me that her employer at the time was not MSNBC, but BNNTV, which had been hired by MSNBC to produce a one-hour segment on the militia movement. When I asked her what she thought of Davis's group, she told me that, although she did not agree with many of his group's positions, she was impressed with Davis's leadership skills and the overall sophistication of the people she met there. As she explained to me in an e-mail, "It turned some of my expectations around. For instance, a lot of these guys are pretty sophisticated. They're reading The Federalist Papers, etc. And they all know the Constitution inside and out."

When Fisher presented her pitch to MSNBC executives, however, she recalled that they were unhappy with her findings. When she told them in a meeting, for example, that many of the patriots she had encountered were sophisticated lobbyists, she told me that one of the executives responded, "We don't want sophisticated. We want unsophisticated. We want the biggest, meanest, ugliest guys you can find, with big guns, that will strike terror into the hearts of every American that holds near and dear those American values we cherish." While Davis was annoyed by the stereotyping Fisher encountered, he was also clearly proud about what it says about his group in particular and about the Kentucky movement in general. As Norm told me, his group did not need guns to change things: "We can go up there and beat 'em [the General Assembly] at their own stuff!"

My experiences in the field buttress Davis's view of things. The Kentucky movement appears to have been so successful exactly because it invoked an above-ground, largely political approach rather than a furtive, underground one. Yet it is important to note that, even though Davis's group clearly defies the stereotypes most people have of the movement, his group is clearly informed by more radical patriots and might easily undo the work Davis has done to build what he sees as TBK's stellar reputation. When I interviewed Davis, he told me that Take Back Kentucky was not a racist organization and that, in fact, he had rebuffed the overtures of a Klan group in the area to join the TBK coalition. Yet as I note above in this chapter, Steve Anderson, a virulent Identity adherent, gave a communications seminar at the April 2001 patriot meeting on Davis's farm. Anderson makes no bones about his Identity beliefs. He has publicly admitted, for example, that he believes Jews are the spawns of Satan. Apparently, Davis did not feel the need to rebuff Anderson in the way he claimed he did with a Klan group. In the short run, Davis's failure to do so allows patriots to discursively link the ideas of white superiority with those of nation, creating a powerful and dangerous right-wing chain of equivalence. In the long run, however, his tacit approval of Identity Christianity (and its growing strength in the movement) means that the Kentucky movement could undergo the same factional splitting that has occurred elsewhere in the country.

Given the political weight Kentucky patriots currently have in the state, I also decided to interview two lawmakers, one sympathetic to the cause and another in opposition to it, to test informally patriot claims about their political influence. My thinking was that supporters would play up patriots' influence, while detractors would downplay it and that, by comparing their claims, I could determine a middle ground that most closely approximated patriot influence. Given Representative Damron's work with the various patriots I interviewed for this project, he was the logical choice among the sympathetic lawmakers. As a counterpart to Damron, I chose Representative Kathy Stein. Stein makes an interesting choice not only because she is in the same party as Damron (both are Democrats), but also because she opposes his work with Kentucky patriots. She was also a good interview because she has experienced their political power up front. Although I interviewed her before the "Free Kentucky" web site posted an Internet death threat against her, that horrible incident verified for me her standing as a good counterpart to Damron. As I was to discover in my interviews with these divergent lawmakers, however, they presented strikingly similar depictions of patriot influence in the General Assembly, although their views of the movement obviously differed substantially.

In addition to lawmakers, I also interviewed Jeff Jones, the commissioner for human rights for the city of Lexington. Jones has also been an activist for the gay community in Lexington and statewide. His contextual knowledge about gay activism in the state was crucial for this project because, as I note in chapter 9, while class and race positioning have long figured prominently in the Kentucky movement's politics, heterosexuality is increasingly becoming an important issue in the movement's identity politics as well.

Finally, in closing this chapter it is worth mentioning the patriot leaders who would not grant me interviews. Two patriots, Rick Tyler and Barry Bright, are clearly important to this study, but I was unable to obtain interviews with either. As I noted earlier, Tyler never refused my repeated requests for an interview, but he did put me off on several occasions and was soon after unceremoniously booted from CCK's ranks. Barry Bright, who has recently become active in KSM, was also masterful at avoiding an interview with me. Given my experience contacting my anonymous informant over the phone, I decided to contact Bright by e-mail. When I wrote Bright, I told him that I was doing research on the Patriot Movement in Kentucky and that I had interviewed several key patriot leaders in the area. I informed him that I was trying to analyze the movement's politics in a more sustained way than the media generally does and that I had identified him as a potential informant after perusing his web site, "Free Kentucky." Bright responded to my first e-mail by asking, "Who's going to publish your book and who's funding your research? Are you being 'fair' and getting info from the hate-watch groups?'" I responded by telling Bright that I was funding my own research and that I had no plans to interview "hatewatch" groups, since I was trying to analyze the Patriot Movement as patriots were constructing it.

In response to this e-mail, Bright suggested I attend a TBK meeting, telling me they were open to the public and giving me directions to their meeting place.

I thanked Bright for the information and asked him again to grant me a personal interview, telling him I preferred talking with patriots individually because each one has his own perspective on the movement. He responded to my question with his own query: "Do you consider yourself a participant in this war we are engaged in or a 'dispassionate observer'?" My response, that I was an academic researching the movement and not a patriot, lost me the interview.

My inability to acquire an interview with either Barry Bright or Rick Tyler is unfortunate, because their views are clearly more extreme than those of other patriots I interviewed. This is particularly important in the case of Bright. While Tyler managed to conceal his beliefs and was ousted from CCK when those beliefs became apparent, Bright is not only up front with his views, but he also provides a written archive of·them on his web page. His views, which contradict the movement as I initially encountered it, high-light the potential points of rupture within the Kentucky version of a mainstream patriot identity politics. Fortunately, despite the absence of his spoken words, he has left a written record from which to draw.

NOTES

1. The term "yellow dog Democrat" refers to a Democrat who votes for the party's ticket without exception. The term originated during the 1928 election season in Alabama from the expression, "I'd vote for a yellow dog if he ran as a Democrat." Alabama Democrats who remained loyal to the party's presidential nominee, Al Smith, a Northerner regarded as hostile to Southern concerns, were called yellow dog Democrats (PBS 2000).

2. I attempted to contact Rowley to determine the exact nature of the meetings she had with the Second Amendment coalition described in this chapter. When I called the NRA, I discovered that she no longer worked there. The NRA's current Kentucky liaison, Nicole Palya, was unable to answer my questions. Palya referred me to the Distilled Spirits Council, where she said Rowley went after leaving the NRA. Representatives in the Council's human resources department, however, have no record of Rowley as an employee of the organization.

3. It is worth noting that, when I interviewed Representative Damron in January 2001, he was fully aware that both Charlie Puckett and Norman Davis were the point people for the Kentucky Patriot Movement. During our interview, however, he never tried to distance himself from them and indicated that he still worked with them on various pieces of legislation.

4. According to the National Institute on Money in State Politics (www.followthemoney.org), the NRA made two contributions to Damron's 1996 reelection bid. The first contribution was $188. The second was $250.

5. See either the Kentucky Registry of Election Finance web site (www.state. ky.us/agencies/kref/krefhome.htm) or the National Institute on Money in State Politics web site (www.followthemoney.org).

6. For a complete list of NRA donations to congressional candidates, see either the Federal Elections Commission's home page (www.fec.gov/) or the Center for Responsive Politics' web site (www.opensecrets.org), which summarizes FEC data for individual candidates. See also Jack Anderson (1996).

7. These links are particularly strong in today's Southern Baptist Convention, which is controlled by fundamentalists within the denomination. In early 2001, for example, longtime Southern Baptist and former president Jimmy Carter left the church in protest of its conservative social positions.

8. While Protestants do not advocate these beliefs, patriots from Protestant backgrounds tend to incorporate the conspiracy theories they encounter in the movement into their religious beliefs. This particular informant, for example, viewed the extraterrestrial Luciferians as evil and told me they were intent on enslaving the world. Similarly, he defended his belief in reincarnation by saying that the missing books of the Bible covered the topic at length.

9. In 1998, Tyler was listed on the SPLC's web site as an identity adherent. He is no longer listed on the center's page of active patriots.

10. Polygamy is not usually associated with Christian Identity. Aho's study of Idaho patriots does note parallels between Mormon theology and the Identity belief system, although he does not cite polygamy, which the Mormon church has banned, as one of them. Tyler's adoption of polygamy is probably best understood as indicative of the fluidity with which Identity adherents borrow from an Identity framework for their own ends.

11. According to the SPLC, the Theatre Command Militia appears to have largely fizzled out in the wake of its ideological feud.

12. Richard Jewel was an early suspect in the bombing of Centennial Olympic Park during the 1998 summer Olympics in Atlanta. He was eventually cleared as a suspect by the FBI.

13. For more recent (and damning) information on Anderson, see the epilogue at the end of this book.

14. See www.freekentucky.com/.

15. See www.takebackkentucky.org/.

6

Hemp and Its Discontents

Patriots have joined a rising number of voices calling for the legalization of industrial hemp (Cheves 1998; Charpentier 1995; NORML 2001; NAIHC 2001). This chapter examines how patriots in Kentucky have made legalizing hemp, traditionally a left-wing or green issue, into a patriot cause. The purpose of this chapter is to analyze how calls to legalize hemp, when framed through discourses of patriotism, address patriots' class-based concerns about rural livelihood. Getting to the meat of this issue, however, requires some context. To understand patriots' claims about hemp, it is first necessary to clarify facts about hemp's character. Is it, for example, the wonder product its proponents claim it to be or just another name for the drug marijuana, as its detractors argue? Second, it is necessary to outline the history of hemp in Kentucky. The breadth of this history helps explain in large part why patriots' have rallied behind this otherwise controversial plant. Finally, because patriots support hemp as an alternative/complement to tobacco, it is also necessary to provide basic information about tobacco production in the state and key issues confronting its future. I begin this chapter, therefore, with a contextual detour, trusting the reader will bear with me for the relevance it brings to the coming analysis.

THE HEMP PLANT

Cannabis sativa is the scientific name of a plant in the mulberry family. It is thought to be indigenous to the temperate, midlatitude regions of Asia. By the colonial era, however, hemp was grown by farmers in Europe and, as early settler accounts indicate, by native groups in the Americas. American varieties of *Cannabis sativa* were called, alternately, flax, hemp, silk grass, and enequen (Hopkins 1998).

There are hundreds of varieties of the *Cannabis sativa* plant. The majority of these varieties may be classified into one of two categories—hemp and marijuana (Thompson et al. 1998; NAIHC 2001). These two categories include plants with quite different characteristics. Hemp varieties tend to have long, sturdy stalks in which strong fibers are found. Hemp fibers have been and continue to be used to make canvas, rope, and clothing. Indeed, the sturdiness of hemp fibers and their use in industrial settings gave rise to the now common moniker applied to hemp varieties of *Cannabis sativa*— industrial hemp. Hemp varieties may also produce seeds for consumption as well as oil for use in hair and body products. More recent studies suggest that hemp may also be used as an environmentally safe form of energy, although at present this potential is largely unproven and thus largely untapped.

Marijuana varieties tend to have less-developed stalks, but larger leaves. The leaves in marijuana varieties contain elements of the psychoactive chemical compound tetrahydrocannabinol (THC). Generally, marijuana plants contain at least 5 percent THC. Marijuana sold "on the street" usually contains around 10 percent and some batches have levels as high as 30 percent (NAIHC 2001). The uses of marijuana range from recreational to medicinal. Marijuana leaves may be dried and smoked, giving the user a chemically induced high. Marijuana may also be used to control asthma or nausea or as a general analgesic (Clark 2000; Voth and Schwartz 1997; Williamson and Evans 2000).

The characteristics of hemp and marijuana are different enough to affect the way each is commonly used. The stalks of marijuana, for example, are not generally cultivated because they produce weak, undeveloped fibers. Likewise, because hemp varieties contain less than 1 percent THC, the only effect a person smoking a hemp cigarette is likely to get is "a big headache" (NAIHC 2001). Low levels of THC in hemp prohibit its use for medicinal purposes as well.

Hemp and marijuana also can be easily distinguished on the ground. Numerous countries that permit the growth of hemp, but not of marijuana, report no difficulties in spotting the difference. Moreover, the illegal growth of marijuana within hemp fields is impractical, because cross-pollination always results in lower THC levels in marijuana, rather than higher levels in hemp (NAIHC 2001).

Hemp and marijuana were both grown in the United States until the mid-1950s. But in 1971, the Controlled Substance Act classified *Cannabis sativa* as a Schedule 1 narcotic[1] and established penalties for its unapproved use. Currently, it is a crime to grow, sell, distribute, use, or possess *Cannabis sativa*, although for most of the 1990s it was not a crime to possess certain products made from *Cannabis*. A 1998 Drug Enforcement Administration (DEA) press release, for example, noted that restrictions placed on the *Can-*

nabis sativa plant "do not include the mature stalks of such plant, fiber produced from such stalks, oil or cake made from the seeds of such plant, any other compound manufacture, salt, derivative, mixture or preparation of such mature stalks (except the resin extracted therefrom), fiber, oil, or cake, or the sterilized seed of such plant which is incapable of germination" (DEA 1998).

Despite these exceptions, in August 1999 U.S. Customs, working on behalf of the DEA, seized a Canadian farmer's twenty-ton shipment of birdseed on the grounds that it was a "controlled substance" (Wren 1999). Although the seeds were sterile (as required by U.S. law), they were confiscated because they contained trace amounts of THC. The DEA also ordered the farmer to recall earlier exports, including hemp oil and hemp straw for horse bedding. It was clearly a "tall order"—the oil and straw shipments had been legally purchased and were already in use. Two months later, the farmer's shipment of birdseed was returned (Mayer 2001), but for many the situation brought to the fore not only the confusion surrounding what is and is not legal, but also the absurdities that arise from vague government policy.

When I began the policy research for this chapter in February 2001, I felt compelled to sort out this confusion. I wanted to do so not only because I hoped to be fair to the government's position (which was not clearly represented in the newspapers), but also because, as I discovered, when hemp is concerned the issues tend to turn on details (scientific and legal) rather than broad points. Unfortunately, my attempt to clarify at least the legal side of the issue (with both U.S. Customs and the DEA) met with limited results (but a handy lesson on bureaucracy). I detail it here to illustrate how the politics surrounding the so-called drug war sustains the outlawing of this plant today, even as a growing body of evidence suggests it could be successfully grown and used in manufacturing.

The U.S. Customs Office was in charge of the 1999 seizure, so I contacted it first. I spoke with Tom Corwin, whose division is responsible for *Cannabis*.[2] Corwin told me that, currently, U.S. Customs operates on a zero-tolerance policy for ingestible products made from hemp. He explained that ingestible products include anything that can be eaten (e.g., birdseed) or absorbed into the skin (e.g., lotion). Any such product coming into the United States is subject to seizure, even when it has only trace amounts of THC. I asked Corwin to explain the rationale for the policy, in light of the fact that not only was the seed intended for birds, but that the amounts of THC were negligible, thus prohibiting any practical use of it as a drug. Corwin told me that the rationale, as he understood it, concerned the DEA's ability to effectively administer drug tests. The use of hemp (with trace amounts of THC) in popular foods and body products weakened the effectiveness of drug tests because a person who tests positive for THC can claim they ate a granola bar made with hemp seed, even if they had actually smoked marijuana. He cautioned me, however, that I should contact the DEA to clarify these policies, since it was the role of U.S. Customs only to enforce the policy, not to set it. He referred me specifically to Martin Pracht, telling me that his office was responsible for the guidelines related to *Cannabis* and products made from it.

When I spoke with Martin Pracht,[3] he declined to answer my questions over the phone, telling me that the DEA preferred to respond to outside queries in writing. He suggested I contact the DEA's Office of Congressional Public Affairs and gave me their phone number. At my request, he also gave me an e-mail address. Given the DEA's preference for written responses, I tried an e-mail query first (DEA1@aol.com). My e-mail bounced back. I tried sending the e-mail again the next day, with the same result. On both occasions, the message from the server cited an undisclosed error message.[4] Having had no luck with e-mail, I called the DEA's Public Affairs Office, where I spoke to Rogene Waite.[5] Waite also refused to answer my questions, telling me that the DEA was currently revising some of its policies regarding hemp and that in the meantime I should refer to their most recent press release (cited above). When I told her the press release contradicted the 1999 birdseed seizure, she referred me to U.S. Customs. I responded, "But they referred me to your agency," adding in a moment of pique, "I'm finding it difficult enough to get a clear answer here. What must it be like for a farmer?" She suggested a concerned farmer should also contact U.S. Customs. In a last-ditch effort to get a handle on the current policy, I asked Waite if she could detail the interim policy currently in practice regarding the importation of hemp-based products. She said she did not know what it was. She then referred me to the Office of National Drug Control Policy (ONDCP), telling me that perhaps they could answer my question.

I followed her advice, even as my annoyance with the DEA's PR tactics rose. At the ONDCP, I spoke with a representative named Jennifer Devallance.[6] When I asked her to explain the current policy for hemp importation, she told me, not surprisingly, that I should speak to the DEA, since it was its responsibility to set enforcement policies. Sensing my frustration, however, she transferred me to Maureen Bory[7] at the DEA, telling me Bory might be more helpful than the people with whom I had previously spoken. Bory finally provided a measure of clarification. She explained that the DEA had drafted new guidelines for importing hemp-based products and had sent them to the Office of Management and Budget, which prints the *Federal Registry.* The new Bush administration, however, had placed a hold on printing the guidelines until they could be thoroughly reviewed. Bory added that only a small circle of people knows what the new guidelines entail. "They're keeping them close to the vest," she explained, "even I don't know what's in them." When I asked her what the current policy regarding importing ingestibles was, she said that current policy did not distinguish between ingestible and noningestible hemp-based products. She cautioned, however, that the DEA currently considers even trace amounts of THC grounds for seizure.

Several months after my initial efforts to get some clarification on hemp products, the DEA issued a press release on its web page summarizing the updated guidelines regarding hemp in the *Federal Register* (for the press release, see DEA 2001a; for the guidelines in full, see DEA 2001b). The press release, published October 9, 2001, on the administration's web page, began by reaffirming the administration's long-standing position that hemp and marijuana are the same plant. Quoting Asa Hutchinson, who had given a press conference on the matter earlier in the day, the press release noted: "DEA Administrator Asa Hutchinson states that 'many Americans do not know that hemp and marijuana are both parts of the same plant and that hemp cannot be produced without producing marijuana'" (DEA 2001a). The press release then moved to the heart of the matter, explaining that the guidelines on the legality of any hemp-based product would from here forward be based on "whether the product causes THC to enter the human body" (DEA 2001a). Under the new guidelines, for example, "foods and beverages that contain THC," such as veggie burgers, flour, and pretzels, are now specifically categorized as illegal. The updated guidelines do, however, make an explicit exception for "textiles" and "personal care products" made with hemp, noting that "the DEA believes [these] 'hemp' products do not cause THC to enter the human body" and are thus legal (DEA 2001a). In a sidebar listing legal products under the new guidelines, cosmetics, lotion, paper, shampoo, and birdseed mixtures are mentioned. The specific mention of birdseed (neither a textile nor a personal care product) was no doubt included to quell the mass criticism the administration received after the 1999 incident described above. The new regulations do, however, leave open the possibility that such products may be outlawed in the future, stipulating that these products would be legal "unless and until [the DEA] receives evidence to the contrary"(DEA 2001b).

Despite the administration's attempt to clarify which hemp-based products are legal and which are not, the government's continued refusal to differentiate between hemp and marijuana leaves a variety of issues unresolved. The Hemp Industries Association, for example, is considering a lawsuit because it feels the DEA's attempt to lump the two plants together, as well as its open-ended phrasing regarding personal care products, presents undue uncertainty for producers and purveyors of hemp-based products. Moreover, Kennex Ltd., Canada's largest exporter of hemp seeds to the United States, has signaled its intent to seek $20 million in compensation from the U.S. government under the NAFTA accords (Mayer 2001). Finally, activists promise to continue their push to have the crops differentiated and the hemp variety of *Cannabis sativa* exempted from the Controlled Substance Act. And they are increasingly collecting at least rhetorical support from elected officials. In response to the DEA's October press briefing, for example, Democratic representative George Miller of California told the press that the DEA decision "undermines the credibility of the so-called war on drugs" and queried sarcastically, "the amount[s] of THC in these food products are so infinitesimally small—are addicts going to carry around barrels of pretzels?" (Miller, quoted in Mayer 2001).

A BRIEF HISTORY OF HEMP

Although hemp is not native to North America, its history there, particularly in the United States, is long. The first American flag stitched by Betsy Ross is purported to have been made of hemp, while Thomas Jefferson is thought to have penned a rough draft of the Declaration of Independence on paper made from hemp. George Washington and Jefferson grew hemp on their Virginia estates and Ben Franklin owned a mill used to process the plant into paper. Hemp even took on a moral flavor during the colonial era, when Britain tried to persuade Virginia farmers to grow it instead of tobacco, which was considered an unseemly crop (Hopkins 1998).

Before the Revolution, the production of hemp was largely concentrated on the eastern seaboard, in Maryland and Virginia, although it was grown as far north as Maine. Generally, farmers grew hemp for domestic use. On occasion, however, they also grew it as a cash crop. The British expansion of its navy in the seventeenth century, for example, created a robust market for the crop, as traders sought fiber for sails and rope. Hemp's durability, long fibers, and resistance to salt water made it an excellent choice. Britain could have looked domestically for their hemp supply—it was grown there at the time—but the cool, wet climate produced an inferior crop. The purchase of better-quality hemp from the Baltic region was also a poor option. Political instability within Europe essentially stifled easy and constant access to the crop. Thus, hemp was introduced as an important crop early on in U.S. history (Hopkins 1998).

As colonial expansion continued westward, hemp production followed. Although *Cannabis sativa* will grow almost anywhere, the successful production of hemp varieties requires more particular conditions. Conditions in Central Kentucky were especially suitable. Hemp thrived in the region's loamy, rich soils, while infrequent droughts meant sufficient water for the thirsty plants. As significant settlement expanded beyond the Appalachian Mountains, hemp came to be associated specifically with Kentucky (Hopkins 1998). Initially, farmers there grew hemp to make clothing, rope, and twine. Before frontier markets had consolidated, hemp also served, like tobacco and whiskey, as a form of currency when cash was scarce.

As the frontier fortified, hemp came to be an important cash crop as well. Fluctuations were common in the hemp market, but for almost a hundred years after the American Revolution Kentucky farmers found hemp profitable enough to grow as a cash crop on at least portions of their farms. The earliest frontier markets for hemp developed when the Mississippi waterway was opened to commercial traffic. This allowed distributors to affordably ship hemp to markets back east that, because of high transportation costs, could not be accessed via cross-mountain routes. As increasing amounts of hemp flowed through New Orleans, a market also developed there for manufacturing hemp fiber for naval uses, such as canvas, sails, and rope.

Kentucky hemp farmers saw a third market emerge in the plantation South. As the European textile market boomed in 1815, cotton production expanded to meet the demand. In turn, cotton producers purchased hemp to make bale bags and ropes for their cotton shipments, creating the largest market to date for hemp grown in Kentucky. From then until the early 1850s, the hemp market became increasingly dependent on the health of the cotton industry (Hopkins 1998). Hemp production in Kentucky reached its peak in the 1850s and went into a slow but steady decline afterward. Several factors contributed to this decline, including the availability of cheaper hemp from Italy and Russia and competition from other states, including Missouri (Hopkins 1998).

Hemp would experience two more booms before it would eventually be rendered an illegal crop. Both of these growth spurts were related to government war efforts, in World War I and again in World War II. As Russian and Italian hemp became unavailable during World War I, Kentucky farmers returned portions of their land to hemp cultivation for the government-driven market for thread for army shoes, twine for grain bags, and caulking for ships. During World War II, similar needs led the government to contract farmers to grow hemp exclusively for government use. Even during the war efforts, however, hemp production never rivaled that of the previous century (Hopkins 1998). And after World War II hemp production declined to negligible levels in Kentucky and other hemp-growing areas, such as Missouri.

Despite its reliance on hemp during World War I, the government began efforts to ban *Cannabis* during the interwar years. In 1937, the government enacted the Marijuana Tax Act, which placed heavy taxes on the growth and distribution of *Cannabis*, making it unprofitable to grow under even the best circumstances. As the name implies, the act also worked to conflate hemp and marijuana varieties, since it regulated all forms of *Cannabis* as marijuana. After 1937, hemp could only be grown with government aid. Indeed, during World War II the government had to offer tax incentives in its contracts to encourage farmers to grow hemp and the government had to pour in huge capital inputs, from free seeds to government-built mills, for production to be profitable (Hopkins 1998). The categorization of *Cannabis* as a controlled substance in 1971 merely sealed hemp's fate, eliminating the final vestiges of a once thriving industry.

The larger context surrounding the outlawing of hemp is complicated. Not surprisingly, there are different explanations for its being outlawed. The government's position in 1937 was that all varieties of *Cannabis* could be potentially used as a drug and that the rising threat of its use in urban areas and among poorer populations warranted its termination as a legal crop. The American Medical Association lent its support at the time, arguing that marijuana was a "menace" worthy of being outlawed (Hopkins 1998). Some at the time, however, thought the government action hasty. This was the case even among those who accepted the premise that hemp and marijuana were essentially one and the same. A 1944 study conducted by the New York City Mayor's Committee on Marijuana, for example, concluded that claims about the spread of marijuana use and its purported dangers were exaggerated (Hopkins 1998).

The positions have changed little since 1937. Over the past ten years, however, grassroots efforts have emerged from a variety of quarters to lobby for the legalization of *Cannabis*. These groups run the gamut, from hippie-identified groups like the National Organization for the Reform of Marijuana Laws (NORML) to farmer-associated groups like the North American Industrial Hemp Council (NAIHC).[8] The efforts of these groups and others have resulted in intense scrutiny of the process by which a once legal and quite common crop came to be outlawed. Perhaps most influential in this regard is Jack Herer's *Hemp and the Marijuana Conspiracy: The Emperor Wears No Clothes*. In its earliest incarnations during the mid-1970s, Herer's book was a self-produced manifesto, passed around informally among promarijuana and hemp advocates and occasionally sold at bazaars, fairs, and environmental gatherings. Today, Herer's book is copyrighted, has a publisher, and is frequently cited as the premier text on social and environmental issues surrounding *Cannabis* (Nazario 1991). The core of Herer's message, however, has remained the same.

At root, Herer sees a corporate-led conspiracy behind the outlawing of *Cannabis*. He argues that during the 1930s timber and chemical companies such as Hearst Manufacturing and DuPont viewed hemp as an economic threat. Both companies knew that hemp had long been used to make paper and that its recent expansion during World War I increased the likelihood it would be again. According to Herer, DuPont was also worried because its engineers had just patented a chemical process to transform wood pulp into paper. The process for turning hemp pulp into paper did not require chemical transformation, so any potential expansion of hemp's production could have made DuPont's patented process irrelevant. New innovations in the processing of hemp also worried the timber and chemical interests. Improvements to decorticating machinery (for extracting fiber from the stalk) and new machines for preserving hemp's high-cellulose pulp content also posed the possibility for its mass manufacture. The good press hemp received in popular outlets was also unnerving. In the mid-1930s, industry heads discovered that *Popular Mechanics* was dispatching a team of journalists to write about possibilities in the hemp industry. The article, which eventually appeared in 1938, after the passage of the Marijuana Tax Act, heralded hemp as the "new billion dollar crop" and an improved decorticator as the machinery to make it happen. In short, moneyed interests had much to gain from outlawing hemp and more to lose from its continued production. Analyzing the impact on Dupont, Herer (1995, 24) estimates that, if hemp had remained legal, "80% of Dupont's business would never have come to be."

Given the relative abundance of hemp and the innovations in its manufacture, companies like Dupont and Hearst were forced to resort to backdoor tactics to engineer its outlawry. According to Herer, the process involved a two-pronged strategy. First, companies privately lobbied government officials to outlaw hemp. Given the breadth and depth of connections between industry and government, as Herer notes, the process was not difficult. Of particular importance in getting the ball rolling was Andrew Mellon, president of Mellon Bank in Pittsburgh and DuPont's chief financial backer. During the Herbert Hoover administration, Mellon was secretary of the treasury. While in this position, he appointed Harry Anslinger, his nephew-in-law and a strong anti-*Cannabis* crusader, to head the freshly reorganized Federal Bureau of Narcotics and Dangerous Drugs. Herer contends that Mellon and Anslinger were critical in establishing within government circles the notion that hemp was a financial threat to business. And their internal lobbying paved the way for a series of secret meetings held in the Treasury Department between 1935 and 1937, under Henry Morganthau's tenure, to devise an innovative strategy for putting a stranglehold on hemp production—regulation through taxation.[9] The bill that resulted, the Marijuana Tax Act, required all growers, sellers, manufacturers, importers, and distributors to register with the Treasury Department. It also levied an occupational tax on growers and placed prohibitive taxes on most *Cannabis* transfers.[10] The effect of the tax was all too clear. At the time, an ounce of "raw drug" *Cannabis* was worth about a dollar, but the bill proposed placing a dollar-per-ounce tax on all sales and transfers. And to ensure the legislation passed through Congress, Treasury had the bill introduced to a "friendly" committee whose chairman, Robert Doughton, a DuPont ally, ensured its smooth sailing onto the House floor.

The second prong of attack, Herer contends, was a smear campaign during the debate stage of the bill. Like the bill's inception, its debate period was tainted by the appearance of a conflict of interest. A key witness in the 1937 debates about the marijuana bill was Harry Anslinger, the Mellon appointee as head of the Federal Bureau of Narcotics and Dangerous Drugs. According to Herer, Anslinger's testimony before the committee relied heavily on a personal "gore file" containing tabloid newspaper clippings sensationalizing marijuana use among minority communities. Indeed, using nothing more substantial than anecdotes culled from the tabloids, Anslinger inaccurately testified that one-half of all violent crimes in the United States were committed by minorities using marijuana. And, lest anyone miss the racial message, Anslinger read aloud for the committee a newspaper clipping about two African American students in Minnesota who supposedly used marijuana to lure a white woman into a jazz club and then seized the opportunity to impregnate her. Anslinger's file also included stories perpetuating the myth of the "lazy pot-smoking Mexican" (Herer 1995, 26). As Herer concludes, Anslinger knew the composition of the committee well—Jim Crow legislators from the Deep South and congressmen from southwestern states who hoped to cash in on a Depression-era backlash against Mexican immigrants—and tailored his message accordingly, assuring its easy passage.

It is worth noting here that even scholars who do not depict Anslinger as part of a wider conspiracy to ban marijuana on behalf of special interests acknowledge the role that racial bigotry played in its outlawing (Keys and Galliher 2000; Musto 1999). In contrast to Herer, Musto (1999), for example, contends that Anslinger was initially uninterested in targeting marijuana because he feared its proscription was a poor strategy for his agency. In particular, Anslinger worried that outlawing marijuana would send too many ordinary people to jail, thereby alienating the judiciary (as prohibition had done in prior decades) and ultimately undermining his agency's budget and power. Moreover, Musto argues firmly that Anslinger did not create the racial scare tactics, noting that it was sheriffs and prosecutors from the Southwest who were clamoring for marijuana regulation so that they could exert greater control over their Mexican migrant populations. Musto does concede, however, that Anslinger was ready and willing to exploit racial bigotry when it became clear that the regulation-through-taxation method was a feasible option for outlawing *Cannabis*.

For Herer and his growing legion of supporters (see Conrad 1994, 1997; Robinson 1997), the damage done by outlawing *Cannabis* has been manifold, ranging from the suppression of inalienable rights and creative expression to the loss of sustainable energy sources and forest habitat. Citing a diverse array of artists, from Lewis Carroll to the Grateful Dead, Herer reminds his reader that *Cannabis* has long helped writers, painters, and musicians to unleash their creative potential. Herer also sings the praises of *Cannabis*'s medicinal potential, arguing that its pharmaceutical properties make it suitable for treating everyday ailments like premenstrual syndrome and migraines. In addition, Herer bemoans the lost environmental benefits that could have accrued from hemp production. He argues that had hemp been legal, much of the destruction of habitat resulting from DuPont and other companies' chemical product development could have been avoided.

For Herer, the solution to this mismatch—between *Cannabis*'s usefulness and its illegal status—is clear. He calls for the repeal of all laws that place prohibitions on any kind of *Cannabis*. And he advocates a broad-based amnesty for all those charged with crimes relating to *Cannabis*, from "peaceful possession" (Herer 1995, 92) to its cultivation and transport. He also believes that those charged with *Cannabis*-related crimes should have the offenses erased from their records and some form of government reparations paid to them. Hemp's outlawing, Herer concludes, is fascist, and the continuing "War on Drugs" against it a "monstrous crime" (92).

While Herer espouses no political affiliation in his book, and in fact attacks Republican and Democratic supporters of the war on drugs with equal force, his analysis represents a fairly typical blending of left-leaning positions. In advocating hemp as a natural solution and juxtaposing it with DuPont's chemical one, Herer stakes out a position consistent with green/ environmentalist rhetoric. His assertion that the drug war assaults human liberty, when coupled with his belief that addicts should be treated rather than jailed, places his analysis solidly within standard left perspectives on the drug war specifically and government repression more broadly (see Bertram 1996). And Herer's criticism of Anslinger's testimony as racially motivated clearly conforms to the left's concern with the role of racism in drug policy (see Lusane 1991; Schneider 1998). Despite the leftist flavor of Herer's analysis, patriots in Kentucky have basically accepted the major premises of his book, from Herer's assertion that *Cannabis* was outlawed as a part of a corporate conspiracy to his declaration that the war on drugs is an affront to our basic civil rights. Yet, as I will demonstrate in the next section, there are critical differences in how patriots and the left interpret and use Herer's analysis. I turn now to the Kentucky patriots, outlining how hemp is defined as a patriot issue and how its adoption by patriots results in a pro-hemp politics quite different from the left's.

HEMP AS A PATRIOT ISSUE

When I first set out to research the Patriot Movement, I read several histories on the movement (Dees 1996; J. Dyer 1997; Junas 1995; Mozzochi 1995; Stock 1996). While the studies I read were diverse, certain issues were repeatedly marked as patriot issues in each study. As I note in chapter 4, gun rights was the issue most often cited as a patriot issue. Many studies, for example, note the importance of the Brady Bill as a galvanizing moment in the Patriot Movement (Abanes 1996; Dees 1996; Mozzochi 1995). The bill, named after

James Brady, the Reagan aide who was shot and paralyzed during John Hinkley Jr.'s assassination attempt of Ronald Reagan in 1981, enacted sweeping controls on firearms. Government actions in the events surrounding the shoot-out at Ruby Ridge and the tense standoff at Waco were also cited as important (Dees 1996; Junas 1995). Commentators and academics alike read them as proverbial straws that broke the camel's back in the Patriot Movement. For their part, patriot leaders proffered these public relations debacles as evidence that gun control efforts should be targeted at government instead of "the people" and that it was incumbent on "the people" to be vigilant in protecting the right to bear arms. Studies also cited the importance of private property battles to the movement's emergence. New government restrictions on ranchers' use of BLM lands sparked "patriotic" responses in the form of wise-use and local control ordinances (Burke 1995). A few studies posited rural restructuring as key to the movement, including J. Dyer's contention (1997) that the farm crisis was pivotal in its emergence (see also Davidson 1996). But with the exception of Catherine Stock's analysis (1996), these studies tend to foreground the loss of farms rather than more general debates about agricultural policy as central to the movement's emergence.

I was, therefore, somewhat surprised to discover such a prominent place for hemp in the Kentucky Patriot Movement. Not only was hemp generally considered a "lefty" or "green" issue, but the plant had also been effectively illegal for thirty years. Yet there it was, packaged as a patriot issue my first night in the field. Indeed, it was while I was waiting for Tom to finish his hot dog that first night that I happened to glance down at a vendor's table and notice a copy of Jack Herer's book for sale. And, as I noted in chapter 1, hemp would figure prominently at the first CCK meeting and make several return appearances throughout my time in the field.

As I was to discover during my research, Kentucky patriots overwhelmingly support the legalization of hemp, although no consensus exists about the legalization of marijuana. When I asked my interview participants what their position on hemp was, they were usually hearty in their affirmative responses, saying resolutely as Norman Davis did, "If it'll help the farmers I'm all for it!" or as Doug Fiedor retorted, "I mean, what's not to like here?" Even patriots who oppose the legalization of marijuana and worry that their support might be taken as pro-marijuana stand in support of hemp. When I interviewed Wasley Krogdahl in the summer before his unsuccessful bid for Kentucky's 6th district congressional seat in 1998 (the same seat Galbraith would run for two years later), I asked him a variation of the same question. "Does your campaign," I queried, "view hemp seriously enough to consider it as an alternative for tobacco farmers?" He responded affirmatively, adding, "If it's possible to be absolutely clear and certain about what is a field of hemp and what is a field of marijuana, then I say, why not let the farmers grow a profitable crop?"

While all of the patriots I interviewed supported hemp, Gatewood Galbraith is clearly its biggest proponent within the movement. Galbraith has a long history of advocating *Cannabis*. Galbraith told me in three of my four interviews with him that he and Jack Herer were close personal friends and that they had worked together for years for the cause. Like Herer, Galbraith also supports legalizing all forms of *Cannabis*. In 1989, Galbraith was interviewed for a *USA Today* article about legalizing *Cannabis* (Kelly 1989). The picture accompanying the article showed Galbraith perched in an illegal "pot patch," a wide grin covering his face (see Galbraith's home page for a good reproduction of the picture). Allowing farmers to grow industrial hemp was also central to his unsuccessful bid in 1983 to be commissioner of agriculture and to his two bids for the Democratic nomination for governor, in 1991 and 1995. Though not central to his 1999 gubernatorial race or his 2000 congressional campaign, *Cannabis* was still present in both platforms—articulated specifically through the issue of medical marijuana, the legalization of which he supported. In short, Galbraith's credentials in the pro-*Cannabis* movement are well established. In a recent edition of *High Times,* a magazine produced by NORML, a "Gatewood for Governor" bumper sticker was featured in the voter's gallery as an option in the magazine's best pro-*Cannabis* bumper sticker competition.

As I will discuss in more detail in chapter 8, Gatewood Galbraith's long associations with NORML and the Democratic Party make him an "odd" fit with the socially conservative, right-affiliated Patriot Movement. Indeed, even during Galbraith's most recent campaign for Congress, when he had fully developed his pro-gun stances and had taken a turn to the right on cultural issues, many in his district continued to view him as the candidate of the far left rather than of the extreme right. In January 2001, for example, Galbraith won the "Best Example of the Vast Left-Wing Conspiracy in the Bluegrass" category in the annual best of poll in Lexington's alternative newsweekly, *Ace Magazine.* When I asked Representative Kathy Stein about this seeming discrepancy, she told me that Galbraith's turn to the right had not been well publicized and that Gatewood was happy to keep it that way. The progressives that voted for him, she said, "haven't picked up yet on the issues, the right-wing issues he has embraced. And he doesn't want those people to pick up on them, because he knows it would alienate them." Indeed, during the 2001 congressional campaign she and another local legislator felt compelled to set the record straight. They sent letters to precincts within their districts where Galbraith had done well in the past, outlining his move to the right. "I hope it helped some," she added.

Despite the seeming incongruencies, Galbraith sees a logic to his move. Indeed, as I describe in greater detail in chapter 8, Galbraith purposefully decided to try to link the otherwise disparate pro-*Cannabis* and patriot constituencies. As he told me in our first interview and reminded me in the two that followed, "You see, I decided a long time ago that I was going to marry marijuana and the militia."

It is perhaps for this reason that while the movement in Kentucky relies heavily on Herer's account to undergird the patriot position on hemp, it interprets the significance of hemp's outlaw in ways that are quite different from Herer's analysis. First and foremost, while Herer's analysis supports hemp for its environmental qualities, Kentucky patriots rarely sing hemp's praises on environmental grounds. Indeed, it was a common occurrence at meetings to hear calls for legalizing hemp juxtaposed with antienvironmental rants such as the one given at the first meeting by Ed Parker, who the reader will recall labeled the 1970s oil crisis a fiction and bemoaned the environmental movement as unchristian. Moreover, while Herer's book spends quite a lot of space deconstructing the racist rhetoric used by people like Anslinger to "sell" hemp's outlawing in the context of the Jim Crow South, I never heard individual patriots decry this aspect of hemp's outlawing. Nor did speakers discussing hemp at CCK meetings ever raise these concerns in their speeches.

Rather, hemp's outlawing was generally couched as a local example of undue government control. This was especially the case at the most general discursive level of the sound bite. Indeed, one of the characteristics I noted early on about patriot leaders was their effective use of sound bites to define their cause, and their hemp position offered no exception. During my time in the field, Gatewood Galbraith's flair with rhetoric provided especially fertile ground for these sound bites. During Galbraith's speeches at CCK meetings and in my interviews with him, the phrase I would hear over and over again in the context of hemp was his snazzy alliteration that "the government should stay out of your billfold, your bladder, your bloodstream, and your back pocket!"[11] While Galbraith's quote was clearly most relevant to the use of marijuana varieties of *Cannabis,* its depiction of government as an intrusive big brother had obvious resonance among even the movement's antimarijuana constituencies because of its simple evoking of antigovernment sentiment.

While sound bites generally took precedence over more in-depth analyses at CCK meetings, a deeper probe of patriot support of hemp indicates a serious desire to address the region's dependency on tobacco in order to secure future livelihood from the land. Yet the patriot position is fraught with an uneasy blending of class-based concerns about hemp (as a potential source of livelihood) with traditional right-wing concerns with "creeping socialism." As I noted in chapter 4, these conflicting concerns have long sat uneasily next to one another in rural America. Farmers often depend on government aid to make farming profitable, but they decry the position of dependency it puts them in.

Not surprisingly, this uneasy pairing is at play in the patriot position on hemp as well. Patriots support hemp in part for very practical reasons. While they may decry its outlawing in order to provide local testimony of an overbearing government, their support is more than a rhetorical weapon. It is based on a desire to provide tobacco farmers with viable crop alternatives. Tobacco is Central Kentucky's number one cash crop and, as it has come under increasing assault by all levels of government, health providers, and insurance companies, farmers have become uneasy about the region's future (Berry 1992; Cheves 1998). Given the history of hemp in the state, patriots feel that if it were legalized it might provide a viable companion crop to tobacco, if not a replacement for it. In my interview with Doug Fiedor, he told me that he even went so far as to suggest to his representative in the General Assembly that the state use hemp for paper production. As he explained it to me, "We have some of the largest printers, magazine printers and stuff, in the world here in Kentucky. We would be able to offer them paper that is better quality than anything we have available now for the same price as newsprint paper." And when I asked Wasley Krogdahl why patriots, many of whom are not farmers themselves, would care about hemp, he gently reminded me, "The disruption of the tobacco industry would create economic havoc in Kentucky. Now none of us wants that. It isn't only the tobacco farmers who will be affected." Patriots' support of hemp is further buttressed by the state's legacy as an internal periphery (especially the eastern coal fields of Appalachia). As Doug Fiedor complained, "It seems that every time Kentucky people get something going, such as the coal mines, they shut it down. Now, its farming things, suddenly they're putting big, big regulations, federal regulations on things. Like now, they're messing with tobacco!"

Yet patriots' concern with farmers' livelihood is clouded by their view of government intervention, even on behalf of farmers, as ideologically repugnant. Indeed, it was routine for patriots I interviewed to constantly remind me of the historical place of hemp's outlawing within Roosevelt's New Deal. Patriots regard the New Deal as socialist and, to them, hemp's outlawing within it represents a government that thought it knew what was "best" for farmers to grow and for consumers to buy (Hearst paper processed with DuPont chemicals rather than local paper made from hemp). It is this ideological grounding that allows patriots to criticize big businesses like DuPont, but renders them unable to follow through on the critique. This became clear to me as I reviewed the transcript of my first interview with Gatewood Galbraith.

The first time I interviewed Galbraith, we had lunch at a local eatery. As we munched on our sandwiches, I asked him general questions about the movement's position on hemp. Throughout the interview, I was struck by his persistent criticism of corporate power, both in terms of hemp's outlaw and more generally in terms of government abuses. One exchange was particularly interesting in this regard. By way of context, I should note that an interview with Gatewood Galbraith is no rote affair. Gatewood is a mercurial conversationalist, charming, witty, and quick on his feet. I frequently found our roles reversed, with Galbraith asking me questions as he worked to prove a point. In this particular exchange, for example, Galbraith leaned forward conspiratorially and asked me, "Who do you think controls the White House?" "Presumably the president," I responded. "No it's not!" He proclaimed. "We don't have any control over it. If I told you that the petrochemical companies did, would you believe that?"

I took a sip of my iced tea to collect my thoughts. It was my first interview and I had not expected such a critical view of raw corporate power. Putting down my glass, I tentatively responded, "Well, you know, it's interesting that you say that because what you are saying is something that a lot of people, I guess you could call them old marxist lefties, are saying about U.S. multinationals today." I bit my lip, apprehensive that he might object to being lumped with "old marxist lefties." Instead, he took umbrage with my comment on entirely different grounds. "They're not American corporations! You think they're American corporations for America? Hell, they're franchises set up around the world, across the globe!"

As the above exchange illustrates, while patriots are disturbed by corporate power and government regulations that benefit capital accumulation by them, patriots fail to see these concerns as class based. This is due in large part to how discourses of patriotism frame the articulation of these concerns. By responding to their class-based concerns on the grounds of nation (rather than class), their penultimate concern becomes reclaiming a time and place where corporations were "American" rather than foreign. So framed, patriots are unable to see their issues as class based, and thus to consider how to address them as such. This became especially clear to me when I asked patriots specific questions about hemp's reintroduction into the state agricultural economy. The introduction of hemp, as I will demonstrate in the next section, is intricately tied to tobacco farming. Any mechanism for reintroducing it as a replacement or companion crop requires addressing the current context, in which tobacco farming is viable, on small-acreage farms. As I will discuss shortly, however, framing hemp production through discourses of patriotism blunts patriots' ability to develop sound solutions for the farmers they wish to help. Before illustrating these discursive twists in some detail, I turn briefly to tobacco farming in Kentucky and highlight structural elements relevant for considering hemp, or any other crop, as a *viable* alternative.

THE TOBACCO CONTEXT

Kentucky's tobacco farmers grow three kinds of tobacco: burley, dark fire-cured, and dark air-cured. Burley tobacco is, however, Kentucky's signature crop: it accounts for over 90 percent of the tobacco produced in the state. Tobacco has a central place in Kentucky's agricultural economy. During the 1990s, its total value averaged over $800 million annually (Snell and Goetz 1997). And currently, tobacco accounts for approximately 50 percent of the state's total crop receipts.

Despite its centrality to the agricultural economy, tobacco is grown on less that 1 percent of the state's cropland, with most grown in Central Kentucky (Raitz 1998). This is due in large part to the relatively high returns per acre that tobacco receives at the market. On average, an acre of tobacco fetches $4,000 in gross returns. Corn, the second-largest cash crop, only brings in around $500 per acre (Snell and Goetz 1997).

Historically, tobacco's high per-acre price is due to the subsidies attached to its production. Tobacco first became a subsidized crop in the 1930s, during the New Deal. Farmers were assigned a tobacco quota for each harvest based on their acreage. The limits on production staved off overproduction, thereby ensuring relatively high prices. The quota system also had the effect of keeping farm size small, because strict regulations were imposed on the sale or purchase of quotas. Today, Kentucky ranks fourth among states in the number of small farms (Snell and Goetz 1997). This trait is frequently lauded as central to the state's culture and the strength of its rural communities (see especially Berry 1992).

The increasingly global nature of agricultural commodity production, however, requires most farmers to diversify their crops in order to buttress themselves against market fluctuations. This is the case in Kentucky, as well, where many tobacco farmers grow fruits, vegetables, and other crops to supplement their income. Many farmers also work part- or full-time jobs outside of agriculture. Tobacco remains, however, a key source of personal income for farmers in Kentucky. According to Snell and Goetz (1997), Kentucky contains seventeen of the twenty most tobacco-dependent counties, as designated by the U.S. Department of Agriculture. The rural nature of Kentucky also means that the majority of these counties are in areas where few off-farm employment options exist.

Clearly, tobacco is a central part of Kentucky's agricultural economy and equally important to the farmers who grow it and the municipalities that rely on tax revenue from it. It was, therefore, with trepidation that Kentucky received the Universal Tobacco Settlement Act[12] proposed by Republican senator John McCain of Arizona in November 1997. Much of the bill targeted the practices of the tobacco industry. The bill proposed regulating tobacco marketing and advertising and establishing guidelines for dealing with tobacco as a public health threat. Particularly relevant to farmers, however, was the portion of the bill that proposed the gradual phaseout of the tobacco quota system. The elimination of subsidies would make tobacco farming unprofitable on all but the largest of farms (Berry 1992). Any attempt to protect small farmers in Kentucky, therefore, must address the issue of subsidies. Furthermore, any attempt to introduce new cash crops must consider whether these crops could be profitable on the small-acre farms that dominate the region. The ominous nature of the bill, however, did present a potential bright spot for those in the state proposing alternative crops. Indeed, eliminating tobacco supports lends an immediacy to considering other crops—a context that simply does not exist when subsidies are intact and market yields are high.

I was therefore surprised that most of the patriots I talked to knew very little about the tobacco context and that few had any concrete proposals for implementing hemp. I was also puzzled when patriots seemed to pay little attention to the McCain bill when it was introduced during the middle of my year in the field. And I was nothing short of astonished that its failure on the floor in the late spring went unnoticed at the following CCK meeting. It is to this seeming paradox that I now turn.

WITHER CLASS?

While I heard a lot about legalizing hemp at CCK meetings and from informants, during my time in the field patriots seemed unable to rally around a concrete proposal for its implementation. This stands in stark contrast to their ability to successfully lobby for pro-gun legislation. As I left the field and reviewed my field notes, I debated whether I should analyze hemp as a patriot issue. Its mention at meetings clearly demonstrated its place in the movement, yet my probing for specifics surrounding hemp's reintroduction resulted in little of substance. Moreover, the deafening silence at CCK meetings about the McCain bill seemed to indicate that hemp was a passing issue in the movement. Indeed, I almost dropped it as a focus for my work because it began to seem insignificant. The more I pondered the issue, however, the more I realized the initial fanfare around hemp, and its slow decline within the movement, was significant in itself. I began to question what it was that kept patriots from formulating a plan that could provide material gain for the region and, conversely, what it was that allowed them to rally around other issues that bore them only symbolic fruit.

In posing these questions, I chose to take the Patriot Movement at face value. That is, while it is easy to write patriots off as ignorant of the "wider" issues, I decided it would be arrogant and foolhardy to do so. Studies on the Patriot Movement indicate that patriots are no less educated than their nonpatriot peers (Aho 1990; Dees 1996). Two of the patriots I interviewed had Ph.D.s and one had a law degree. Patriots were also willing to get into the nitty-gritty of what seemed to me obscure legal questions. They could cite passages from *Black's Law Dictionary* and the Uniform Commercial

Code and hold forth on them as well. Moreover, many of the patriots I interviewed had devoted several years to the cause, making it virtually an unpaid, full-time job. This commitment, I believe, compels me to take their claims seriously and ponder their inability to address the problems they identified in their own meetings.

As I was to discover through probings about hemp's potential reintroduction, discourses of patriotism thwarted patriots' ability to address livelihood concerns in a variety of ways. First and foremost, discourses of patriotism obscured class positioning as a point of reference, replacing it with "nation." So framed, patriot responses tended to advocate the integrity of the free market over the well-being of farmers, even though they presumed to speak for farmers. This became particularly apparent to me when I queried patriots about the issue of subsidies. While subsidies were widely supported in Central Kentucky, and are necessary for small farming to continue, patriots seemed unable to develop a coherent position on the issue. This is not to say that patriots should be pro-subsidy. Indeed, they could reasonably take either the pro position, arguing that subsidies protect farmers, or the con position, arguing that subsidies inhibit the introduction of hemp. When I asked patriots about tobacco subsidies, however, patriots framed their responses (whether pro or con) in terms of what was best for the American "system," which they defined as a capitalist hegemon (though not using those words). And when capital's interest conflicted with those of farmers, as they inevitably do, patriots championed the system over its producers. The result was the deafening silence that I initially found so hard to understand, given patriots' overwhelming support for hemp.

Several of the patriots I interviewed were opposed to subsidies. When I asked Joe Burton about subsidies, for example, he responded forcefully, saying that he was categorically against them. When I pressed him to explain his opposition, given the importance of subsidies to farmers, I found his concern for nation trumped that for the farmer. And because nation in patriot discourse is equated with capitalism, at times his position seemed to work directly against farmers' interests. The exchange below highlights this seeming incongruency:

> *Gallaher:* What about subsidies and things like this which come from the federal government and which protect farmers from the free market?
> *Burton:* "Subsidies" is another word for "socialism," you know that right?
> *Gallaher:* Well . . . .
> *Burton:* It is, it really is.
> *Gallaher:* Well, it depends on how you define it, but the reason I'm asking this question is because in Kentucky the big issue is tobacco farmers, right?
> *Burton:* Uh huh.
> *Gallaher:* And you want to protect tobacco farmers if you're gonna, you

know, do anything in Kentucky, if you're gonna run for office, if you're gonna have any sort of groundswell [of] support. But if you get rid of subsidies in Kentucky for the farmers, the small farming is gonna fall apart. Because they can't really grow anything else in those small lots, so what could happen is land consolidation and people getting de facto booted off their land because they can't afford to grow crops without subsidies.

Burton: Well, the subsidies came into existence during the dust bowl days, which was a good thing at that time for facing hardships, but it was never removed. And the reason, there was a design intent, and that was moving us into socialism, OK? What should have happened is once those hardships were over people were put back on their own to raise their crops that they could raise and sell at a fair market value. But the markets became so controlled at that time that the markets actually became a way to control people.

Gallaher: But if the markets are now controlled by agribusiness, then how can a Kentucky or Tennessee tobacco farmer compete with tobacco grown in Brazil?

Burton: He can't, he can't.

Gallaher: But the subsidies are the only way they can compete. If you get rid of tobacco subsidies, there goes the tobacco, there goes the small-time tobacco farmer.

Burton: Because we put him in that spot. We put him there. Had we not opened up the world's borders, OK, to where essentially anything goes, or what's best for the rest of the world. America's had it so good for so long, let's take from them and give to the rest of the world. OK? Which is what's happening. OK? Be it coal, or tobacco, or just about anything you can name.

Gallaher: So, the answer is?

Burton: The answer is to have not allowed the big conglomerates. See, at one time you couldn't do that, you couldn't have one telephone company, you know, that regulated everything. You couldn't have one corporation come in and regulate everything.

Gallaher: As in the antitrust laws?

Burton: Yes, the antitrust laws, but now somehow you can do that, see, and the little guy can no longer compete with the big guy. It used to be if you worked hard, you could produce and you could grow and become that big guy. Now, the big guy is suppressing and putting out of business mom and pop and the little guy.

I must admit to having been frustrated as I talked with Joe Burton that day. Of course, I tried not to show it at the time. I realized early on in my research that interviewees are more likely to share their perspectives when they do not feel on the defensive. Moreover, Joe Burton was, like all of the patriots I interviewed, extremely courteous to me. I had trouble, however, reconciling what seemed to me a glaring contradiction in his position, and one I had tried to no avail to coax him to explain. That is, while he supported "mom and pop" stores and even bemoaned their loss, he was unable to support government structures that enabled them in the first place. As I reviewed my research notes and gave the interview some more thought, however, I realized that the discourses through which Burton framed his view of the problem and solutions to them stymied his options. Discourses of patriotism, as they are currently constructed, view American dominance as a direct result of capitalism. Other forms of political economy, such as socialism, are the inferior "others" against which the land of the free and the powerful is defined. To accept subsidies on this rigid discursive terrain would be to fundamentally call into question the otherwise presumed "truths" that the American capitalist system accrues equally to everyone and that the so-called evil empire, the Soviet Union, was without merits.

Other patriots supported subsidies. They did so, however, on pragmatic grounds and they were quick to note their general dislike of such interventionist measures, arguing that they ultimately undermined the integrity of the system. My interview with Wasley Krogdahl is particularly illustrative here, not only because he was quite good at articulating his position, but also because he actually seemed to know details about the proposed McCain bill. When I asked him whether or not he supported the bill, he responded,

> There is a kind of vexing problem here. The quotas are what allow the small tobacco farmer to compete with those who might grow much more. In other words, the market has been bypassed. If you are going to support a product at anything but the free-market price, then you have to regulate the quantity. Otherwise, the government will be in a position of having to buy an unlimited amount of tobacco with nothing to do with it.

While his comments indicated an understanding of the difficulty tobacco farmers faced, he told me he thought tobacco would eventually lose its subsidy, as would other crops, and that it was mostly useless to fight it:

> No one wants to say we should drive anyone out of business, but I would hope that the problem is a temporary one. Hundred and fifty years ago, 85 or 90 percent of all Americans lived on a farm. Today, 2 percent. What's happened? They have left the farm and gone to the city. Now, I don't think there's any way that Congress can actually forestall an economic movement afoot. In other words, are they going to pass a law and say let's keep those 2 percent on the farm, no matter what, even if we have to pay them outright to stay there? So we would hope that a lot of the farmers will voluntarily turn to other crops or leave farming altogether.

Given his take on the sustainability (or unsustainability) of family farming, I asked him why he supported maintaining tobacco subsidies:

> Well, I would have to continue the present system until the sentiment of the farmers themselves changes. The government itself has created this dependent

class. It goes way back, sixty years or more, to the Agricultural Adjustment Act [New Deal legislation]. So the government has to assume responsibility for its actions. What is ideal and what is actual are two different things. And I think that time will eventually cure things.

While Krogdahl supports subsidies, his support is limited. Ideologically, he faults subsidies because they create a dependent class that is at odds with the free market. This underpinning explains why he can posit time as the solution rather than present any specific plan for preserving small farming—whether of tobacco or hemp. Indeed, while Krogdahl casts his support behind subsidies, his support is stymied in much the same way that Burton's analysis is when cast through the lens of "patriotism." Invoking a local version of Thatcher's "There is no alternative," Krogdahl's first priority becomes preserving the integrity of American capitalism rather than preserving the farmers for whom hemp's legalization is advocated in the first place. In this framework, farmers, for whom Krogdahl's patriot campaign presumes to speak, have very little to rally around. It is interesting to note further that, in Krogdahl's campaign literature, there is no mention of subsidies, either pro or con. This is significant, considering that the McCain bill was being debated in Congress within six months of election day and that the local papers had given significant attention to the issue (Gibson 1998; Patton 1998).

A second way that discourses of patriotism work to obfuscate patriots' class positioning concerns the interplay of nation and locality within patriot discourse. As I discovered through the process of my fieldwork, there is a constant tension within patriot rhetoric between patriots' allegiance to nation and their insistence that the local always trumps the federal. Patriots, for example, heartily embrace national signifiers. They decorate their meeting halls, as CCK did, with grandiose pictures of founding fathers, they say the pledge of allegiance before all meetings, and they define themselves and their actions as on behalf of the nation. Yet most patriots I interviewed believed the county was the highest order of power in the United States and the sheriff was the county's official arbiter. Accordingly, Kentucky patriots believe the sheriff has the constitutional right to prohibit federal action within county borders and the federal government has no constitutional basis for challenging such restriction. Indeed, all of the patriots I spoke to believe that the federal government has jurisdiction over only the District of Columbia and a smattering of protectorates, including Guam and Puerto Rico. As chapter 5 illustrates, these are well-established patriot principles stemming from the farm crisis (J. Dyer 1997), if not before (Diamond 1995; Stock 1996).

In regard to the hemp issue, this tension played out in a very intriguing manner. As I noted earlier, CCK was unable to put forward a cohesive position on subsidies or develop a plan for hemp's successful reintroduction. However, two of the patriots in my interview pool—Doug Fiedor and Gatewood Galbraith—had developed their own plans for hemp's reintroduction. Their plans, which were quite similar, illustrate this tension well. I focus first on Fiedor's plan.

In my interview with Doug Fiedor, he told me that he did not support tobacco subsidies, but that he did support subsidies for hemp. As he put it, "Well, I don't think anything should be subsidized, but I would support a state subsidy for the hemp growers because we want to get them going." To reconcile his opposition to subsidies with his desire to help hemp production, Fiedor told me that he had developed a plan to subsidize farmers at the state level, without getting the federal government involved. "My proposal," he explained,

> is that they not license people, I'm against that, but to contract with certain farmers who wish to be part of this, to grow only industrial hemp and only sell to the consortium that's going to sell to the mill that makes the paper. The paper will only be sold to Kentucky printers: 100 percent Kentucky, 100 percent! Federal regulators have nothing to say about it because nothing goes across state borders until it is a finished magazine. And you can't do anything about it. So it would be strictly Kentucky, 100 percent. Nothing else, and it would be regulated in a fashion, in that they're required to sell to only one place. That's terrible to do that. It's really terrible, but we got to get a foothold here.

Galbraith's plan was similar. He argued that the state of Kentucky could establish a guaranteed market for hemp by contracting small tobacco farmers to grow certain amounts each year. The government could then use this hemp to produce the paper it needs and sell the rest. In this manner, Kentucky would not only be less dependent on goods produced outside of Kentucky and in fact the country, but it would also be less reliant on the petrochemical companies.

When I heard Galbraith and Fiedor's plans, I was surprised at their apparent "socialist" nature. These plans represented the first concrete evidence that at least some patriots in the Kentucky movement were willing to step back from their full-fledged support of the free market and recognize the need for intervention. Yet the viability of their plans for addressing working-class concerns is mitigated by the discursive constraints imposed on them by their attachment to the local and their exclusion of other scales. Indeed, their plans are undergirded by a containerist logic (see Luke and O'Tuathail 1998). In the case of Kentucky patriots, however, they have reduced the spatial area encompassed by the "container" from the national to the state level. So bounded, patriots are unable to see how their rural, working-class concerns are linked to those of other rural peoples, both in the United States and abroad. Yet it is exactly these kinds of cross-scalar linkages, and the ability to see them as important, that are necessary to confronting the "spatial fix" employed by corporations (and supported by state-led neoliberalism) in the search for ever-expanding profit. Thus while these plans represent a step toward a class-positioned politics, the success of such a politics is blocked by the bounds of the container—which, as Doug Fiedor would say, is "100 percent Kentucky! 100 percent!"

Indeed, the attachment to the local (or in this case the state) is such that even between patriot groups the local always supersedes other scales of interest or decision making. The Theatre Command Militia, which I discussed briefly in chapter 5, is one of the few umbrella patriots groups that actually operates at the national level. When I discovered its existence, I queried several patriots about its purpose and level of power within the movement. Several patriots, such as Dan Wooten, told me they went to meetings quite regularly. Even Wooten, however, who seemed to have the most consistent attendance record, was careful to emphasize to me that

> the Theatre Command does not have any authority over local groups. It's mainly a communications network, a support network where if something goes down, then around 70 percent of the militias in this country would fall into place and organize their efforts and their resources together. But if something went down here in Central Kentucky, the people calling the shots would be the local groups controlling the territory. Only the locals would be giving orders!

Doug Fiedor's response was even more telling, and it indicates the power of the attachment to the locality to divide even the movement: "The militia is supposed to be local, and that's why you don't see any coordination between efforts anywhere. The ones that make all the noise about coordinating between efforts, the Theatre Command, they're wrong. And they're not gonna get anyone to back them up!"

While patriot discourses tend to obscure class positioning, and cross-scalar activism on its behalf, as I will demonstrate in the next chapter, discourses of patriotism are effective for buttressing cultural anxieties—about race, gender, and sexuality—by funneling them through safe, nationalistic coding. It is to a detailed example of this characteristic that I now turn.

NOTES

1. Controlled Substance Act, U.S. Code, title 21, sec. 802 (16) (1996).
2. I spoke with Corwin on February 15, 2001.
3. I spoke with Pracht on February 15, 2001.
4. I called Pracht the next day to tell him the e-mail I sent to the address he gave me had bounced. I asked him if the address was correct. He said that it was. While I

have no reason to doubt Pracht's sincerity, I must admit that I find it odd that a government agency like the U.S. Justice Department, where the DEA is housed, would use a commercial Internet provider instead of the government network (which usually carries a ".gov" ending).

5. After several days of phone tag, I finally spoke to Waite on February 26, 2001.

6. I spoke with Devallance on February 26, 2001.

7. I spoke with Bory on February 26, 2001.

8. Some groups, like NORML, support legalizing all varieties of *Cannabis*. Others, like NAIHC, advocate only the legalization of its hemp varieties. NAIHC officially takes no position on the legalization of marijuana, although it does warn on its Internet home page that it "will oppose anti-marijuana advocates who fail to distinguish industrial hemp from marijuana."

9. Herer claims that taxation was first used as a means to control human behavior during the 1930s. The strategy was tested around the Firearms Act, which withstood constitutional scrutiny in 1937 before the Supreme Court. Herer notes that a mere two weeks later the Marijuana Tax Act was introduced in Congress.

10. A few *Cannabis*-based products, such as birdseed, were exempted from the transfer tax, although growers were still required to pay the occupational tax (DEA 2001b; Musto 1999).

11. In the course of writing this book, I have been asked by several people whether Gatewood (and other patriots) think a woman's uterus should also be off limits to government meddling. Despite the social conservatism of most patriots, at present there does not appear to be a larger political will to make pro-life a rallying point for the movement. For example, when I asked Gatewood during his 1999 gubernatorial bid where he stood on the issue, he told me that, while he thought abortion was morally wrong, he also supported a woman's right to choose: "In essence, I believe in *Roe* v. *Wade*. I believe that there has to be some relief from the back alley butchering that women have been subjected to."

12. Universal Tobacco Settlement Act, Senate Bill 1414, 105th Cong., 1st sess.

7

Biosphere—Not in My State!

One of the key issues that galvanized Kentucky patriots during my time in the field was the designation of a biosphere reserve in the Land Between the Lakes region in southern Kentucky (figure 7.1). Compared to their drive to legalize hemp, patriots were effective at producing results on their biosphere initiative. As I note in the previous chapter, their crusade for industrial hemp largely fizzled out because discourses of patriotism work to mask class positionality as a category for social action. Patriots were unable to formulate a coherent position on subsidies, which are crucially tied to hemp's potential reintroduction into the state economy.

As I demonstrate by analyzing patriot opposition to biospheres, however, when patriot discourses are used to address cultural anxieties related to globalization, they allow greater successes because cultural anxieties (about race, ethnicity, and global cultural dominance) are given expression through the more palatable codes of nation and patriotism. Establishing "palatability," as I note in chapter 4, was a pivotal maneuver that allowed white supremacists to expand their cause into a movement with national impact. As I demonstrate in chapter 5, it was also crucial in facilitating Kentucky patriots' efforts to meet their goals through mainstream channels. Indeed, patriots' successes around the biosphere issue were succinctly captured by an employee of the Land Between the Lakes (LBL) Biosphere who told me that "With these guys around, its been hard to get anything done down here"!

While biospheres may appear to be an environmental issue, the crux of the patriot opposition to them is culturally based. Their opposition hinges on the association of biospheres with the United Nations, an organization patriots view as representative of culturally inferior people. Patriots believe that a UN takeover of the Land Between the Lakes Biosphere is imminent and that the biosphere's impending seizure represents a tragic loss of U.S. sovereignty. Because patriots identify biospheres so completely with the UN, and

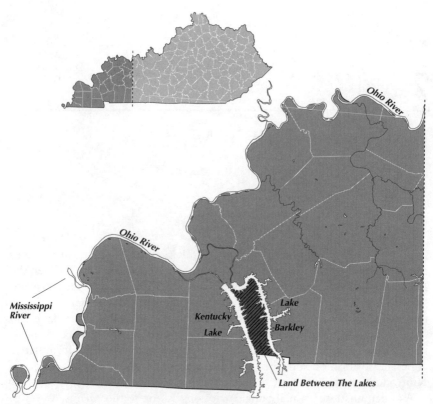

Figure 7.1   The Land Between the Lakes Region

because they make a variety of claims about these linkages, I begin this chapter by describing the biosphere concept and the logistics involved in operating biospheres. This factual information provides a necessary backdrop for understanding and evaluating patriot claims about them. I then outline the specific history of the LBL Biosphere, noting the historical tensions that predate its designation and exacerbate its operation today. In the third section, I outline patriot opposition to the LBL Biosphere. As I demonstrate, much of this opposition is based on erroneous assumptions about LBL's structural connection to the UN. In the fourth section, I describe how patriots once again used the General Assembly to address their concerns, analyzing a patriot-inspired bill about biospheres and the positive momentum it has built for the Kentucky movement. Finally, I examine what Kentucky patriots' opposition to the LBL Biosphere says about the way discourses of patriotism function in the movement.

MAN AND THE BIOSPHERE

In 1968, the United Nations Educational, Scientific, and Cultural Organization (UNESCO) convened a Conference on Conservation and Rational Use of the Biosphere in Paris, France. Its purpose was to systematically address threats to global ecosystems, while at the same time facilitating the material needs of the globe's growing population, much of which lived in undeveloped countries. As UNESCO posed the question at the time, "How can we reconcile conservation of biological resources with their sustainable use?" (UNMAB 2001).

The 1968 conference resulted in the UN's decision to launch a Man and the Biosphere Programme (UNMAB). The program's goal was to develop a series of broad protocols for how to meet development needs while also preserving the environment for future generations. Its signature program, the biosphere reserve, was developed and formally initiated in 1974. At root, UNMAB envisioned creating at least one biosphere in each of the world's major biogeographical regions; it viewed the biospheres as "experimental sites" where protocols could be "tested, refined, demonstrated and implemented" (UNMAB 2001).

Biospheres are organized into three basic areas (see figure 7.2). The first, an inner area called the "core," functions as the nerve center of the biosphere. In it, the wealth and diversity of the biogeographical region represented should be in abundance. In order to protect the flora and fauna there, human activity in the core area is restricted to research and monitoring. The core area is also required to have domestic legal protection, so that disruptive activities such as mining, drilling, and human settlement may be prohibited and enforced by law (UNMAB 2001).

Buffer zones are the second area of a biosphere and, as their name implies, they are meant to serve as a buffer between the reserve's prized biological treasures and human activity that might harm or disturb them. Buffer areas are frequently used for experimental research on the management and use of natural resources as well as rehabilitation of damaged ecological systems. Some human settlement, as well as tourism and recreational activities, may occur in buffer zones, although human settlement at high densities is not encouraged. The outer edge of buffer zones may also contain human activity related to economic development. As with core areas, however, buffer zones are required by UNESCO to have legal protection so that human activity considered disruptive may be legally regulated (UNMAB 2001).

The outer edge of buffer zones, where some economic activity may occur, is designed to blend into the third area, the zone of transition.[1] Here, economic development is encouraged, although development is intended to be sustaining, as best as possible, of the ecosystem. As UNMAB (2001) explains

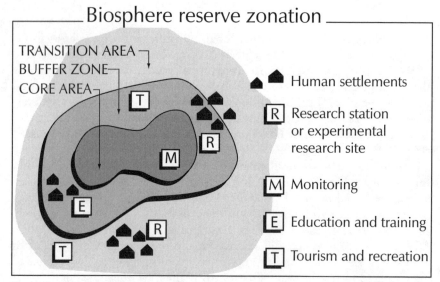

Figure 7.2   Biosphere Prototype
Source: "Biosphere Reserve Zonation" © UNESCO reproduced by permission of UNESCO.

it, "It is here that the local communities, conservation agencies, scientists, civil associations, cultural groups, private enterprises and other stakeholders must agree to work together to manage and sustainably develop the area's resources for the benefit of the people who live there." It is important to note, however, that UNESCO does not require the zone of transition to have protected legal status (whereby human activity and land use may be curtailed by law). While a biosphere reserve may demarcate a zone of transition on its maps and other printed material, it does not necessarily own the land or have legal control over land-use activities within it. This is frequently the case in countries with strong private property protections. None of the biospheres in the United States, for example, own the land in their zones of transition. Rather, land in these zones is privately owned. To make the zone of transition a viable part of a biosphere in this sort of context, managers are expected to establish voluntary cooperation with the landowners in it.

To jump-start the biosphere concept and to make it a reality, UNESCO established broad guidelines in the early seventies for reserve formation. Given the UN's organizational structure, these guidelines were designed for implementation at the state level. UNESCO requires national governments interested in creating biospheres to establish a domestic MAB program. Generally, national governments are encouraged to house their MAB programs within an existing agency and branch of government. The United States, for example, housed its program, USMAB, in the State Department.

In 2000, USMAB was moved and placed under the jurisdiction of the U.S. Forest Service. Once established, a national MAB is expected to select (or accept applications for) potential biosphere designation and to nominate them to the UNMAB committee responsible for awarding designation status. Currently the United States has forty-seven sites with a UNESCO biosphere designation.[2]

There are a variety of ways in which biospheres may be crafted. Typically, a state government will nominate an existing national park or reserve for biosphere designation. This method is the most common way to craft a biosphere reserve, because existing reserves, such as national parks or game reserves, already have the extant space necessary to meet UNMAB guidelines, the domestic legal code to protect them, and existing limitations on human activity within them. In these cases, the national government in question owns the biosphere reserve and charges an appropriate government agency with operating it. The Denali National Park in Alaska is a good example of this kind of reserve formation. The U.S. government has owned Denali since 1917, when it was established as a national park (then called Mt. McKinley National Park). In 1976, the USMAB program applied for and received UN biosphere designation for Denali. The National Park Service is currently in charge of its administration.

Biospheres may also be crafted on private land, although this type of formation is less common than the national park model. Generally, the owners of these biospheres are nongovernmental organizations with environmental mandates. The biosphere reserve on the eastern shore of Virginia, for example, is privately owned by the Virginia Coast Reserve, a project of the Nature Conservancy (Virginia Coast Reserve 2001).

Finally, biospheres may also be crafted from a combination of government and privately held lands. The Golden Gate Biosphere reserve in the San Francisco Bay area, for example, comprises land owned by nine different parties, including the University of California, the Audubon Ranch Society, and the City of San Francisco (GGBR 2001).

As the previous examples indicate, biospheres are owned by national governments or private entities within them. As I note above, however, in the United States ownership only covers the core and buffer zone areas of the biosphere. Zones of transition, because they have no legal status or protection, are only governed by federal laws and applicable laws of the state in which a reserve is located. Landowners in zones of transition may use their land however they choose within the law, unless they voluntarily submit to a reserve's land-use suggestions.

What this arrangement means is that while the biosphere concept is the brainchild of UNESCO, it does not operate, manage, or otherwise control individual biospheres. UNESCO's only power over them is its ability to extend and revoke designation. Indeed, at a UNMAB conference held in Seville, Spain, in 1995, biosphere managers from around the globe estab-

lished a statutory framework in which this arrangement was specifically codified (UNMAB 1995). In article 2, section 3 of the agreement, the UNMAB
program specified that "Individual biosphere reserves remain under the sovereign jurisdiction of the States where they are situated. Under the present
Statutory Framework, States take the measures which they deem necessary
according to their national legislation" (UNMAB 1995).

While the above specifications clearly denote the sovereignty of individual
nations over biospheres within their borders, as I demonstrate in the following two sections, a variety of opponents within the United States believe that
biospheres are spaces subject to "multilateral jurisdiction." This is certainly
the case among patriot opponents of the Land Between the Lakes Biosphere
in southern Kentucky.

CONTENTIOUS TERRITORY: THE MAKING AND REMAKING OF A LITTLE SWATH OF LAND BETWEEN TWO RIVERS

Land Between the Lakes is beautiful. There is no doubt about it. The area is
covered by a lush broad-leaf forest and surrounded on either side by long,
deep blue lakes. Thousands of tourists visit each year to hike and camp in its
forests and to fish, swim, and boat on its waterways. Despite its natural
beauty, Land Between the Lakes is an artificial landscape—it is the by-
product of a damming project undertaken by the Tennessee Valley Authority
(TVA), a government agency created during the Franklin Roosevelt administration in the 1930s.

In the early thirties, during his first administration, Roosevelt launched an
ambitious plan to develop the Tennessee Valley by harnessing the Tennessee
River and its tributaries to produce electricity and spur economic development. The valley was an ideal site for such a project. Not only did the region
have plentiful water, but also its local population was in dire need of aid. At
the time, most of the region's inhabitants still lived without electricity and,
although the area's soils were highly fertile, overfarming in the area had seriously depleted the soil, leading to a serious problem with erosion. When set
against the backdrop of the Great Depression, these problems took on
heightened significance (Callahan 1980; TVA 2001). Roosevelt saw his plan
as a way to meet the needs of a regionally strapped rural population while
also bolstering the overall quality of the nation's infrastructure. Winning the
rapid support of the region's congressmen and business interests, Roosevelt's
proposed legislation, the Tennessee Valley Authority Act, was passed into
law on May 18, 1933.

While the TVA Act provided a variety of benefits for the region's strapped
farmers, from electricity to access to nitrogen-based fertilizers, it was not
without its detractors. Indeed, the backbone of the project entailed damming

large parts of the Tennessee River and resettling thousands of resistant residents. That the TVA had the power of eminent domain[3] at its disposal did little to alleviate criticisms of the plan as heavy-handed.

The initial development of the TVA was focused in central Tennessee and northern Alabama. In the late fifties, however, northern stretches of the Tennessee River in the state of Kentucky were incorporated into the plan as well. Since Kentucky is north of Tennessee, the general east-west orientation of the Tennessee River (whose headwaters are in the Appalachian Mountains) and its confluence point on the Ohio River to the north mean that the portions of the river in Kentucky are downstream from Tennessee (see figure 7.3). The site considered for development in Kentucky was a stretch of land in southern Kentucky where the Tennessee River and the Cumberland River flowed within a few miles of one another. At the time, the region was known locally as "land between the rivers." The TVA's plan was to dam both rivers at their closest point, joining them by a narrow channel and creating two finger lakes extending along each river's original basin. In 1959, the TVA began work on the project, creating Lake Barkley from its dam on the Cumberland River and Kentucky Lake from its dam on the Tennessee.

Unlike earlier TVA projects, which were designed to produce electricity and spur industrial development, however, the Kentucky project was designed to stimulate economic development through tourism. It was to be the first venture of its kind, focusing on building a tourist economy around a protected wildlife area. As the LBL (2001a) home page describes it, "LBL was formed to demonstrate how an area with limited timber, agricultural, and industrial resources could be converted into a recreation asset that would stimulate economic growth in the region. LBL is the country's only such national demonstration area." After construction on the project was completed in 1963, President John F. Kennedy designated the area a "National Recreation Area," which is roughly synonymous in legal terms with "national park" designation.

Visitors to LBL may engage in a variety of tourist-related activities, but the region's protected status means that certain activities are prohibited or controlled. For example, hunting certain animals, such as turkey, is prohibited after established kill quotas are met and, while visitors may gather mushrooms, nuts, berries, and fruits, they are prohibited from taking other flora or fauna from the park. LBL also permits only limited timber cutting on its land, the majority of which is used to thin forests in order to prevent forest fires (LBL 2001b).

In the late 1980s, the TVA decided to nominate a portion of its LBL land for biosphere designation. LBL's protected status and its lush broad-leaf forests, which have suffered from pollution in more densely settled areas in central Tennessee, made it an ideal choice for nomination. In 1991, the area nominated received official designation from UNESCO and currently it is

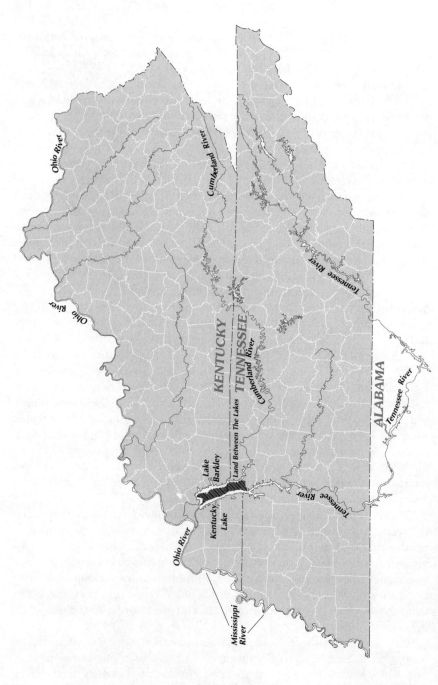

Figure 7.3   Land Between the Lakes in TVA Context

listed on both the UNMAB and USMAB web sites as a biosphere reserve. Only 25 percent, or 42,500 acres of LBL land, however, bears the biosphere designation (LBL 2001b). Also, the geographic layout of the reserve is a bit unorthodox. To work around the existing tourist facilities, the reserve's core area is composed of several noncontiguous sites (figure 7.4). And, as with other domestic reserves, the LBL biosphere does not have a zone of transition with legal protection. In 1999, the TVA transferred ownership and operations of LBL (and the biosphere reserve within it) to the U.S. Forest Service.

Despite the international prestige associated with having biosphere status, neither LBL's promotional literature nor its web page foregrounds its biosphere designation. Indeed, on LBL's extensive web page, only two references are made to its designation and they are made in passing. The first mention is buried in a subsection of the LBL web page about its forests (LBL 2001b). At the end of the page, the reader is informed that 25 percent of LBL land is designated as a biosphere reserve and that forest management (such as forest thinning) is prohibited on it unless nearby residents or LBL buildings are in immediate danger (recall that human activity in core areas is restricted to research and monitoring). The second reference is on the LBL rules and regulations page, where LBL is listed as one of three hundred biosphere reserves in the United States. Significantly, none of the biosphere's scientific projects are mentioned in the context of either USMAB or UNMAB goals. Moreover, while LBL has several maps posted on its web page, none of them depict the parcels with biosphere designation. Indeed, the first such map was published in May 2002, over ten years after LBL first received official biosphere designation.

This absence stands in stark contrast not only to UNMAB guidelines, but also to the common practices of other U.S. biospheres. According to UNMAB guidelines, designated reserves are "encouraged to publicize their biosphere reserves, for example, with a commemorative plaque and distributing information material indicating this special status" (UNMAB 2001). Among U.S. biospheres, it is also common for reserves, especially those that are also national parks, to display their designation prominently. Denali National Park in Alaska, for example, advertises its biosphere status prominently on the top of its web page (NPS 2001a). A variety of other biospheres do as well, including reserves as diverse as the Everglades National Park in southern Florida (see NPS 2001b), the Golden Gate Biosphere Reserve in California (see GGBR 2001), and the Big Bend National Park in southern Texas (see NPS 2001c).

Much of this absence can be attributed to the contentious nature of the LBL biosphere designation in Kentucky. As I note below, the Patriot Movement in Kentucky has made LBL's designation a point of contention in state politics and attempted to void its designation in the General Assembly and inhibit its ability to forge constructive relationships with landowners in its

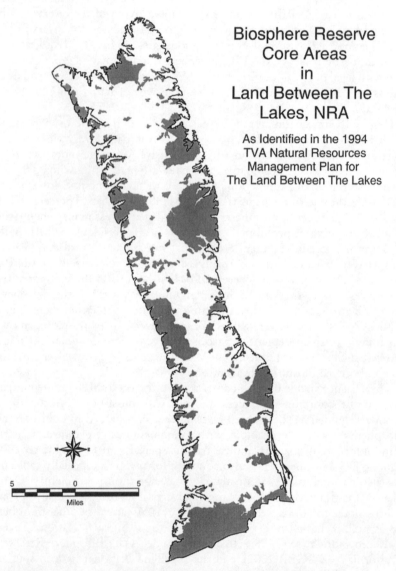

Biosphere Reserve
Core Areas
in
Land Between The
Lakes, NRA

As Identified in the 1994
TVA Natural Resources
Management Plan for
The Land Between The Lakes

Figure 7.4   Core Parcels in the Land Between the Lakes Biosphere

Source: This image appears courtesy of the U.S. Forest Service.

zone of transition. While patriots' opposition is largely based on cultural grounds, it is important to recognize that the opposition to the reserve that patriots have mobilized is built on a continuing anger and mistrust over the original TVA project, which entailed significant social and economic disruptions (see Chandler 1984; Havard 1983).

As it did in the thirties, the TVA used eminent domain to acquire the land it needed to create the LBL recreation area, and in the process it fueled the anger not only of the landowners that occupied affected areas, but also of neighboring people who would see their entire landscape change in a short period of time. In the LBL region, 788 families (about three thousand people) were removed from their land; the opposition was so strong that some had to be removed by force (see Chandler 1984; Havard 1983). The TVA also evoked the wrath of locals by limiting and in some cases bypassing local involvement in the agency's decision to dam the Tennessee and Cumberland Rivers. Indeed, for many, the first time they heard about the TVA's plans for LBL, it was presented as a done deal. Responding to this context, and the anger that it produced, Congress held TVA Oversight hearings in 1975. One of the former landowners in the LBL region, Corrine Whitehead, urged Congress to democratize the organization, noting that it had inordinate power over people's everyday lives:

> The people most vitally affected by the fickle and unresponsive policies of TVA must have a voting voice in the selection of the TVA Board members. If the people of the Tennessee Valley and the nation are capable of electing governors, congressmen, senators, and other representatives, then it stands to reason the people have the capacity to elect their choice of a representative to the TVA Board. TVA yields more power over their lives than any other agency in the United States' Government. (Whitehead, quoted in Chandler 1984, 173)

Residents were no less angry with the TVA for its morally dubious claims that it was preserving a delicate ecosystem. Residents noted with irony that the TVA's environmentalist agenda left them landless so that thousands of tourists from across the country could get away from life in polluted cities for a few days. The process even disturbed environmentalists in the region. John Egerton, an environmentalist who used to own land in the area, described LBL this way in his book, *The Americanization of Dixie; The Southernization of America:*

> The Land Between the Lakes is a "national demonstration" of the destructive consequences of bureaucratic insensitivity and greed, an example of cold and impersonal manipulation to create a controlled environment in which the past is obliterated and all human activity is regulated. It is a concept of urban renewal writ large across a rural landscape. (Egerton, quoted in Havard 1983, 312–13)

As I note in the following section, these sentiments, expressed succinctly here, infuse the patriot politics against LBL's biosphere designation. The heart of the *patriot* politics on the issue, however, has less to do with former landowners and their descendants' claims to the land than it does with patriot anxiety about globalization. Indeed, the extant tensions in LBL become a convenient screen on which patriots project their anxieties about global "others," which are collectively personified by the figure of the UN. In the next section, I outline Kentucky patriots' opposition to biospheres, demonstrating how patriot antagonism toward biospheres is based on presumed links that biospheres have to the UN—links, which as I demonstrate, are not substantiated by the factual record.

BIOSPHERES AS A PATRIOT ISSUE

Patriots oppose biospheres for a variety of reasons. As I would discover, however, patriots seemed to know very little about the actual LBL reserve and appeared to misunderstand key components of its structural organization. Indeed, while it is difficult to assess whether patriots were purposefully misconstruing the facts or were unwittingly working from inaccurate information, it is clear that the bulk of their opposition is based on incorrect information that is taken as fact.

In Kentucky, patriots oppose biospheres on three interrelated grounds. Unlike other complaints, their first complaint with the reserves is not based on a faulty factual base. Rather, their belief that biospheres are "antihuman," falls into that politically gray area where perspective is vitally important. The reader will recall from chapter 1 that, when Norman Davis took the stage at the first CCK meeting to talk about the LBL biosphere, he sternly warned the audience members, "They're gonna take care of the bugs, but not you!" When Henry Lamb gave his two guest lectures to CCK, he made comparable statements. Opening his speech about biospheres at the June 12, 1997, CCK meeting, Lamb told the audience, "Lafayette Park is full of homeless people trying to get out of the snow and we want to give a spotted owl money." When he got into the meat of his speech, he also warned the audience that the biosphere concept is dangerous because it is based on the idea that the needs of plants and animals should prevail over those of humans.

While statements like these make most environmentalists cringe, they are not uncommon in rural areas where environmental restrictions are read, and rightly so in many cases, as paternalistic. In the case of LBL, the triumphalism of the TVA's environmental mandate, which was crafted with little input from the surrounding population, means messages like Lamb's can find a sympathetic ear. Indeed, for a region that was required to sacrifice itself for an environmental agenda not of its own making, Lamb's words ring true.

As I discovered during my interviews, patriots were well aware of this latent anger and they couched their opposition to the LBL designation in terms that appealed to it. As Norman Davis explained to me in our interview, speaking of the people living near LBL, "They was scared to death [the TVA] were going to take more [land]. They already took property once . . . paid them twenty-seven bucks an acre. That was from the thirties to the sixties. They closed off roads to churches, to cemeteries, and all this stuff under this biodiversity crap!" Wasley Krogdahl framed his resistance to LBL in historical terms as well. As he did when we discussed the tobacco issue, he also linked the problems at LBL to bad precedents set during the New Deal: "It goes back into the Roosevelt Administration, which initiated the TVA. So these people have been moved once on the grounds of public necessity, which was dubious even then." Doug Fiedor also placed his opposition to the LBL designation in context of the area's history:

> The problem is the TVA moved all of those people out of there in the sixties or seventies. People that had lived there for generations, and they said they wanted to use the land for the TVA. Well, excuse me, twenty years later and it's not used. Now they want to hand it off, because they don't want to pay for it anymore, hand if off to UNESCO. People want their land back. I don't blame them. Why not?

As Fiedor's comments imply, patriots also oppose biospheres because they believe that UNESCO will soon own the deed to LBL property. As I note in the previous section, however, UNESCO does not own or control any of the more than three hundred biosphere reserves in the world today. Rather, most biospheres are owned by national governments, while the remainder are held by private interests. In the case of LBL, the TVA owned the reserve until 1999, when it was transferred to the Forest Service. It is, therefore, the property of the U.S. government. Yet, the patriots I interviewed routinely referred to one of two scenarios. The first held that the UN owned the reserve. Patriots usually reserved this contention for public appearances, when they were trying to sell their position with catchy sound bites. The second scenario, which was the rendition I commonly heard in my interviews, held that the U.S. government owned the reserve but was preparing to transfer its ownership to the UN. In my interview with Dan Wooten, for example, he presented UN takeover as imminent and warned me that things would get ugly when it happened:

> If the United Nations takes that land from the Tennessee Valley Authority, there's going to be a fight down there. And the ridge runners, and the militia down there, they could handle the whole thing themselves. But its gonna be large. And, you know, here's the issue. If they show up with troops, in uniform, in United Nations uniforms, everyone of them is gonna go back in a box. I'm

not issuing that [command] in any way, but its an invasion of this country. They have no right to do that, and anybody who places those men there, and puts them in danger—where they ended up coming back to their families dead—will be considered a criminal. In other words, the people that established that United Nations territory, they broke the law.

Wasley Krogdahl also presented a UN takeover as looming, but as a politician running for office, his presentation was more measured than Wooten's: "The TVA wants to give that land—from which they actually removed these people—to the United Nations for a biosphere reserve and to exclude all human activity. Well, in the first place, they can't do it. I mean, constitutionally they can't do it."

As I was to discover during my interviews, patriots also had a well-stocked arsenal of patriot propaganda to use in making their case. There are now a variety of patriot-inspired businesses that produce, market, and sell professional and scientific-looking documents that local groups like CCK may use to legitimize their agenda. Of particular note was a map that I would see frequently, both at CCK meetings, where it was for sale, and in my interviews, where patriots produced it as visual evidence of their claims (see figure 7.5). The map is produced by Environmental Perspectives, Inc. (EPI), a patriot organization in Bangor, Maine, whose mission is to document trends leading to "one world government" and provide "scientific" information to assist those opposing it (EPI 2001). The map, entitled "Simulated Reserve and Corridor System to Protect Biodiversity," is a spatial representation of information from over five different data sources concerning environmentally protected land in the United States. The data, when considered as one set, is logically incompatible because some data sources refer to lands with extant legal protection, while others refer to sites proposed for protection but with no current legal standing. The map may be considered a propaganda map because it takes data not coded into biosphere categories and "reinterprets" them through this framework. The result is a map that presents the United States as one giant biosphere with the majority of land coded into core and buffer regions where little to no human settlement will be permitted. When I saw this map in the field, it was in color, with "core" areas shaded red and "buffer zones" shaded in yellow. EPI also produces a black and white version, which is reproduced here.

During my interview with Wasley Krogdahl, he produced the EPI map when we were discussing the LBL biosphere designation, asking me, "Have you seen this map, here? Now, the red areas are called core areas. No human activity will be allowed. It will be closed off to the public. Look at the western United States. . . . [A]pproximately 50 percent of the land area of the United States will be closed to the citizens of the United States." Joe Burton also produced the EPI map during our interview. Pointing at it, he said,

Simulated Reserve and Corridor System to Protect Biodiversity
As Mandated by the Convention on Biological Diversity, The Wildlands Project, UN and US
Man and Biosphere Program, and Various UN, US Heritage Programs, and NAFTA

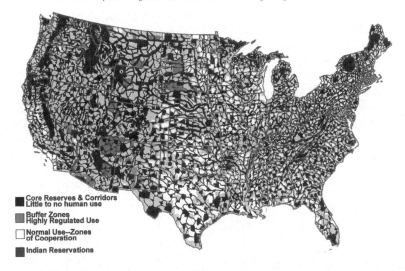

Core Reserves & Corridors
Little to no human use

Buffer Zones
Highly Regulated Use

Normal Use--Zones
of Cooperation

Indian Reservations

Taken From:The United Nations Convention on Biological Diversity, Article 8a-e; United Nations Global Biodiversity Assessment, Section 13.4.2.2.3; US Man and the Biosphere Strategic Plan, UN/US Heritage
Corridor Program, "The Wildlands Project", Wild Earth, 1992,. Also see Science, "The High Cost of Biodiversity," 25 June, 1993, pp 1965-1871 and the Border 21 Sidebar of NAFTA. The very high percentage
of buffer zone in the West is due to the very high percentage of federal land. NOTE: Do not use for real estate purposes.   Copyright 1996, Environmental Perspectives, Inc. (207) 945-9878

Figure 7.5   Patriot-Produced Biosphere Propaganda Map
Source: This image appears courtesy of Environmental Perspectives, Inc.

"There are huge areas, the red areas, where no humans will be allowed to go into. The yellow areas are the buffer zones, you'll be able to go in during the daytime but you'll have to come out at night." As Burton's comment indicates, he and many other patriots fear that once the UN gains ownership over biosphere land in the United States, it will begin to resettle people living in core areas and restrict access to buffer areas surrounding them. At the first CCK meeting, Norman Davis made the same claim, telling the audience that when biospheres are handed over to the UN people will be "herded onto reservations."

These fears explain a third reason why patriots oppose biospheres—they view their control by the UN as an infringement of U.S. sovereignty. Indeed, the crux of patriot opposition to biospheres, and what allows them to discursively define the issue as a "patriot" one, is their belief that biospheres are multilateral spaces controlled by supranational entities lacking constitutional status or democratic mandate. As Gatewood Galbraith explained to me in our second interview, the U.S. government

> entered us into the biosphere treaty, where large acreages are going to be set aside and used as biosphere areas, . . . and we resist that because it is the UN.

. . . The Constitution says that no part of the state may be sold or given away except by consent of the legislature. So it violates the state Constitution to have any of these areas given over to a place where the Constitution does not exist. And when the UN takes over these areas, the United States Constitution is superceded by UN regulation. . . . [I]ts obviously a Constitutional issue to which patriots are much attracted.

Other patriots even went so far as to claim the UN was engaging in preparations for invasion operations from within the confines of the reserve. When Henry Lamb was invited to CCK's June 12, 1997, meeting, for example, Charlie Puckett told a reporter covering the event that armed UN troops were protecting the reserve's perimeter and that UN employees had infiltrated surrounding areas with special vans and were waiting for the go-ahead to tear up roads, eject landowners, and destroy entire counties (see Becker 1997). He did not, however, produce any evidence to substantiate his claims.

ANOTHER PATRIOT INITIATIVE MEETS
THE GENERAL ASSEMBLY

There are two things that are particularly striking about Kentucky patriots' opposition to the LBL Biosphere. First, while patriots have been vociferous opponents of LBL's biosphere designation, their opposition to it came several years after the original designation had been granted. LBL received its designation in 1991, nearly four years before the Kentucky Patriot Movement emerged. Their actions against the LBL reserve, therefore, have focused on discrediting the reserve among the local population and making it difficult for its managers to foster cooperative projects in its zone of transition. Second, while patriots' opposition to biospheres is grounded on factually incorrect information, they not only went to the Kentucky General Assembly with this erroneous information, but they also found a receptive ear for it once they arrived.

In 1997, the Kentucky General Assembly held a special legislative session, opening chambers for a month-long session in May and another in September. During the May session, Senator Virgil Moore, a Republican from Leitchfield, introduced Senate Resolution 35. The resolution stated the General Assembly's opposition to both the USMAB program and biosphere designations within U.S. borders and urged the U.S. Congress not to ratify the UN Convention on Biological Diversity.[4] The resolution passed unanimously by a voice vote on May 29 and was placed on the legislative record. By order of the resolution, copies of SR 35 were also sent to President Bill Clinton, Secretary of State Madeleine Albright, and the Kentucky delegation in Congress.

As with the concealed weapons bill in 1996, the links between the passage of SR 35 and patriot efforts on its behalf are clear. Before the resolution's passage in late May, speakers at CCK made public references to their efforts on its behalf. When Henry Lamb gave his first speech at CCK a few weeks after the resolution's passage, he publicly praised CCK's efforts, congratulated them for the passage of SR 35, and noted its success as a national model.

A perusal of the resolution's sponsors also indicates clear links to the Patriot Movement. The resolution's primary sponsor, Virgil Moore, is widely regarded in patriot circles as a patriot-friendly legislator. At the end of my interview with Norman Davis, for example, he suggested I call Moore, adding "I work with him all the time." As I note in chapter 5, Senator Moore and Representative Perry Clarke were the featured guest speakers at Davis's most recent patriot gathering on his farm in April 2001. Patriots also frequently mentioned Senator Richard "Dick" Roeding, a Republican from northern Kentucky and one of the resolution's cosponsors, as supportive of patriot causes. Still another cosponsor, Barry Metcalf, campaigned at the first CCK meeting for his bid to become the Republican nominee for the U.S. Senate. Of course, as I was to discover over time, establishing such links required little investigative work. Patriots and legislators alike acknowledge they work together. When I interviewed Norman Davis, for example, he told me that he wrote portions of Resolution 35 for Senator Moore and produced a copy for me to take home. When I called Senator Moore's office, Moore confirmed the collaboration, adding "You can pretty much trust anything Norm Davis tells you"![5]

The passage of the biosphere resolution by a voice vote in the General Assembly was significant for the Kentucky Patriot Movement at a variety of levels. From a mobilization standpoint, it demonstrated that patriots were serious about their efforts to operate above ground and through political channels. When viewed in conjunction with their success around the 1996 concealed weapons bill, the 1997 resolution also helped established a lineage of legislative successes that patriots may point to as they expand their movement.

The resolution was also significant because it established patriot claims about biospheres as findings on the legislative record. Indeed, despite the factual inaccuracies that undergird patriots' opposition to the biospheres, Resolution 35 established several of these erroneous claims as "fact."[6] Most notably, the resolution found that "the Biosphere Program threatens to place millions of acres of land under the control of the United Nations viz. agreements and/or executive orders," even though UNMAB guidelines explicitly acknowledge the sovereignty of individual nations over biosphere reserves within their borders (UNMAB 1995). The resolution also found that "the use of land in biosphere areas for ordinary commercial or agriculture purposes may be severely restricted or eliminated," even though such restrictions are not enforceable in the zone of transition, where private property ownership occurs and restrictions on core and buffer areas were in place through TVA long before biosphere designation was granted. Finally, the resolution found that "biosphere reserves are, by definition, designed to continually expand each of the three zones," even though there are no protocols in either the UN or USMAB guidelines requiring individual biospheres to expand their acreage. Establishing expansion as mandatory, however, justifies patriot theories that the UN will seize U.S. land and put its citizens on reservations.

Finally, the passage of Resolution 35 may be regarded as significant because the mainstream right has invoked it in its own fights over the biosphere program. During the 105th Congress in 1997, for example, Congressman Don Young introduced House Resolution 901, a part of which concerned biosphere reserves.[7] In his bill, Young stipulated that the secretary of the interior would no longer be permitted to nominate any sites within U.S. territory for biosphere designation and that the secretary would be required to nullify existing designations unless state legislatures in affected states voted to maintain designation by 2000. The bill was sent to the Senate but was never brought to the floor for a vote.[8] While the bill was being debated in Congress, however, Congresswoman Helen Chenoweth, a Republican from Idaho who has ties to militia groups in her home state (see Dees 1996), referenced the Kentucky resolution in her floor speech supporting Young's proposed bill. A letter to the editor of the *Kentucky Post* several days later highlighted her reference, proudly noting the *national* impact of Resolution 35. The writer, Craig Brown, wrote,

> While [the cosponsors'] efforts have gone almost unnoticed by the media in Northern Kentucky, they haven't escaped the attention of Congress. During the debate on HR 901, which will abolish the Biosphere Reserve and Heritage River programs pushed by the Environmental Protection Agency, Congressman George Miller of California rose in defense of the EPA program. Part of his argument was that the people of Kentucky were wildly enthusiastic over the biosphere program and all the "benefits" it would bring. That was the signal for Congresswoman Chenoweth of Idaho to rise and read to the unenlightened congressman a unanimous resolution by the Kentucky Senate. (Brown 1997)

While the significance of such invocations should not be overstated, they are important because they represent a process of discursive equivalence making between far and more moderate right-wing positions—one that is made all the easier by their "legitimate" packaging by patriots.

RACE, CLASS, AND A REALLY
SMALL BIT OF LAND

There is a clear disconnection between the LBL Biosphere as it is and the LBL reserve as patriots see it. In fact, it is worth reiterating here that, despite patriots' claims to the contrary, no one in the LBL region has lost property or seen added restrictions placed on their land use since the 1991 biosphere designation. Nor have UN troops practiced maneuvers on the land in an imminent bid for a takeover, as Charlie Puckett claimed in both my interview with him and in an interview he did with the *Herald-Leader* in 1997 (Becker 1997).

This is not to say, of course, that patriots are purposefully manipulating the facts in a cold or calculating way. Indeed, while it is difficult to definitively tell whether or not patriots knew their factual claims were inaccurate, it is clear that most patriots see the LBL Biosphere as a real threat and view the issue as local evidence of well-established patriot theories about UN aggression. Indeed, if a patriot already believes these theories, it is not a stretch for him to accept claims about a UN takeover at LBL. Moreover, when I confronted patriots about their factual inaccuracies regarding land-ownership on the LBL reserve, they seemed untroubled, brushing aside my objections and telling me, as Steve Kelly, Norman Davis, and Joe Burton all did, that the only reason the UN did not own the land was because patriots had stopped the UN in its tracks.

This is also not to say that patriots or locals in the area should support the biosphere designation. The history of LBL's creation warrants a healthy dose of skepticism about the biosphere and, for a state that is plagued with a chronic lack of well-paying jobs, it is reasonable to expect residents to be offended by calls to save the environment when such calls might prohibit industry from moving to their area. It is worth noting, however, that none of these concerns were raised in either patriots' public opposition to the LBL designation or in their interviews with me about it.

Given that biospheres are not a threat in the way patriots claim they are, and given that few seem worried about the more traditional concerns listed above, it is worth asking what concerns their efforts do address if not these. As a point of entry for such an analysis, a thorough unpacking of the patriot view of the UN is clearly in order.

My background research on the Patriot Movement prepared me for the anti-UN sentiment I encountered during my research. I must admit, however, that I found myself continuously surprised by patriots' constant references to the dangers the UN supposedly posed. Housed in a university setting, I was more accustomed to the academic view of the UN as a powerless and in some cases inept organization. And, while I knew going in that the UN was commonly portrayed as the command center for the new world order in patriot rhetoric, I still had trouble understanding why an organization so far removed from the daily lives of my informants could inspire such fear, anger, and vitriol in them.

I began every interview, therefore, with a variation of the same question. "What," I queried my informants, "is it about the UN that makes patriots

so uncomfortable?" As time went by, I came to realize that the UN represented a "global other" for patriots, an other onto which they could cast
their anxieties about globalization and through which they could restore an
eroding sense of superiority for themselves.

When I asked my UN question to my informants, for example, they usually began their responses with reference to globalization, which they
referred to alternately as "globalism," "internationalism," or the "new
world order." While these terms can have slight variations in meaning within
patriot rhetoric, in general, when patriots used them in their interviews with
me, they were usually referring to economic and political integration at a
global scale. While patriots' responses varied, from the eloquent to the blunt,
they also all indicated a basic unease with the forces they associated with
globalization.

When I asked Wasley Krogdahl to explain why the UN was such a flash-
point in the Patriot Movement, he focused on political integration, telling me
simply, "The UN has programs that would harm the United States of
America and its citizens." When I asked Steve Kelly the same question, he
responded more bluntly, "It's because Paul Patton [the governor] is siding
with the globalizers, that's why!" Galbraith's response to my question was
more lengthy:

> The real question is sovereignty. That's the real question. Do you understand
> what sovereignty is? It means the rule. Whoever is my sovereign is my leader,
> my ruler. Its where my rights, where my citizenship comes from, OK? Now
> the Constitution and the Bill of Rights set up the United States and conse-
> quently we are the sovereigns of the United States, that's our sovereign. If we
> take on another sovereign, then all of a sudden we are outside the blanket pro-
> tection of the Constitution and the Bill of Rights. If we give over the decision-
> making processes about our private lives, our environment, our economy, and
> other things, then what? . . . The UN has become, through their actions, an
> attempt at supersovereignty over the whole planet! And people like myself are
> afraid that for that to take place the UN wants us to abdicate the Constitution
> and the Bill of Rights.

When I pressed patriots to explain themselves further, however, I realized
that even though patriots have economic fears about globalization, when it
came to their concerns about the UN (and thus its place in a patriot politics)
it was mostly cultural anxiety they were addressing. Indeed, while the UN
was the brainchild of the United States, and has since its inception been an
organization for all nations, patriots view the UN as representative of inferior nations and peoples and resent being grouped with them. When I asked
Wasley Krogdahl, for example, what he thought the purpose of the UN was,
he responded, "They are trying to primitivize the entire world! Now, in the
third world that doesn't take too much, but in the advanced countries that

means completely redistributing the population." He reiterated his point a little later in our interview: "The United Nations and its supporters in this country are trying to take this country back to the condition which existed in 1492. They come out and say that."

I would also discover that patriots' sense of the UN as culturally inferior was tinged with racial undertones. Indeed, while none of the patriots I interviewed used racialized language, their choices of examples was telling and indicated that race was for them the most telling marker of that inferiority. The following exchange, initiated in response to Krogdahl's comments about primitivization, excerpted above, illustrates this point.

> *Gallaher:* When I first started getting into the background research on the Patriot Movement, I discovered that the UN was a target of the movement's anger, fear, and whatnot, and I found this interesting because people in the quote-unquote third world feel the same way, but with a twist. They are saying that the UN is controlled by the U.S. So my question for you is twofold—how would you address those concerns and do you think the third world has a right to want some of the wealth that was taken from them many eons ago?
>
> *Krogdahl:* Wait a minute now, if you are talking about resources, like gold, diamonds, iron ore, timber, whatnot, the United States, in particular, and the Western World, didn't take it, they paid for it.
>
> *Gallaher:* During colonialism?
>
> *Krogdahl:* Yeah, take South Africa, for instance. The South African mines hire native labor.
>
> *Gallaher:* Well they hire them now, but they used to use slave labor.
>
> *Krogdahl:* Well, no there wasn't actually any slavery. People weren't indentured. There was never slavery as such. Its true, they paid low wages, and in fact in South Africa the white labor unions used every trick in the trade to exclude black workers. Not just from the mines but from everything. So, in that sense there was very overt discrimination against blacks. But, in any case, black or white, the gold was mined. The mine owners bought the property and employed the workers and sold the products around the world. So, I don't quite understand what their complaint is about exploitation. What they usually mean is that if it had been in this country they would have had to pay them more. That's true. That's absolutely true, but it just shows they don't understand how wages are set.

While Krogdahl does not use overtly white supremacist language to make his point, the underlying discursive equation in his words is troubling. In order to support his assertion that the UN represents the primitive (and thus has goals harmful to the United States), Krogdahl paints a picture of "primitivism" that not only represents a selective reading of history, but also relies on a well-worn racial trope of the African "other" to give it form (see Morrison 1992).

My anonymous informant, while certainly not representative of the middle of the movement, relied on a similar (if somewhat wackier) trope to define the UN. When we initially discussed the UN in our interview, Lee, like several of my other informants, told me that the UN was the organizational center of the new world order. When I asked Lee to identify the key leaders in the new world order, he mentioned several then current leaders, such as Boris Yeltsin and Bill Clinton. He told me they were not, however, humans. Rather, they belonged to an alien race known as the Luciferians who hail from the fourth dimension. "The Luciferians want to enslave the world's population," he claimed forcefully, adding, "they're an evil breed of space aliens." While such comments may be rightly read as indicative of paranoia or mental instability, they are also illustrative of how white, Western othering of people of color may become dangerously dehumanizing when allowed to fester through an antagonistic framing of difference.

Of course, the power of these discursive chains of equivalence, where the UN as other is equated with people of color (and even aliens), is that they are encapsulated within nationalistic rhetoric that allows those using it to divorce themselves from charges of racism. Constructing their position this way, patriots may define their cause in broader terms that they use to draw people to the patriot cause who would not otherwise join an openly racist organization. Indeed, Gatewood Galbraith, in my first interview with him, would succinctly illustrate how this discursive framing works. After Gatewood finished his response to my UN question, excerpted above, in which he linked his opposition of the UN to American sovereignty, he paused. We were, after all, eating lunch and Gatewood had barely had time to take a bite of his food. Before I had an opportunity to respond to his comments, he added (perhaps in reaction to a confused look on my face—a look I wore frequently during that first year of research),

> You see, Carole, I'm not xenophobic, and I'm not racist, I'm a nationalist. I will play golf with these other countries, I will trade with them, I will sit down to dinner with them, but until they institute their own Constitution and their own Bill of Rights which gives them the individual rights that I have, they are not my political equal! And I'll be damned if I'm gonna abdicate, or be a part of abdicating, that which sets this country and its citizens apart from the rest of the world in order to achieve a parity.

As I would discover over time, Galbraith's comments were a telling indicator of how patriot discourses work. As I have noted time and again in this book, patriots routinely stressed to me in our interviews that they were *not* racist and they were adamant that the patriot groups to which they belonged shunned a racist agenda. Many also did so without prompting from me. Indeed, while I felt it was important to ask questions about race given the history of the movement, patriots usually addressed the issue, as Galbraith did, before I even had a chance to bring it up.

While intellectuals and others should deconstruct patriot rhetoric to show its discursive underpinnings, what is ultimately significant about patriot discourse is not so much that it is based on supremacist logic (the movement was, after all, begun by white supremacists, so these foundations are not surprising), but that it allows patriots themselves to express their race-/culture-based anxieties without having to confront them as such. Rather, patriots are able to see themselves and their concerns as "national."

This discursive framing obviously gives pause to anyone concerned about the poisonous role that racism plays in American politics. Indeed, if the whiteness literature tells us anything, it is that whites must recognize their race before a dialog on racial discord and healing may begin. Patriot discourses, constructed as they are, prohibit such fundamental moments from occurring, yet they provide race-based anxieties a channel for expression—one that reasserts a dominant positionality within the nation (white) and the nation's dominant positionality within the world (Western).

Equally important, patriot discourses tend to divert attention away from class-based issues through which working-class whites may begin to see points in common with other workers, both within their country and outside of it. While patriots' current opposition to biospheres is cultural, for example, the simmering anger in the area could be mobilized around more fruitful class-based issues. Indeed, as in many areas where tourism is trumpeted for bringing economic development, the "beneficiaries" of the mostly low-end service sector jobs there might beg to differ with such triumphalism.

The national frame patriot discourses provide, however, make such articulations difficult to sustain. As both the previous chapter and the exchange with Krogdahl above illustrate, the portrayal of "America" and "the West" as culturally dominant is based on a presumption that free-market capitalism is *the* superior form of economic organization and that those in the third world (or the United States) who oppose it do so not because they are exploited but because they fail to understand the system.

In ending this chapter, it is important to note that while discourses of patriotism as they are currently constituted buttress cultural fears and provide symbolic solutions for them, the "cultural" victories patriots have won are mostly hollow. Despite the passage of Senate Resolution 35, the LBL Biosphere maintains its designation. And although patriots have made it difficult for LBL's managers to establish collaborative projects in the area, their efforts have not resulted in former landowners getting their land back.

In sum, there is a substantial gap between patriot rhetoric surrounding the LBL Biosphere ("We stopped it in its tracks") and the reality on the ground (the biosphere still exists and former landowners still do not have their land back). This is an important gap, both because it illustrates the failure of the Patriot politic to deliver on its promises and because it points to a discursive rupture where the progressive left could insert itself, and to much better ends. Indeed, while it is highly unlikely that any group, left or right, could arrange a return of LBL land to its former owners, the left could (and should) concern itself with the larger question of who benefits (and who does not) from the economic development LBL is purported to bring. Such questioning would likely resonate in LBL as well. Families who gave up their land were told it would benefit the public as a whole, but many in the area now feel that the so-called public good LBL generates is primarily for outsiders (environmentalists, scientists, and visitors), who enjoy its natural beauty at their expense. Considering how that public good (jobs, profits, use, land) might be more equitably distributed, then, provides at least one way to direct the area's long-simmering discontent along more productive lines.

NOTES

1. The zone of transition is also commonly referred to as the "zone of cooperation."

2. Information about the organizational structure of USMAB may be found at www.usmab.org/general_information/geninfo.html. For clarification on finer points of the program's organization, I conducted a brief phone interview on June 22, 2001, with Jack Wade, MAB's acting director in the U.S. Forest Service.

3. The power of eminent domain allows government agencies to acquire privately held land for public uses (such as dam building or highway construction) in exchange for fair compensation to affected landowners.

4. For specifics on the convention, see www.biodiv.org/. The United States has not signed on as a party to the convention. Earlier attempts to ratify the treaty in Congress have failed.

5. I spoke with Senator Moore by phone on June 26, 2001.

6. The entire resolution is available for download on the Kentucky Legislature's web site. See www.lrc.state.ky.us/record/97ss/SR35.htm.

7. House Bill 901 was introduced during the first session of the 105th Congress. Representative Don Young, a Republican from Alaska, was the primary sponsor. The house bill passed on October 9, 1997, and was referred to the Senate Committee on Energy and Natural Resources. For a full text of this bill, see the House of Representatives legislative web page, www.house.gov/house/Legproc.html, where bills may be tracked by a variety of means.

8. Because the Senate Committee on Energy and Natural Resources took no action on the bill, it was never allowed to continue through the legislative process. Representative Young and his backers in the House of Representatives, however, introduced an almost identical bill, HR 883, during the 107th Congress. A Senate version of the bill, S 510, was also filed in the Senate during the 107th Congress.

8

On the Road (Again)

Willie Nelson's little ditty about being in love with life on the road is an apt way to begin a review of the political career of Gatewood Galbraith. Although he's never won any of his five elections, Gatewood keeps going back for more. He is, as one journalist described him, like the energizer bunny—"he just keeps going and going and going" (Gerth 2000).

Gatewood, who is in his mid-fifties, has a lot in common with the elder Willie Nelson. Both have had their financial troubles and it is hardly a secret that both are known to enjoy the pleasures of a good marijuana cigarette. At some point, the two even became friends. When Galbraith launched his 1995 gubernatorial campaign, Nelson played two benefits for him; in 1999, Nelson returned to play an outdoor gig for Galbraith at the Red Mile, a stadium for horse racing in Lexington. Both are also iconoclasts in their own right. Talk to anyone in the country music world and you'll here references to "Willie"—not Willie Nelson, not Mr. Nelson, just Willie. It's the same with Galbraith in Kentucky. There, people just refer to him as "Gatewood," even though his last name lends an alliterative flavor to his full name. When I have been in public with Gatewood, I have heard people shout, "Hi, Gatewood!" from passing cars and seen strangers at restaurants politely interrupt to say "Keep up the good work, Gatewood!" Even his campaign bumper stickers do not use his last name. The bumper sticker for his 1999 gubernatorial campaign read simply "Gatewood." The idea of referring to Gatewood as "Mr. Galbraith" is a little like addressing Madonna as "Ms. Ciccione." It is unnecessary and it sounds strange, too. In Central Kentucky, Gatewood is big enough not to need a last name.

While Gatewood may seem like an odd fit in the stuffy world of politics, he is, in many ways, an odder fit in the patriot circles in which he now travels. A pro-marijuana and hemp activist for almost twenty years, and a loyal Democrat until a few years ago, Gatewood hardly fits the prototypical image of a patriot as someone who moves from white supremacist activity into patriot politics. The purpose of this chapter is to detail Galbraith's political transformation and to analyze the implications of bringing a patriot politics into the political mainstream in Kentucky. To do this, I examine Galbraith's 1999 bid for governor.

Galbraith began his campaign as an independent. Realizing the limitations of running without a party affiliation, however, Galbraith sought out and received the Reform Party nomination for his gubernatorial bid. This campaign, and his congressional bid the following year, mark not only Gatewood's break from the Democratic Party, but also his attempt to mainstream the Kentucky Patriot Movement by building on its legislative successes. As I note in chapters 4 and 5, while often overlooked, the above-ground portion of the Patriot Movement has significant influence. It has brought a patriot sensibility to mainstream politics, pulling, along with other branches of the political right, the so-called political center even further to the right, while simultaneously providing a mainstream outlet for the far right.

While Galbraith's campaign provides a useful site from which to observe the Patriot Movement's effective manipulation of the political mainstream, his story is also compelling for what it says about, and can say to, the progressive left. In many ways, Gatewood is a Tom Watson figure,[1] albeit with much softer edges. A former Democrat who espoused liberal social positions and had a penchant for sticking up for the little guy, Galbraith has transformed himself into a populist with conservative social values and a healthy skepticism toward government. His transformation embodies the fluid nature of identity politics and illustrates not only the constructed nature of political identity, but also its contingency and potential reversibility.

Like the transformation of Watson before him, Galbraith's political transformation in Kentucky has been labeled by people on both sides of the political fence as disingenuous. When I interviewed Representative Stein, a liberal Democrat, she expressed disappointment with Gatewood—"He was a progressive" she told me. She also questioned his motives:

> Unfortunately, when advocates for issues get involved in the political arena, or the public arena, and they're trying to garner support, they sell out to groups . . . whom they perceive political power will come from. And, I'm afraid that Gatewood picked up on the militia groups, those unsettled individuals, and they are shaping him far more than I would like to see.

Many on the right are equally skeptical, continuing to see him as a "pro-drug" candidate. When Galbraith was running for governor in 1999, the *Courier-Journal* in Louisville did a story on Galbraith's push to win political respectability (Gerth 1999). The reporter noted that, despite the strides Galbraith had made—"from someone viewed as a pro-marijuana crackpot to a broad-based politician with a firm grasp on numerous issues"—he had a tough legacy to live down:

> And then there's the marijuana issue. Although Galbraith is not the one-issue candidate he was in 1983, shaking that image has been tough. That's what made him famous in Kentucky, and that's what people continue to remember about him. That issue stuck with him when he ran for governor as a Democrat in the 1991 and 1995 primaries, and it continues to dog him today. "I don't even want to see it," said Jim Tucker, when Galbraith tried to hand him campaign literature on a campaign swing through Northern Kentucky. "You can just take it somewhere else." Galbraith made the mistake of trying to win the vote of a drug investigator for the Kenton County sheriff's office. "I just don't like what he stands for," Tucker said.

While it is difficult to assess Galbraith's sincerity, as I demonstrate below he constructs his move to the right as driven by a discursive narrowing within the Democratic Party—one that squeezed out his support for hemp/marijuana on the grounds that it was "pro-drug" and turned its back on the little guy when it chose to support corporate-driven rural development. While progressive outlets on the left were drying up, however, there was no dearth of openings appearing on the right. As I note in chapter 4, white supremacists-turned-patriots adroitly exploited this discursive void in rural areas during the farm crisis. And as they crafted their identity politics they left it intentionally broad and pliable so that individuals and groups across the country could adapt it to their local circumstances. In Kentucky, Gatewood found these openings on the right as doors on the left were closing to him and, although his politics are not virulent in the way earlier versions of the patriot politics have been, his long-standing concerns, when framed through patriot discourses, go unresolved.

This changing discursive field has implications well beyond the figure of Gatewood Galbraith. Indeed, whether Galbraith is an "opportunist" who has sold his political soul or an honest person who has had a sincere change of heart, the discursive shrinking on the left and its corresponding expansion on the right also frame the choices of white working-class folks who are the most likely to be drawn to the Patriot Movement. As such, opportunist or not, Gatewood serves as a useful proxy for understanding the wider implications of the patriot push into politics.

I begin this chapter with a brief overview of the "old" Gatewood, recognizable then for his left-wing positions and hippie demeanor. In the second section, I detail Galbraith's transformation from left-wing to right-wing populist, focusing in particular on how he constructs his move. I then examine Galbraith's 1999 bid for governor, noting points of continuity between the "old" Gatewood and the "transformed" Gatewood as they developed through his platform. As I demonstrate, Galbraith has discursively linked class-based concerns, articulated through the thwarting discourses of patriotism, to conservative social causes, creating a chain of right-wing, essentialist, equivalencies. In the final section, I assess the impact of Gatewood's efforts to mainstream the patriot politics, examining in particular the effects that his discursive links have had on the movement in Kentucky.

THE "OLD" GATEWOOD

Gatewood was born in 1947 in Nicholas County, at the beginning of the baby boom. His mother was a schoolteacher and his father held a variety of jobs, from car salesman to restaurateur (Gerth 1999). When he graduated from high school, Galbraith went to the University of Kentucky, where he earned a bachelor's degree in general studies in 1974 and a law degree three years later. After passing the Kentucky bar exam, Gatewood worked as a trial lawyer in Lexington, representing people in both civil and criminal court. While he has tried a variety of cases, Gatewood has largely focused his practice on defending people indicted on drug charges, including minor possession offenses as well as more serious distribution charges. More recently, he has begun defending people indicted on weapons charges. In my third interview with Galbraith, he told me about his new focus, informing me by way of illustration that a current client of his was a young man charged with illegal possession of a firearm. "I'm going to get him out of it!" he told me.

While Galbraith has put his law practice on hold during his numerous campaigns, he clearly enjoys practicing law. In my third interview with him, held shortly after his 2000 congressional race, Galbraith seemed blue as he told me that he was trying to regroup from his latest unsuccessful foray into politics. When I asked him what he was doing with himself since the election, however, he grew animated, telling me about his plans for the aforementioned case. "Do you want to hear how the opening statement goes?" he asked me, adding, "Juries love me!" I did, of course. Listening to a Galbraith speech, whether an opening statement or a stump speech, was watching a master at work. It is easy to see why he likes politics and why he is a hit on the campaign trail, even among skeptics. He is comfortable being in the limelight and he is undeniably endearing as he spins folksy yarns, cracks jokes, and makes deliciously barbed comments about the absurdities of Kentucky politics (Gerth 1999; Poore 1995).[2]

Galbraith launched his first campaign in 1983, when he ran on the Democratic ticket for agriculture commissioner. His campaign was largely built on a one-issue platform. In it, he proposed legalizing marijuana and hemp so that family farmers could have an alternative (or companion) crop to tobacco. Although his prolegalization stance was set in an economic framework, he was widely painted as a "pro-drug" candidate. His public admissions of regular marijuana use (he uses it to control his asthma) did not help his credibility as a serious politician, either, and he lost the election by a wide margin. During the campaign, he did, however, earn an enduring nickname—"Gateweed." Today, many of his college age fans, who are too young to remember his 1983 campaign, affectionately refer to him by the name.

In the early nineties, Galbraith once again decided to make a go at politics. In 1991, he entered the Democratic primary for governor and hired Dan Wooten to be his campaign manager. Although he was running for a different office, one with a larger mandate, Galbraith again ran on a platform cornerstoned by his support for legalizing marijuana and hemp and, lest anyone miss the point, he campaigned across the state in his "hempmobile," a Mercedes-Benz that ran on fuel made from the plant. He was also fond of telling people on the stump that the suits he wore were made from hemp fibers (Schaver 1999). He lost by a wide margin, gaining only 5.3 percent of the total votes, well behind the three front-runners—Floyd Poore, who secured 26.8 percent of the vote; Scotty Baesler, who received 30.3 percent; and Brereton Jones, whose 37.5 percent made him the Democratic candidate for governor.

Although Galbraith was the clear underdog, his 5.3 percent was well above the predictions, which speculated he would win no more than 1 percent of the total vote (AP 1991). It was also close to Galbraith's personal goal of 6 percent, the amount he vowed to earn or quit politics for good. Given the higher than expected returns on election night, Dan Wooten also backtracked for his boss, telling the press, who were curious to know if Gatewood would keep his promise, "You don't want to make that decision on the night of the election. I'm sure he'll look at this very logically" (AP 1991). Showing persistence in the face of his second defeat, Galbraith also stubbornly reiterated the centerpiece of his platform when he conceded, saying, "We tried to speak the truth . . . and the truth is that marijuana is necessary as a medicine to hundreds of thousands of Kentuckians who could benefit within the next five minutes over its application" (AP 1991).

In 1995, Gatewood Galbraith once again entered the Democratic primary for governor. As with his prior bids for public office, legalizing marijuana/hemp was a central part of his platform. Of course, with two unsuccessful bids under his belt, he broadened his campaign platform to include other issues. His choice for lieutenant governor, for example, a former labor leader named Jerry Hammond, infused his campaign with a decidedly broader appeal, helping Galbraith reach out to urban workers as well as the farmers he had long courted.

Galbraith also made an issue out of the state's new campaign finance reform program, which gave $1.2 million in matching funds to any candidate who raised $600,000. As a long-shot candidate with no corporate sponsors, Galbraith argued that he would find it difficult to raise $600,000 from his typical donors, who could afford on average a ten- to twenty-dollar contribution, and he refused to participate in the program (Armstrong 1995). He also opposed the new system on ideological grounds, arguing that special interests should stay out of politics and that the state should not encourage the participation of interest groups by "matching" their funds. Indeed, Galbraith and Hammond refused on principle to take money from NORML, the National Organization for the Reform of Marijuana Laws, even though Galbraith was a former board member and the organization was clearly eager to contribute to his campaign. As NORML's deputy director, Allen St. Pierre, lamented to the *Herald-Leader* reporter doing a profile on Galbraith, "He wins all the elections in the marijuana movement . . . [and with our money] they could have filled their coffers many times over 800,000 dollars" (Poore 1995).

Also evident in Galbraith's 1995 campaign were the first hints of his political transformation to come. In one stump speech, for example, he told the crowd assembled, "I'll be damned if we're going to let this 'new world order' tell us what the internal development process of the state of Kentucky is going to be!" (Poore 1995). In an interview with the *Kentucky Post*, Galbraith was also heavily critical of the government. At one point, he described it as "an overburdening cloud that people have to fight all their lives," prompting the interviewer to respond, "Aren't you sounding like a Republican?" (Armstrong 1995).

Despite Galbraith's efforts to moderate his position and expand his base, he lost his second primary bid for governor much as he lost his first, coming in last place among the four contenders, which included winner Paul Patton, runner-up Bob Babbage, and Eck Rose. In contrast to his first run, however, Galbraith earned a respectable 8.6 percent of the vote and the margin between Galbraith and his nearest competitor, Rose, was just slightly more than 12 percent.

Galbraith vowed to continue fighting for the principles on which he had run. A few weeks after the primary, he joined a local talk radio show on WVLK as a regular Wednesday guest, promising to discuss "constitutional and civil rights issues" (Crane 1995). And, in October, he and Hammond decided to launch a write-in campaign, agreeing to pay the state board of elections to count their votes (Staff Reports 1995). In the final election, however, Galbraith's returns were negligible, well under 1 percent of the total votes cast.

Galbraith's first three campaigns had a decidedly populist flavor, in the tradition that Stock (1996) identifies as producer radicalism. Indeed, while Gatewood was often portrayed as a one-issue candidate, and in fact often encouraged these portrayals by his own actions, the "marijuana" politics of his early campaigns was underlain by a critique of political and economic structures that favored corporate interests over those of small and medium-sized producers.

The crux of Galbraith's support for legalization is based on a theory he developed during law school that he calls "the synthetic subversion." "I wrote a[n unpublished] book on the topic," he told me, adding, "I can get you a copy if you want to read it." As I was to discover, Galbraith's theory is critical not only of the structural arrangements that benefit large producers over small and medium-sized ones, but also of the havoc these arrangements have wreaked on small communities, families, and the environment. Below is Galbraith's description of the synthetic subversion from our first interview:

> Now, the way the synthetic subversion works is, and what it's done, is this. One-hundred and fifty years ago the farmer raised all the fiber, all the fuel, all the medicine, and all the food. That's what farming is—you raise those four basic commodities from the land and when you use land as a means for producing wealth, the wealth flows back to the land, it goes back to where it was produced. We had nuclear families, you could be raised on a farm and grow up, and the mom and dad could leave it to you and you could leave it to your children. You could be born in a small town, grow up, raise a family, fall in love, and live and die in a small town because the economy would support you. We didn't have all the environmental problems that we have today, and that's because the farmer produced the fiber, fuel, medicine, and the food—150 years ago. Today, 150 years later, the farmer doesn't produce any fiber, and if they do it's cotton, which accounts for 50 percent of the pesticides and herbicides used in the agricultural sector. The farmer doesn't raise any medicine because its been monopolized by the pharmaceutical companies. The farmer doesn't raise any fuel—its all been monopolized by the petrochemical companies. Now, if you go to a grocery store, and look at the ingredients on the package, you'll find out how rapidly farmers are being displaced from food production. It's all been taken over by the synthetic manufacturers and producing the synthetic products creates a toxic waste, hazardous by-product with which we have had such a tough time. And it didn't happen because of the consumer's demand. Or supply or demand. It happened because of specialized legislation [the New Deal] which gave certain synthetic producers a monopoly in the production of basic commodities.

While Galbraith was already a self-identified patriot when he outlined his theory of synthetic subversion to me, I would hear him invoke the theory less and less frequently as I charted Galbraith's foray into the Patriot Movement. Indeed, for a man who had self-consciously staked his reputation on his support for legalizing hemp and marijuana, it was a surprise to see such a diminutive place for the issue in his 1999 gubernatorial campaign. It was equally troubling to see what sorts of issues would take its place. Before examining the nitty-gritty of Galbraith's two most recent campaigns, I turn first to the transformation itself, noting the discursive turns that mark his journey.

A POLITICIAN REBORN

If you ask Gatewood Galbraith to explain his transformation from a left-oriented populist to a right-leaning patriot, he will tell you he has always been a conservative. When I interviewed Galbraith in the summer of 1999, for example, a few months before his gubernatorial race in November of that year, I asked him to comment on his political transformation. "I think it's fair to say," I said to Gatewood, "that your record on paper, at least, looks sort of erratic. So do you think your political path has changed, or is there a stream that's run through it all along the way?" He responded, "Of course there is—trying to find the conservative voice! . . . Even when I ran before, it was publicly stated that I was looking out for the conservative voice in the Democratic Party." When I protested, pointing out that the pro-marijuana/hemp position was left identified and noting that the war on drugs, while garnering bipartisan support, has been championed by some of Congress's most right-leaning members, Galbraith strongly rejected my depiction: "The whole war on drugs, that's not a conservative war. That's a tax-and-spend liberal agenda. . . . We [marijuana lobby] have been conservative all along."

If you talk to Galbraith's former political allies, however, you will hear a different story. Representative Stein, a friend of Galbraith's, sees a stark change in his political position. Remarking on Galbraith's protest of the UN float in the 1995 Fourth of July parade, she recalled,

> I remember seeing him, you know, with his face twisted in anger and hate, as he was trying to stop that parade. And that frightened me, that all of a sudden someone who had been a progressive, and who had been for a lot of issues I agreed with, began taking a turn to the right—one that has only continued since then. . . . It just completely blew me away that Gatewood all of a sudden started talking about those sorts of issues.

When pressed, Galbraith will also acknowledge that he has made some tactical changes pertaining to his political career, even as he continues to hold that his underlying philosophy has remained constant. Indeed, as I would discover, there was a well-developed plan behind Galbraith's political transformation—a plan that was clearly based on reconciling his past positions with a body of decidedly more conservative views. As Galbraith explained to me in our second interview,

> About three years ago, I set out to marry marijuana and the militia. And I did that. Went to the militia and said . . . "Look, the Republicans are talking about

the big tent theory, but we already have a big tent, its called the Constitution. And whatever our individual differences are, on homosexuality, education, abortion, etc., . . . we do agree on 90 percent of the other stuff, including that we have a common enemy, which is domestic fascism." . . . [Then] I went over to the marijuana smokers and said, "Look, we ought to get these guys smoking as much pot as we can."

Galbraith's plan to "marry marijuana and the militia" is perhaps most clearly observable in his (re)interpretation of the hemp conspiracy outlined in chapter 6 of this book. Recall that Herer argues that it was during Franklin Roosevelt's administration that the government first began using taxes as a way to control human behavior. He also contends that the Roosevelt administration first tested its "regulation through taxes" scheme by proposing the Firearms Act in 1934. Herer notes that two weeks after the Firearms Act was upheld by the Supreme Court in 1937, the Marijuana Tax Act was introduced in Congress. Herer does not, however, fundamentally link the loss of liberty surrounding the production of *Cannabis* to a loss of liberty vis-à-vis access to weapons. Rather, Herer makes only two connections between the issues—a structural one (both acts allowed Congress to "regulate" activity through taxes) and a temporal one (Roosevelt waited until the Firearms Act was upheld to introduce other prohibitive taxes). This is not to say that Herer is either for or against gun control. Herer has not written on the subject, so I have no idea where he stands on it. What is clear, however, is that in his work he does not present limitations on firearms as of equal importance with those placed on hemp.

When I interviewed Galbraith for the first time, by contrast, he presented the two issues as linked within a larger conspiracy that depicted the government as intent to seize one fundamental right, access to weapons, in order to thwart resistance to its seizure of a second fundamental right, access to the "natural," the "God-given." As Galbraith explained it to me:

Now, if you'd just taken over the country with a sweeping New Deal, a sweeping New Deal between business and government, what's the first law or thing you want to do? Well, you want to locate the automatic weapons that are out there. Right? Sure, you want to know where them tommy guns are. OK? You can't tell people they can't have them, but there's a two hundred dollar tax on them. And, if you don't pay that tax then by God we're gonna take it away from you. What is the second law that they passed? The 1937 Marijuana Tax Act. Now tell me something. You've just taken over the largest, most powerful country in the world, and the first thing you do is locate the automatic weapons, then why would the second thing you do be to put a tax on marijuana? There's not a market there—it had been miniscule, miniscule. It was the first time they ever told you you couldn't plant a seed in God's green earth and consume a green natural plant.

The answer for Galbraith's query was, as I detail above, the "synthetic sub-version" facilitated by the Roosevelt administration at the behest of the pet-rochemical companies. As I note above, however, regulating firearms was not an integral part of Herer's theory on hemp's outlaw. The issue of gun control was, however, significant to the then burgeoning Patriot Movement in Kentucky and, in the context of Galbraith's outreach to it, discursively linking the two issues had obvious appeal.

As I remark above, it is difficult to assess Galbraith's interior motives regarding his move to the right. My personal belief is that Galbraith is a complicated person and so it is pointless to put his political turn into either the "opportunist" or the "heartfelt" category. Indeed, from my interviews with Galbraith I would say both elements were at play. On the one hand, it is clear that Galbraith felt betrayed and shut out by the Democratic Party, whose concern for working men and women had been replaced by its efforts on behalf of "special interests." Yet, on the other hand, it is obvious that Galbraith's decision to seek the Reform Party nomination for his 1999 gubernatorial bid was a politically expedient choice—one based on the hard realities of running an election in a big money environment, rather than on a sense of loyalty to Ross Perot or his party.[3] As Galbraith explained it,

> Let's go back to the '95 race. You know, we got outspent in that race, we got outspent three hundred to one, but only outvoted eleven to one. Big money dominated again, even under the campaign finance reform. If there was any hope that leveling the playing field through campaign finance reform would keep the special interests out, that hope was dashed when the point man for special interests in this state [Paul Patton] got elected governor. And they did it through the same old same old: the same good old good boys network, the same old payoff system. So finally I became convinced, I mean, I'm a pretty stubborn guy. When I give my loyalty to something and get behind something, I mean you very well have to just smack me in the face to keep me from defending that position to the end. Even if it turns out to have clay feet, even if it turns out to be someone who's let us down or something, you know. When I get behind somebody or something, I just defend it with force. But at some point there comes a time when you've got to call a pile of shit a pile of shit. Sorry, there's no euphemism for it. And it became painfully obvious that neither major party is capable of producing a candidate that will address the chronic problems that this state has had. And we're a microcosm of the national aspect of it.

As a politician looking for a constituency and a party, Galbraith was in search of open doors and he found them on the right. As I document in chapter 5, in Kentucky the Patriot Movement was creating discursive openings at both the social movement level and in the General Assembly. Indeed, by the mid-nineties patriots had formed a variety of local patriot groups, from Norman Davis's Kentuckians for the Right to Bear Arms to Charlie

Puckett's militia. They had also organized their respective "constituencies" into a sophisticated political coalition, as the passage of the 1996 concealed weapons bill demonstrated. By the time Galbraith became organizationally involved with CCK, the Patriot Movement had become a consolidated social movement and was on its way to becoming a political force to be reckoned with in the state.

At the same time, however, there were no comparably strong or broad outlets on the left. On the party front, the Democrats had closed the door on a class politics by adopting a neoliberal strategy of development. As I detail below, the current governor, Paul Patton, has implemented a variety of neoliberal "reforms" for the state, from trimming workers' compensation benefits to establishing tax incentives for industrial chicken- and hog-farming operations considering a move to the state. These policies have alienated both workers and farmers, traditionally the two largest and solid constituencies of the Democratic Party in Kentucky. Moreover, while farmers and their supporters (especially in Central Kentucky) have kept the pressure on state government to legalize hemp, even securing the help of actor Woody Harrelson, who planted four hemp seeds on a farm to protest its illegality, they have largely confined themselves to the one issue—an approach with which Galbraith found little success. Finally, like the left in the United States as a whole, progressives in Kentucky are largely divided into narrowly focused interest/identity groups. While the relations between them are cordial, there is little collaboration. As Jeff Jones, the human rights commissioner for Lexington and a long time gay activist in the state, put it:

> What you could call the left in Kentucky is largely built around particular constituencies organized around an issue or issues of interest. While almost all of the groups that I am familiar with discuss the need for allies and supporting progressive causes, the structure of largely volunteer, time-consuming efforts on what is near and dear to oneself often leaves little time and energy to learn about and support other issues. So there are environmental groups with a clear focus on stopping coal mining in sensitive areas or passing a bottle deposit bill. Although many but certainly not all may support equal rights for gay people, most are not members of Fairness [the statewide organization for gay, lesbian, bisexual, and transgendered (GLBT) rights]. Similarly, many gay people are not as actively engaged with environmental, antiracism, or antideath-penalty groups.

For a hopeful (and progressive) politician, such a context can be daunting, and it could drive all but the most stalwart to look for other venues to express working-class concerns. More importantly, however, nonpoliticians who are looking for similar venues have few progressive outlets available to them. Thus when someone like Galbraith attempts to address long-standing concerns about structural inequality through available (and welcoming) right-wing discourses, a dangerous discursive chain of equivalence may be forged between class-based concerns and conservative social positions—a chain of equivalence that thwarts class-based solutions and encourages social and cultural antagonisms.

POINTS OF CONTINUITY, POINTS OF RUPTURE

Galbraith's first three campaigns are relatively easy to overview. Their platforms were, after all, built largely around one issue. Galbraith's most recent, patriot-inspired bids for political office, however, are more complicated. Indeed, since 1995, Galbraith has matured into a serious third-party candidate. And with that maturity has come the responsibility to stake out positions on a variety of issues that fall outside of the direct purview of the Patriot Movement. In this section, I outline the predominate issues in the 1999 gubernatorial race and the views Galbraith articulated about them. I also note the points of continuity with, and moments of rupture from, the producer politics of the "old" Galbraith.

The 1999 gubernatorial race was an interesting one for Kentucky. Unlike previous campaigns, the 1999 race had four contenders—Democratic incumbent Paul Patton, Republican nominee Peppy Martin, Natural Law Party candidate Nailah Jumoke-Yarbrough, and third-time contender Galbraith, now running on the Reform ticket. In addition to the large field of candidates, the race was also interesting because the Democratic incumbent, front-runner Paul Patton, considered Galbraith's third-party bid a more substantial threat than that of the Republican nominee (Cross 1999b). Peppy Martin barely won her primary bid, even though her opponent did not actively campaign, and she alienated the state's most powerful Republican, Senator Mitch McConnell, when she pejoratively referred to his wife Elaine Chao[4] (who was born in Taiwan) as his "Chinese connection" (Cross 1999b, 1999c). While analysts viewed Galbraith's strength vis-à-vis Martin as an embarrassment for the Republican Party, they also saw it as indicative of serious discontent within the Democratic Party. As Paul Blanchard, a political scientist at Eastern Kentucky University, put it, "A lot of people believe that Gatewood Galbraith is a much more respectable candidate than Peppy Martin is, but I still think Gatewood, should he even come close, would be a huge embarrassment to the Democrats" (Gerth 1999).

As Blanchard's assessment indicates, the political battle within the 1999 race had more to do with tensions within the Democratic Party than those between the parties. These tensions largely revolved around the party's appeals to big business, and Galbraith adeptly tapped into the current of discontent resulting from this appeal. Indeed, while governor's races often concern issues of local interest (Should the state fund a road here? Should teachers get a raise?), Galbraith made opposition to what he called "corporate welfare" a central theme in his campaign. His favorite stump sound bite, for example, was any variation of his stated opposition to the "petrochemical-pharmaceutical-military-industrial complex." And, when he made such claims around pertinent issues in the campaign, it was easy to see the producer politics of the "old" Galbraith at work.

Galbraith articulated his opposition to corporate welfare most forcefully around the issue of workers' compensation, focusing specifically on a revision to the program initiated by Governor Paul Patton during his freshmen year as governor. After taking office in 1996, Governor Patton called on the General Assembly to reform the state workers' comp law. He argued that the system was rife with excess and abuse and that these breaches were critical because they hurt existing businesses in the state, particularly the coal industry, and discouraged new ones from coming in. Patton proposed streamlining the claims process (the state would reduce its involvement and workers would no longer need a lawyer to represent them in workers' comp cases) and trimming the costs (the state would reduce or cancel compensation for lesser injuries). The program, Patton argued, would cut workers' comp costs in the coal industry by 22 percent and in other industries by 11 percent (Collins 1996; Wolfe 1996).

Not surprisingly, Patton's bill was widely opposed by organized labor in Kentucky, which is centered in the state's eastern coal fields. Most disturbing to the region's mine workers was a provision in the bill that proposed limiting compensation for black lung, the leading source of comp claims made by miners, to those who could demonstrate a breathing impairment greater than 20 percent. The former standard, X-ray evidence of black lung, would no longer be considered sufficient evidence for compensation. Moreover, some forms of black lung were excluded from compensation altogether (Chellgren 1999).

While organized labor in the state would have been opposed to the bill regardless of its sponsor, labor was particularly offended that the bill had been initiated by Governor Patton. After the 1995 gubernatorial primary, in which Galbraith had run, Patton faced a tough battle against his Republican opponent, Larry Forgy. To pull ahead, Patton drew heavily on his roots in eastern Kentucky to establish his empathy with workers, and he called on his contacts with organized labor there to bring out the voters on election day. His decisions to introduce the reform package so soon after the election and to include a provision directly impacting the workers in his home district incensed them.

Despite these views, Patton viewed the bill as a signature moment in his first term as governor. Indeed, a week after the bill passed, Governor Patton used an announcement of a new manufacturing plant in Hopkinsville to trumpet up the likely success of his program. Standing in the capital press room with company officials and Hopkinsville leaders, he told those assembled, "It's the first example of the job growth we expect because of the new workers' compensation system. We have a tremendous central location, a good work force with a good work ethic, a lot of advantages. But workers' compensation is a real cost to any business, and it had been holding us back" (Wolfe 1996). Patton's announcement, however, looked more like political maneuvering to the press. As an Associated Press reporter noted,

> The plant . . . will have about 90 employees at peak production. Nothing to scoff at, certainly, and Patton said the new jobs figure to pay well. But announcements of plants on that scale are usually handled with news releases from the Cabinet for Economic Development. This announcement came from Patton personally, and it was at the Capitol, not in Hopkinsville. (Wolfe 1996)

The announcement also left labor warning of reprisal. Ron Cyrus, the Kentucky AFL-CIO executive secretary-treasurer, warned Patton that the bill "would be a 'unifying measure' for labor" (Wolfe 1996).

The reform of workers' compensation was, in many ways, a tailor-made issue for Galbraith's old-style producerist politics. As Cyrus's comment above indicates, the bill had obvious producerist appeal. It was widely regarded among labor and its supporters as a sellout to big business. Senator Benny Ray Bailey, a Democrat from eastern Kentucky and an opponent of the bill, succinctly captured that sentiment when he sarcastically told the legislature after the vote that he heard "the sound of the champagne corks being popped in the mega-corporations of America and the first floor of the Capitol" (Collins 1996).

Galbraith was clearly cognizant of Patton's loss of credibility among labor and he made overhaul of the new workers' comp system his top campaign platform priority. During the televised gubernatorial debate,[5] for example, Galbraith used his opening statement to foreground the issue in his campaign and to chastise the Democratic Party for its abandonment of the state's working people:

> Kathy[6] and I have both been members of other parties before. But at the end of the '95 election, we believed that both parties had deserted the principles which made them great. I've been a Democrat all my life. When I was in the Democratic Party, through that time they always represented the working man and woman, the middle class, the miners, and the farmers. But I've sat by over these last eight years and watched the leadership of that party destroy the party and move it away from the traditions and principles which made it great. . . . The working men and women in this state have had workers' compensation, the most basic protection for them on the job, removed from underneath them.

Galbraith's foregrounding of the workers' comp issue was a smart move. Several United Mine Workers' locals in eastern Kentucky broke with both their national union and the AFL-CIO to endorse his campaign (Estep 1999)[7]. The issue was also clearly on the minds of the panel convened to formulate and deliver the questions at the gubernatorial debate. Indeed, the first question, by Judy Jones of the *Courier-Journal*, was about the controversial reform measure. As the question and Galbraith's response to it indicate, the issue was ready-made for a candidate intent not only to distance himself or herself from Patton, but also to make a pitch for class-based concerns in the context of an unpopular issue.

> *Jones:* In 1996, Governor Patton led the General Assembly in a massive overhaul of workers' compensation in Kentucky based on what he and others described as excesses of awards for coal miners in this state. Since that time, a series of hearings and a number of media reports have revealed that disabled workers have been driven into poverty by this new system. Does the state workers' compensation need another overhaul and, if so, how would you affect the necessary changes?
>
> *Galbraith:* I think everyone agreed four years ago that workers' comp needed to be revised. There is no doubt, however, that in that revision that this present administration threw the baby out with the bath water. There was room for improvement by removing the administrative layers, by removing some of the attorney's fees, by removing all the administrators and regulators from the basic system and still having the ability to pay the injured worker from the employer. Once we removed all of the administrators, all of the clerks, all of the courts, all of the bureaucrats, and all of the patronage from that system, the system that should have remained intact was the basic and just compensation to the injured worker. That got thrown out along with all the rest of them. The Galbraith ticket is committed to putting a *compassionate* workers' compensation system in to adequately protect the injured working man and woman, and miners, and farmers, and other people injured in the course of employment, and offer them a basic safety net of relief!

It is worth noting here as well that the Republican nominee in the race, Peppy Martin, was equally critical of Paul Patton's workers' compensation reform package. Clearly agitated by the issue, she scolded Patton, telling him,

> You consider those hurt and injured people who cannot get any kind of [other] help just a nuisance. You were poor at one time and there's nothing wrong with that. But you are turning a deaf ear to the poor and injured. These people are injured once on the job, and their entire families get injured [by your reforms]. I know people, I have names and phone numbers of people who are starving because they cannot get any help. And it is a shame that you can stand before the people of Kentucky and claim any kind of compassion whatsoever!

Galbraith's calls to overhaul Patton's reforms are important at numerous levels. As I note above, they demonstrate the carryover of class-based concerns in Galbraith's personal political transformation from left-leaning to right-leaning populist. They are also important for what they say about the discursive void on the left regarding class-based issues. Indeed, Galbraith and Martin's comments are a disturbing indicator that, in Kentucky at least, William Greider (1997, 36) is correct when he argues that "the right has seized the revolutionary banner from the left."[8] Finally, and perhaps most importantly, in the right's hands class-based concerns become articulated in tandem with conservative, antagonistically constructed social positions, creating a volatile chain of right-wing equivalence. In his 1999 campaign, Galbraith staked out two positions in particular that not only solidified his place in the ranks of the Patriot Movement, but also bore the markings of antagonism as well.

Not surprisingly, one of the social issues around which Galbraith articulated an antagonistic position was gun control—a hot-button issue in the Kentucky Patriot Movement. His campaign literature listed "protecting Second Amendment rights" as a top priority. And when he framed his position on the stump, in interviews, and during the televised gubernatorial debate, he did so through a patriot frame, calling the issue a constitutional matter. Indeed, he rarely mentioned guns in the context of "safety," which even Representative Damron did when he first introduced the 1996 concealed weapons bill. During the gubernatorial debate, for example, when television reporter Mark Hebert asked the candidates a question about gun control, Galbraith never referenced any of the more traditional anti–gun control arguments (people need guns for self-defense, hunters need access to guns, widespread gun ownership deters crime), hammering home instead his opposition "on constitutional grounds." As Galbraith's response indicates, he was also willing to abandon patriot ideals about the power of the local when it suited patriot ends, demonstrating that in patriot politics the federal does trump the local when gun rights are involved:

> *Hebert:* Right now, Kentucky has a law that bars cities and counties from passing any tougher gun control ordinance than the state has. Would you favor a repeal of that law which would allow local government to approve their own gun control ordinances?
> *Galbraith:* Certainly we would not, Mr. Hebert, and I'll tell you why. That is a federal, constitutionally protected right, to be able to bear arms, and to have local municipalities acting politically to arrange some sort of piecemeal or quilt laws concerning firearms or guns would be unmanageable, costly, and people wouldn't know from one city to the next what they could do with their weapon. It's a federally, constitutionally protected right, and we are the strongest proponent for the Second Amendment in the state of Kentucky.

Of course, by the time of the debate, Galbraith's Second Amendment credentials had been well established. He was recognizable not only from his affiliation with CCK, but also from his association with Norman Davis, a patriot point man in the state and Galbraith's campaign manager as well. Indeed, well before the gubernatorial debate, the Gun Owners of America, a Second Amendment lobby generally considered more conservative than the NRA, had endorsed Gatewood's campaign. And it is likely that if the NRA worked with third parties ("They never endorse a third party candidate," Norman Davis told me), Galbraith would have received their support as well. Indeed, the NRA steered clear of the Republican candidate,[9] whose pro-gun image was in doubt even before hackers broke into her web page and accused her of being a closet advocate of gun control (Cross 1999a).[10]

It is important to note here that, while I present Galbraith's embrace of the gun issue as indicative of the "new" Galbraith, I do not mean to imply that support of the Second Amendment, or gun rights more generally, is necessarily a right-wing position. Indeed, marxists have long argued that access to weapons by "the people" is a necessary defense against state ownership of the means of violence. In the United States, radical elements of the left-oriented Black Power movement, including the Black Panthers and factions of the Nation of Islam, have made similar arguments.

Moreover, while the gun control lobby likes to argue that the case law on the Second Amendment is definitive (the amendment does *not* grant an individual the right to bear arms),[11] these claims are not entirely accurate. There is a growing body of legal scholarship on the Second Amendment that argues that the historical record does indicate the founders intended the Second Amendment to grant an individual right to own weapons. This body of thought is generally referred to as the Standard Model (see Halbrook 1984, 1989; Levinson 1989; Malcolm 1994, 1995; Reynolds 1995). The model is clearly controversial. It also has a variety of detractors. The gun control lobby, for example, has dismissed the model's proponents as politically motivated, while historians have criticized its key scholars, who hail largely from the legal field, for using outdated norms of historiography (see Cornell 1999; Higginbotham 1999). Nonetheless, there is clearly a healthy debate on the issue and it is difficult to dismiss, given its discussion in peer-reviewed academia, where even politically motivated work must stand up to theoretical and methodological scrutiny.

In this context, what makes Galbraith's support of the Second Amendment problematic is its antagonistic deployment. Indeed, the history of the "gun issue" in the Patriot Movement, both nationally and in Kentucky, indicates that it became a convenient screen onto which patriots could project not only their anxieties about the new global order (and their new place within it), but also their eventual triumph over the challenge the new world order presented. As the reader will recall from chapter 4, while patriots have often articulated their position on guns through the lens of Ruby Ridge and Waco, the context in which they have done so was "global." They explained the bungled operations in conspiratorial terms, insisting that the government had been "occupied" by members of the new world order, who were planning a coup in the world's remaining superpower in order to enact global communism. Indeed, in the wake of Ruby Ridge and Waco, patriot leaders like John Trochmann and Norman Olson began making the rounds of the patriot circuit, lecturing audiences about the impending takeover and instructing people how to prepare for it.

I witnessed one of these appearances firsthand when I attended a Preparedness Expo in Indianapolis in the fall of 1996. I received word about the expo from the Militia of Montana, whose mailing list I was on during the early stages of my research. The mailing, a small booklet on news-grade paper, billed itself as "The premier consumer show of it's [sic] kind, dedicated to educating and preparing people for the future possibilities that may lie ahead; economic instabilities, natural disasters, political unrest, threats to our personal freedom, health and well-being." In addition to purchasing survival gear, such as freeze-dried food, first-aid kits, herbal remedies, and air purification systems, visitors could also attend the expo's premier event, a panel discussion entitled "Gun Control: The 2d Amendment under Fire" (see figure 8.1). The expert witnesses read like a who's who of the movement at the time—J. J. Johnson, Mark Koernke, Jack McLamb, John Trochmann, and Bo Gritz.[12]

As I wandered around the large expo hall waiting for the panel discussion to begin, I happened upon the Militia of Montana booth. John Trochmann was manning the station and an attentive crowd had gathered around him as he spoke gruffly, occasionally striking his hand in the air for emphasis. As I moved closer to better hear him, I heard him mention UN troops in the United States. "Where are they?" a young man asked. "Take a look in here," he said, holding up a large, three-ring binder filled with pictures, "they're all over the place." The notebook contained scanned copies of pictures showing troops, tanks, and helicopters. The pictures were grainy and, being a novice on military hardware, I was hardly able to evaluate what I was looking at. The notebook had the appearance, however, of legitimacy. It was neatly assembled and jam-packed with "evidence"—each picture documented for date, time, and location. It looked as if Trochmann might take it to court the next day to argue an important case.

Like Trochmann, patriots in Kentucky also frequently discussed the gun issue in relation to the UN. Indeed, it is worth noting that when Galbraith ran his 1999 campaign there were no pending threats to gun ownership or use. At the time, neither the Kentucky General Assembly nor the U.S. Congress had any significant gun control legislation pending, yet "preserving Second Amendment rights" occupied a central place in Gatewood's campaign platform.

As I document in chapter 5, the local push for pro-gun legislation has

PANEL DISCUSSION

GUN CONTROL

The 2nd Amendment
Under Fire

Sydicated Talk Show Host
STAN SOLOMON

CRIME, TERRORISM & YOUR RIGHT TO SELF-PROTECTION

Americans' fear of Terrorism rises · Clinton wants a stronger BATF,
The media villianizes the Militias· How will your rights be affected?

Hear The Experts & Voice Your Opinion!
FRIDAY, SEPTEMBER 6TH, 7:00 P.M.
Indiana State Fairgrounds
Requires General Admission to Expo of $6

J.J. JOHNSON
Founder of **Citizens Defense League** and spokesman for the **Georgia Militia** J.J. was a guest speaker at the "Committee of 1776 Pro-Gun Rally" in Washington, D.C. and testified as a Militia panelist before the United States Senate Sub-Committee on Terrorism.

MARK KOERNKE
A former Army Intelligence Analyst, Koernke is best known as **"Mark from Michigan"** as this is how he has authored his best-selling video **America In Peril** and **A Call To Arms**. Mark is the host of **The Intelligence Report** short wave radio talk show.

JACK McLAMB
Director of the **American Citizens' and Lawmen's Association** and editor & publisher of **Aid & Abet Police Newsletter.** McLamb is the highest decorated police officer of the city of Phoenix, twice-earning officer of the year.

JOHN TROCHMANN
John Trochmann, co-founder of the **Militia of Montana,** has been instrumental in networking American Patriots together for a number of years. He has appeared often as a guest analyst on **This Week with David Brinkley.**

BO GRITZ
America's most decorated Green Beret Commander and Commander of Special Forces in Latin America. Bo conducted four POW rescue missions into Communist Asia. He is the author of **A Nation Betrayed** and **Called to Serve.**

Figure 8.1   1996 Patriot Expo Speakers' Forum

more to do with perceived international threats than domestic ones. My discussions with Norman Davis, for example, indicate that the patriot push to have a concealed weapons bill passed was rooted in conspiracies about the UN. Moreover, when patriots articulated their opposition to the Land Between the Lakes Biosphere, they did so by making erroneous claims that the UN would use the spot to launch a takeover of Kentucky. And as I detail in my discussion about patriot opposition to the LBL Biosphere, when I pressed patriots to describe *why* they thought the UN was a threat, they inevitably resorted to antagonistic tropes about cultural and racial inferiority of the so-called third world (equated in their rhetoric with the UN) to make their point.

The second conservative social position Gatewood advocated in his 1999 gubernatorial campaign was opposition to gay rights. The issue became relevant during the summer campaign season, when a gay rights bill was introduced at the June 21 meeting of the Lexington city council.[13] The bill had been forwarded to the council by the Lexington Human Rights Commission, the city agency responsible for monitoring discrimination. The bill, referred to as the Fairness Ordinance, offered wide protections for the GLBT community, banning discrimination in employment, housing, and public accommodations (restaurants, parks, stores) in the city on the basis of sexual orientation and gender identity.[14]

The ordinance passed the city council on July 8 by a 12–3 vote. The wide margin of victory, however, belied the intense debate around the bill. Before the final vote, only two of the fifteen council members had indicated public support for it and three had pledged to vote against it. The other ten wavered publicly, with some expressing exasperation that they had to grapple with the issue at all. At the council's July 2 meeting, where the bill received its first public reading, tensions were high. Large crowds for and against the bill squeezed into City Hall and overflow crowds milled around in the building's lobby and on the sidewalk in front of it. Not surprisingly, given the religious context of the area, many of the bill's opponents decried the bill on moral grounds. When the council opened the floor for public comment, for example, an insurance agent took to the microphone to scold the bill's proponents, saying, "What are you going to do when you're dying of AIDS? What are you going to do when you're dying because of your immoral lifestyle?" (George and Mulvihill 1999). Another opponent, a reverend at a local Christian church, was equally harsh, warning the bill's supporters, "God has spoken clearly about human sexuality. The sin that invited that judgment was the sin of homosexuality!" (George and Mulvihill 1999). As I sat in City Hall that night watching the debate unfold, I wondered if the bill would pass. There was no doubt that Lexington had a politically active gay community. Indeed, while it might surprise those living in urban settings like Los Angeles, Washington, D.C., or New York, many medium-sized cities with large rural hinterlands develop thriving gay cultures in spite of their size. Growing up gay in rural areas can be difficult, and research has shown that gay youth (or older persons just coming out) usually head to the nearest city looking for a community, in the process creating a critical mass for it to develop (see Fellows 1998; Howard 1999). Yet Lexington also had a well-developed, politically active, conservative Christian community. And while many people in Lexington would not consider themselves fundamentalists, the city is hardly a hotbed of liberalism.

After the bill passed, I asked Jeff Jones, at the time the cochairman of the Lexington Fairness Campaign, how his organization had pulled off the bill's passage. "Tireless lobbying and stealth tactics," he told me. Jones explained to me that the Fairness Campaign knew the Conservative Christian lobby was more powerful than Fairness was. Therefore they did most of their lobbying quietly, intentionally avoiding the press so as not to alert their opponents to their activity. They also lobbied the Human Rights Commissioner to introduce the bill near the end of the council's summer session, so members would have little time to drag their feet on the issue and give the conservative Christians time to mobilize opposition.

While the Fairness Ordinance was a local affair, Galbraith was unable to avoid the issue. As a longtime resident of Lexington and a gubernatorial candidate, it would have been difficult to do so. Stories about the ordinance were making front-page headlines in the *Herald-Leader* (George and Mulvihill 1999; Mulvihill 1999) and the issue was set to become statewide the following year. Earlier that summer, representatives Kathy Stein and Mary Lou Marzian, a Democrat from Louisville, prefiled a similar bill for consideration in the 2000 General Assembly. The state-level showdown that was sure to come had the gay community on its toes. The *Letter*, a statewide newspaper for the GLBT community, contacted the gubernatorial candidates' campaign headquarters and requested that each lay out his or her position on the Lexington Ordinance and the prefiled motion in the General Assembly.

Galbraith's campaign was the first to respond to the *Letter*'s inquiry. In his response, Galbraith informed the paper's editor that his campaign was opposed to both the Lexington ordinance and the prefiled statewide initiative. And as he did when he laid out his opposition to gun control, Galbraith articulated his opposition on constitutional grounds, arguing that the measures granted "special rights" thereby violating section 59 of the Kentucky Constitution, which holds that "in all other cases where a general law can be made applicable, no special law shall be enacted."[15]

Galbraith was careful, however, to clarify that his opposition to the measures were not "antigay," insisting instead that it was based on constitutional grounds. His response to the *Letter* began by making that point, which was reiterated several times during the course of the letter:

The Galbraith/Lyons Reform Party slate for Governor and Lt. Governor has been asked its position on gay rights legislation from several interested groups. Some of these inquiries have been reasonable while others have sought to couch the question in the form of "Are you for the legislation or are you anti-gay?" This latter question is unreasonable and illogical because it does not axiomatically follow that someone who opposes this legislation is anti-gay. The answer is that we are opposed to gay rights legislation because it is special legislation which is prohibited by Section 59 of the Constitution of Kentucky. This does not mean that our slate is anti-gay but that special legislation is not the answer to discrimination. Kathy and I stand shoulder to shoulder under the Constitution for any group to be free from unfair discrimination but we cannot do so under the auspice of special legislation which is specifically prohibited by Section 59 of the very document with which we intend to protect the rights of all Kentuckians.

It is important to note that while Galbraith opposed the measure, even the *Letter* did not view his opposition as "antigay." Rather, the paper expressed formal disappointment in the Galbraith campaign and took exception with Galbraith's depiction of the Fairness measures as "special legislation." As the editor, David Williams, wrote in his September column covering the issue,

The Marzian-Stein proposal would apply to all Kentuckians because it adds to existing civil rights laws the category of "sexual orientation" (homosexual, bisexual, or heterosexual), not just homosexual orientation. For that reason, Fairness activists assert it's not special legislation because it would extend the same right to all citizens. (Williams 1999)

In a private letter to Galbraith, Williams reiterated the same point:

Mr. Galbraith,
Thank you for your response. We differ substantially with you on your interpretation of the Kentucky Constitution. We feel that gay civil rights legislation is no more "special legislation" than was civil rights legislation protecting citizens on the basis of their religious beliefs, race, etc., back in the 60s. We will therefore actively work towards passage of this legislation in the 2000 General Assembly. . . . As staunch proponents of the US and Kentucky Constitutions, we do respect your right to your viewpoint and would stand shoulder to shoulder with you and Ms. Lyons in defending that right. Given your analysis in your email [response], we in no way consider you or Ms. Lyons to be anti-gay— just misinformed.[16]

While Gatewood's positions on both the Lexington and statewide fairness ordinances were not couched in traditional antigay rhetoric, his position stood in stark contrast to his progressive past. And as I would discover when I pressed Galbraith on the issue, it bore the markings of antagonism.

When I discussed the Lexington Fairness Ordinance with Gatewood in the summer of 1999, it had just become law. Galbraith had not yet released his statement to the *Letter* publicly opposing the ordinance. I was, therefore, unsure how Galbraith would approach the issue. On the one hand, I knew that the Patriot Movement was not known for its tolerance of gays and lesbians. Yet, on the other hand, I thought he might support it, given that it was a local control measure. Indeed, the bill's advocates were careful to position the issue as a "local matter," arguing that it was something the citizens of Lexington wanted and thus right for the city. Its progressive flavor notwithstanding, it was a good example of local people defining the contours of local life—an ideal long espoused by patriots.

When I interviewed Galbraith, however, I came to realize that, as with the gun issue, patriot invocations to local power were becoming increasingly expedient, rather than ideologically grounded. Indeed, Galbraith was quite adept at deploying various scalar arguments to explain his opposition to the Lexington Fairness Ordinance. In his explanation to me, he switched back and forth between a constitutional framework (localities cannot make "special" legislation, only states can) to an individualistic one (religious landlords should not have to rent to gay people just because the state says so). Below is an excerpt from our conversation about the ordinance:

> *Galbraith:* I do not support it [the Fairness Ordinance]. It's special legislation. It's unconstitutional. Section 59 of the Kentucky Constitution says that you cannot give special legislation to any particular group of people.
> *Gallaher:* But what would you say if I told you that you can discriminate against some people but not others. If you're a landlord, for example, and a prospective renter comes along with his boyfriend, you can say "We won't rent to you because you're gay," and that's legal. Right now that's legal.
> *Galbraith:* That's right.
> *Gallaher:* So, if you make that action illegal are you actually giving someone a special right or are you giving them equal protection under the law?
> *Galbraith:* You're giving someone a special right. The landlord's got his property. That landlord bought the property. That landlord may have religious convictions about it. Religion doesn't stop at the church door. You know? Here's the deal, the city of Lexington already has a landlord/tenant law that has a religious exemption, which means that if your religion thinks homosexuality is a sin, why should any government body be able to tell you you've got to turn your personal property over to people who you think are engaged in living in sin?

The shifting grounds of Galbraith's argument are important for a variety of reasons. First, as with the gun issue, they indicate not only the limits of the "local" in patriot discourse, but patriots' willingness to use whatever scale suits their particular need. In Gatewood's case, it also indicates the limits that patriot discourse places on his previous aversion to meddling in "other people's bedrooms." Indeed, while he never admitted it, I believe patriot rhetoric, and Gatewood's adoption of it during the 1999 campaign, forced him to stake out a position with which he was rather uncomfortable. He told me, for example, that he supported the Kentucky Supreme Court's 1992 decision to strike down the state's sodomy law. It was, he told me, a good move that protected gays without giving them special rights. When I brought up the ordinance in our second interview, he told me, as he did the *Letter,* that he wanted me to know he was not "antigay"—a position no other patriot ever felt compelled to establish with me when the Fairness Ordinance came up in conversation. "Hey, I have a lot of gay friends," he told me, "this is strictly a constitutional argument I'm making."

Of course, none of this can prove that Galbraith is not antigay. Indeed, it's a common joke in oppressed communities that the biggest homophobes/racists/sexists are frequently the ones who will tell you "I can't be homophobic/racist/sexist—I've got gay/black/female friends!" In Gatewood's case, however, his position seems especially odd given his progressive past. When I spoke to the editor of the *Letter,* for example, he told me that when Galbraith first announced his candidacy, older folks in the GLBT community, who remembered his activism from the 1980s, were excited by the prospect of it. "He was as left as you ever get in Kentucky," Williams explained to me.

It is important to reiterate here, however, that regardless of the motives driving Gatewood's stance, the politics he helped craft (and bring to the mainstream) through his gubernatorial bid framed how white working-class people (the main target for the Patriot Movement's mobilization bids) will see the issue. And, as I note in the following section, while Gatewood lost his gubernatorial bid, his efforts to cast the Constitution as a catchall signifier for conservative social positions led, in Kentucky, to a particularly virulent piece of legislation that succinctly captured the two positions discussed in this section.

A LOSS, BUT A POWERFUL ONE

On November 2, 1999, Gatewood lost his third bid for governor and his fourth statewide election. Unlike his earlier efforts, however, the press viewed his 1999 loss as respectable. When Galbraith lost his first gubernatorial bid in 1991, the press made light of his campaign, doing an affectionate story on the one political district he did win, under the headline "Gov. Galbraith No Pipe Dream in Aylesford," in reference to his pro–marijuana/hemp platform. Aylesford is a Lexington neighborhood in between the University of Kentucky and downtown. It houses students, blue-collar workers, and professionals and it was the only precinct in the entire state that Gatewood won. Andy Mead, the staff writer covering the story, queried, "What is this, a hippie haven?" The former president of the Aylesford Place Neighborhood Association responded, "We've always just been a progressive neighborhood. The neighborhood is great because it's so diverse. I think that's why it's such a fun place to live, because you're never bored" (Mead 1991). When Galbraith lost his 1999 bid, by contrast, the *Herald-Leader*'s cover story, "Galbraith Sends Message," cast his bid as politically significant. Galbraith's election returns, 15 percent of the vote, were, as the paper remarked, a record amount for any third-party gubernatorial candidate in the state. His bid was also presented in the paper as a message to the Democratic Party. As the reporter noted, "Patton angered some labor interests in his first term by pushing changes in workers' compensation rules that limited payments for injured workers. Some United Mine Workers' locals in eastern Kentucky endorsed Galbraith" (Estep 1999). There is no doubt Galbraith felt positive about his strong showing as well. A few months later, he announced that he would be running for the Central Kentucky 6th district congressional seat, again on the Reform Party ticket. No one laughed this time around. Gatewood was now an official contender. And while he lost that seat as well, he again earned a respectable, even noteworthy percentage of votes—12 percent.

While these measures are significant in their own right, Galbraith's electoral strides are also important for what they say about the effects of bringing a patriot politics to the mainstream. In the context of Galbraith's particular bid, the effect was, as I note in the previous section, to link class-based issues with antagonistic social positions (a move he continued in his 2000 congressional bid). The absences are equally important, and the most compelling one in Galbraith's 1999 gubernatorial bid was a heretofore campaign mainstay—legalizing marijuana/hemp.

This is not to say that the issue did not make the final cut on Galbraith's platform. It did. Gatewood's 1999 platform advocated "legalizing the medical use of marijuana." Galbraith's previous campaigns, however, had supported legalizing the *growth* of industrial hemp and the *use* of marijuana, thereby casting the issue in a political and economic frame, as well as a civil liberties one. The absence of hemp in his 1999 platform is important because it indicates *how* patriot discourse narrows the possibilities of addressing class-based concerns through patriot discourse. As I note in chapter 6, while patriots support legalizing hemp (some oppose legalizing marijuana, others do not), they were unable to articulate a political response to it in the same way that they did with concealed weapons and the LBL Biosphere. This was a result of their inability to tackle the dicey issue of subsidies, which facilitates small farming in the state, but also obviously links it to the government. Unlike many patriots, Galbraith (who introduced most patriots to the issue in the first place) was well aware of the important role of subsidies, and the government more broadly, in ensuring the future of small farming in the state. During my first interview with Gatewood, for example, I asked him how he thought hemp could be reintroduced to the state's economy in a manner that would ensure its viability for small farmers. "Licensing and regulation," he succinctly told me. And, as I note in chapter 6, when I asked him to explain what he meant by that, he told me it would be similar to the way tobacco farming is kept viable in the state today. Farmers could apply for a license to farm hemp, but there would be acreage limits in place so that large growers, such as agribusinesses, could not receive the licenses, thereby keeping hemp in the hands of the state's small farmers.

When I asked him about the plan in my second interview, held in the summer before the gubernatorial race, however, he cautioned me: "You understand this is my idea, but this isn't a campaign platform we're talking about. I'm describing a program I wrote in 1977." Moreover, when I asked him about the McCain tobacco bill, asking him how he would respond as governor were it reintroduced (recall the bill would have eliminated tobacco subsidies), he protested my description of Kentucky tobacco as subsidized. He told me that because farmers do not receive a direct cash payment, "I don't see that as a subsidy"!

While Galbraith opposed eliminating the tobacco subsidy program, telling me, "If it's gonna hurt the tobacco farmers in the state of Kentucky, you bet I will oppose it," his unwillingness to tackle the issue on its own terms is significant. Indeed, his ability to discuss the important role that government plays in protecting small farmers is hampered by the discursive constraints that guard against using the very words that describe that help. And while I was unable to receive an adequate answer for why the issue was dropped from the campaign platform, its absence there is logical given the discursive constraints inherent to the patriot frame. Indeed, Galbraith's support of workers' comp was only able to elude this discursive trap because even in the old system the employer, not the state, paid the benefit.

Galbraith's failure to win the gubernatorial race was also significant because his efforts to use the Constitution as a catch-all signifier for a variety of antagonistically constructed social positions had the effect of formalizing opposition to gay rights as a patriot issue. Indeed, while white working-class, heterosexual males are not necessarily known for being especially tolerant of gays and lesbians, it was not a foregone conclusion that the movement would adopt the issue as a patriot one. Indeed, for most of the movement's history its adherents have been concerned, on the cultural front, with race and ethnicity, whipping up opposition to causes such as immigration or Holocaust remembrance. Therefore, opposition to gay rights required discursive articulation to become a part of the patriot politic—and

Galbraith's campaign, while not solely responsible, set important ground-work for it to become so.

Galbraith's use of the Constitution to ground his opposition to gay rights also allowed the position to be linked with a more established patriot issue—gun rights. And, in the hands of other patriots, this discursive equation took a vitriolic turn. Of particular note is a bill Representative Bob Damron intro-duced in the 2001 General Assembly. The bill, House Bill 49, proposed expanding the legal use of deadly force. Currently, Kentucky law allows people to use deadly force to defend themselves from possible death, serious injury, forced sexual intercourse, and kidnapping. Damron's bill proposed adding to that list burglary, robbery, and deviate sexual intercourse.[17] Cast-ing the bill as citizen friendly, Damron told the *Herald-Leader* the day after it was introduced: "This bill basically gives civilians more rights to protect themselves. People should have the right to defend themselves and their property, and this puts more teeth into self-protection. For example, if someone is trying to break into your home, I certainly think you have the right to defend yourself" (Brammer 2001).

Despite Damron's benign descriptions of his bill, its detractors described it variously as "dangerous," "unnecessary," and "a serious threat." Of par-ticular concern among its critics was the clause in the bill allowing deadly force in cases of "deviate sexual intercourse." Historically, Kentucky stat-utes have defined deviate sexual intercourse to mean sex acts common in (but not exclusive to) the gay community, such as anal sex. Jeff Vessels, the execu-tive director of the American Civil Liberties Union (ACLU), argued that the bill would sanction violence against gays. Referring to the Wyoming gay col-lege student who was brutally beaten and left to die by his assailants after allegedly making a pass at one of them, Vessels argued "a Matthew Shepard could be murdered in Kentucky and the law would give his killers a cover" (Brammer 1999). Jeff Jones, the Lexington Human Rights commissioner, raised a similar concern in my interview with him. He said the bill's wording, which did not include the word "forced" before the term "deviate sexual intercourse," begged the question of whether a person engaged in consensual gay sex could be murdered and the assailant let free because of the clause.

When I interviewed Bob Damron, I asked him to explain why he intro-duced House Bill 49. His initial response was similar to the one he gave the *Herald-Leader* reporter a few days prior:

> What House Bill 49 is, is it's an attempt to clean up Kentucky's use-of-deadly-force statute—when you, as a victim of a crime, can defend yourself and use deadly force to do so and when you can't. And Kentucky's law is not very clear on that right now. And so I had looked at the statutes in Tennessee and Mis-souri, Indiana, and Illinois, which are border states, and they provide some pretty specific defenses for you to use deadly force—if it's a break-in into your

home, which is burglary, or robbery, which is by use of a weapon. And I brought in sodomy as one of the crimes against which you can use deadly force to protect yourself.

Despite Damron's depiction of "sodomy"—another term historically used in Kentucky legal statutes to describe gay sex acts—as a crime, it is not a criminal act. As I note previously, the Kentucky Supreme Court ruled that the state's sodomy law was unconstitutional in 1992.[18] Given the legality of sodomy, I felt compelled to ask Damron why he included the "deviate sexual intercourse" phrase in his bill:

> *Gallaher:* Now, I have to ask why the final [sodomy] clause? Was there a constituency or an element of your constituency that was clamoring for that to be added?
> *Damron:* Not the sodomy issue, no. But, I did have the issue raised to me by an individual down on the Tennessee line, who lives in Bell County, and his brother lives in Tennessee . . . and we were having lunch one day in Bell County, and he said, you know, we don't have the same rights that they have in Tennessee. And so we got to looking at the rights they had in Tennessee and he's right. We don't.

Not satisfied with the answer, given that it did little to explain why his bill proposed allowing someone to use deadly force against a noncriminal act, I pressed him still further, repeating my question and adding, "And why that particular wording?" Below is our exchange:

> *Damron:* Well, because when the statutes were written, we just talk about sexual intercourse. Kentucky statutes define sexual intercourse as the normal sex acts. And we don't consider the other to be normal in Kentucky, so we then have a separate definition for sodomy that says that it's deviate sexual intercourse. When the self-protection act was written a long time ago, deviate sexual intercourse was not included in the statutes. Uh, and so, we didn't have that included, and it's not included in the public self-protection provisions for using deadly force. Technically, a person that's being sodomized can't use that as a defense.
> *Gallaher:* So, this is designed to protect a gay constituency?
> *Damron:* Uh huh. Uh huh. Or a heterosexual constituency that is being sodomized.
> *Gallaher:* So, what would be the circumstance under which you could use it? It wouldn't be, uh, the only example I can think of is a Matthew Shepard sort of example, where a guy makes a pass at another guy and then gets shot?
> *Damron:* That's not deviate sexual intercourse because it requires force, it requires compulsion, and making a pass at somebody doesn't meet those tests, which is the argument made by the ACLU in Louisville, who anytime they see anything that looks homosexual, runs to its quick aid and defense without read-

ing or looking at what they're doing. They never contacted me. If they'd contacted me, I could have kept them from looking like a fool.

Gallaher: So, have you talked to them now? I mean, do you foresee the more liberal wing of your party opposing the bill because of that particular wording?

Damron: I don't think they're gonna necessarily oppose it. The bill, when they recognize what it actually does, uh, I think the extreme liberal wing of the party, when they recognize that sodomy, sodomizing, you know, one homosexual sodomizing another one by force, is not covered and [the law] doesn't provide them the ability to defend themselves, I think they probably will support adding that language to it. It's just ignorance from their standpoint of what's actually in the statute.

When I asked Representative Stein about the bill, she told me she would not support it. And when I explained Damron's justification, she took umbrage with his comments, arguing,

He is *not* opening up a way for gay people to protect themselves. Certainly, if you stretch it, that argument could be made, but based upon Bob Damron's philosophy, his voting record, and statements he has made both on the record and off the record—they all indicate that he does not, excuse my language here, give a rat's ass about the lives of any gay or lesbian individual. . . . You know, Bob Damron was against gays and lesbians being included in our Domestic Violence emergency protective statutes. Now, if you want to afford a defense to somebody, then you are not opposed to their being able to take advantage of civil protection.

Moreover, as Representative Stein reminded me, the wording of Damron's bill describes sodomy as a crime, even though it was decriminalized in 1992. Referring to the phrase "deviate sexual intercourse," she told me, "In Kentucky those are code words, OK, because in 1992 our Supreme Court outlawed the crime of sodomy. . . . You know, that is just a code word, a way to expand the use of what I perceive to be gun violence and also open it up to a class of individuals much maligned and much hated by this group of religious, political extremists."

While I have no way of assessing Damron's personal feelings about gays, given his depiction of gay sex as "abnormal" and his pejorative depiction of the ACLU as blindly beholden to a "homosexual agenda," it was hardly a difficult step for me to arrive at the same opinion as Stein—that the bill is an antagonistic measure aimed at the state's GLBT community. Indeed, other patriots I spoke to after Galbraith's 1999 election were quite frank about their new focus against gay rights. When I interviewed Norman Davis, for example, he told me that one of the areas Take Back Kentucky focused on was "morality," and when I asked him what some of the issues were, he responded, "Well, we call them the queers, the homosexuals, whatever you

want to call them. We work on that. No special laws for anybody. We're all
the same. We're all people, we're all equal. You got your rights, why do you
want special ones?"

Homophobia is nothing new in the United States. Neither are efforts to
discredit gay people and to thwart their efforts to gain equal protection
under the law. In that regard, the Patriot Movement's opposition to gay
rights is hardly special or innovative. Indeed, even its depiction of gay rights
as special rights is a well-established argument on the mainstream right (see
Diamond 1994; Goldberg 1995; Nakagawa 1995). What is significant about
patriots' opposition to gay rights is its placement within the same discursive
frame as opposition to gun control. It is just this sort of framing that allows
a bill about two otherwise unrelated topics to be linked together. And in
their linking, protecting one "right" (deadly force) comes to be equated with
the right to take the life of another (an "other"). And, while Damron's bill
was indefinitely tabled in committee, the discursive framework is in place for
another try at the measure.

So crafted, the patriot politics becomes a metapolitic in which essentialist,
antagonistically constructed social positions are connected with important
class-based concerns. That patriots are willing to constantly shift the spatial
grounds of this metapolitic, arguing for the power of the local when it suits
their needs, supporting the state or federal scale when the local works against
them, only makes their politics more dangerous. Indeed, it is a vitriolic politics made all the more potent by the mobility of its spatial grounds. It is
important to note, however, that it did not have to be this way, nor does it
have to be this way in the future. This is the case both in terms of Gatewood
Galbraith and the rank and file of the movement. It is to these potential
openings that I now turn.

NOTES

1. Tom Watson was an early leader in the populist movement. He went from
championing a biracial farmers' alliance to espousing a politics of racial bigotry. The
best-known biography of Watson is Comer Vann Woodward's *Tom Watson: Agrarian
Rebel,* first published in 1938.

2. In the 1995 primary season, for example, Galbraith had a field day with the
FBI's BOPTROT sting, which resulted in twenty high-ranking state employees
being indicted and later convicted for taking bribes from agents posing as horse
industry lobbyists. In a speech before the AFL-CIO, Galbraith reminded his audience that his three opponents were in the capital at the time and drew hearty laughter
and thunderous applause when he told the audience, "There's only two ways you
can look at that. Number one, these three men knew what was going on up there and
didn't have the backbone to stand up and point it out to us. Or number two, these

three men did not know what was going on up there, which makes them all three too damned dumb to be governor" (Poore 1995).

3. The Reform Party, first established by Ross Perot in the 1992 election, has never had a coherent political ideology. Ross Perot's showing in the 1992 and 1996 elections, however, secured the party access to federal campaign funds, making it an attractive political vehicle for hopeful politicians of various ideological stripes. In the 2000 election, the party's incoherence eventually led to its undoing, as an internal feud, waged on the convention floor and in the courtroom, demolished what little unity the party did have.

4. Elaine Chao is the U.S. secretary of labor. She was nominated to the position by George W. Bush in 2001.

5. Kentucky Educational Television (KET) sponsored and filmed the debate, which was held on October 25, 1995. All candidates' comments included in this chapter were transcribed directly from a videocassette of the debate purchased from KET.

6. Galbraith's running mate for lieutenant governor was Kathy Lyons, a farm activist from western Kentucky.

7. The AFL-CIO does not usually endorse third-party candidates. In the 1999 race, they endorsed Democrat Paul Patton, prompting Galbraith to criticize the organization: "The AFL-CIO is a bunch of prostitutes, and I'm not talking about the members. I'm talking about the leadership. . . . Paul Patton is anti-union, anti-membership. He's a scab coal miner!" (Gerth 1999).

8. In 2002, the Kentucky General Assembly approved a bill to liberalize the 1996 program. The data collected after 1996 demonstrated just how hard it was to get compensation. Only eleven claims, approximately one in ninety, were honored. Chastened, Patton even led the push to have the new bill introduced (Staff Reports 2002a, 2002c).

9. The National Institute on Money in State Politics, a group that collects campaign donation data and compiles them by election, records no donations to Martin's campaign from the NRA.

10. The individual or group that hacked Martin's web page also accused her of being "pro-gay" during their brief hijacking of her campaign page.

11. Gun control advocates argue that the Second Amendment only confers on states the right to keep and bear arms, pointing to the clause "A well regulated militia being necessary to the security of a free state" to prove their point. They argue that the National Guard is a "regulated" militia and thus constitutional, while patriot militias are neither regulated nor state-sanctioned and thus unconstitutional. Gun rights advocates point to the clause immediately following the "well regulated militia" phrase, which reads "the right of the people to keep and bear arms shall not be infringed," arguing that the amendment holds gun ownership as an individual right.

12. J. J. Johnson is one of the Patriot Movement's few black leaders. He testified along with John Trochmann and Norman Olson at the 1995 Senate hearings on militias. Mark Koernke is a patriot gadfly who was active at the time in the Michigan Militia Movement. Jack McLamb is an Arizona police officer who has publicly endorsed the militia movement.

13. The Lexington city council is officially termed the Lexington Fayette Urban

County Council, because it governs the city of Lexington and Fayette County, in which Lexington is located.

14. The most contentious part of the bill concerned the phrase "gender identity." After much debate, the final bill defined the term as "having a gender identity as a result of a sex change surgery; or manifesting, for reasons other than dress, an identity not traditionally associated with one's biological maleness or femaleness" (Mulvihill 1999).

15. The Kentucky Constitution may be read in its entirety on the Kentucky Legislative Research Council's web site at www.lrc.state.ky.us/Legresou/Constitu/list1.htm#Legislative.

16. Williams posted his personal response to Lambdanet, a listserv for GLBT students, faculty, and staff at the University of Kentucky. Jeff Jones forwarded me the e-mail, with the permission of the editor, for my research.

17. House Bill 49 reads: "Amend KRS 503.050 relating to the use of physical force in self-protection to authorize the use of deadly force against criminal homicide, burglary, robbery, and deviate sexual intercourse and the attempt to commit such crimes, in addition to current authorized use of deadly force."

18. The court ruled 4–3 that the state's sodomy law was unconstitutional because it singled out gay people. The court noted that the state did not outlaw sodomy (called "deviate sexual intercourse" in the statutes) for heterosexuals, concluding, "If there is a rational basis for different treatment it has yet to be demonstrated in this case. We need not sympathize, agree with, or even understand the sexual preference of homosexuals in order to recognize their right to equal treatment before the bar of criminal justice" (Tolliver and Grelen 1992).

9

Looking Ahead

The third time I interviewed Gatewood Galbraith, it was a blustery January day. The weather forecasters were calling for snow later in the day—the kind of storm that leaves its icy remnants on the ground and roads for days as testimony to its strength. It was, I thought while preparing for the interview, the kind of day tailor-made for playing hooky from work or school and settling down on the sofa with a good book. Given the looming storm, it was gracious of Galbraith to agree to meet me that morning. I appreciated it all the more because I knew we were set to talk about a topic potentially depressing for him—his fifth electoral loss, this one in the 2000 race for Central Kentucky's sixth district U.S. congressional seat.

We started our interview in Galbraith's downtown office, sitting across from one another at his large, mostly empty desk. He had just moved into the office from a larger one down the hall where he had headquartered his 2000 campaign. His mood seemed to match the scarcity of his surroundings. He told me somewhat glumly, "I've decided I'm unelectable." No mean statement from a man who had kept his eyes on the prize for almost twenty years. Given his longtime political aspirations, I was curious to know what he would do next. "Well," he told me,

I'm going in several other directions. First, I'm going to appear every place I can, get out there on the speakers' tour. I'm giving a talk to a nine hundred-level graduate course at the College of Justice over here at Eastern [Kentucky University] in about two weeks. And, since I'm going to have as much time as I want, I'm going to take that time and put together as close as I can the quintessential political position from an historical, psychological, political base. I'm gonna educate these folks [about] from the time we crawled out of the chemical soup and became more than single cell amoebae. We're gonna start at that and talk about the human nature and the drive for intoxication and how that is controlled and who controls it, and what's the political basis for it, and how those decisions are made, who makes them, and how that affects us. And, I'm gonna videotape them, run them on TV.

As I listened to Galbraith plot out his postpolitical life (which if history tells us anything, may not be "post" for very long), I was struck in particular by two things. The first was Galbraith's plan to develop the "quintessential political position." The second was his strategy for getting the message out, appearing and speaking wherever he could and using television for places he could not. He was, I realized, trying to address his concerns on a dual front—an ideological one and a popular one—and attempting to do so simultaneously. His two-pronged approach, although different politically from mine, encapsulates the strategy of this book, which is theoretical but also, by virtue of the story it tells, political. I end this book, therefore, by reviewing these goals as I've addressed them here, noting where I think I have succeeded and where more work is clearly in order.

WHAT CAN THE PATRIOT MOVEMENT TELL US ABOUT THEORIZING IDENTITY?

A few years ago, David Harvey participated in an author-meets-critic forum, published in the *Annals of the Association of American Geographers*, on his then new book *Justice, Nature, and the Geography of Difference* (1996). While his book was wide ranging, many reviewers in the forum expressed particular dissatisfaction with Harvey's use of the fire at the chicken processing plant in Hamlet, North Carolina, to make a point about the left's fascination with identity politics. One of his critics, Bruce Braun, accused Harvey of engaging in an unfair blame game and took exception with his attempt to reinsert class as a central element of the leftist project:

> Harvey places the blame for the lack of attention to the fire—even the fire itself, if we accept his argument that the weakening of working class politics contributed to the tragedy—at the feet of feminist and racial politics. . . . Harvey is simply wrong to imply that class is the difference that mattered in Hamlet. Surely the lesson in all this is that the disproportionate number of deaths among women and African Americans requires additional forms of explanation and politics to those based solely on class. . . . Class-based politics may have addressed the exploitation of workers, but processes of domination and oppression based on racialized and gendered identities and geographies were not peripheral in these tragic events, and, moreover, they could very well continue apace, regardless of the success of class-based politics. (Braun 1998, 715)

In response to Braun and others like him, Harvey (1998, 726) noted that his critics "have collectively spent far more ink expostulating about those ten pages than they have spent on the rest of the book in toto," and concluded, "methinks they all protest a bit too much." Indeed, Harvey was stubborn in his insistence that the fire did have a lot to say about the lack of a class politics on the left today and he speculated that something important was behind the "raw nerve" he clearly touched:

> Behind it lies, I suspect, a struggle to account for much of our recent intellectual history. We must obviously come to terms with the whole push into identity politics (of various sorts often associated with a wide variety of so-called "new social movements") and the capturing of academia by a whole set of trends that varied from post-modernism and post-structuralism to strident claims about non-communicability and separation as fundamental to the recognition of particularity. Such trends were quite strong for a while and indeed threatened to engulf the whole academic left. I think it would be a churlish exaggeration to say that I depict these movements as useless or "mere diversions," for I think it clear that I believe they all had something important to say. But insofar as they were viscerally opposed to Marxism—and I submit that a lot of them were—they were devastating for conceptions of class politics as well as for serious development of the tradition of Marxian critical examination of a rapidly transforming capitalist political economy. (Harvey 1998, 726–27)

Braun and Harvey's comments indicate the breadth of the divide that separates poststructuralism from Marxism in the academy. As the reader is by now well aware, I am not a neutral observer in this debate. Indeed, Harvey's insistence that a class politics is of fundamental importance to leftist theory and politics drives this book and gives it its overall flavor. My concern with the role of racism in the Patriot Movement and my witness to its growing influence in the Kentucky movement, however, keeps me equally interested in analyzing oppression that stems from other social positions. In short, you could say I am interested in using both perspectives and doing so simultaneously.

I believe these two analytic models can, however, be fruitfully merged and I believe the Patriot Movement provides an excellent site from which to conceive how this can be done. As I have noted numerous times in this book, perhaps even a bit redundantly, patriots occupy conflicting social positions. On the one hand, their class positionality, which leaves them captive to the ebb and flow of the global market, creates the context for their oppression as workers. On the other, their dominant racial and gender positions oppress by virtue of their normativity, even if the individuals in question do not set out to do so. Standing on the fault line of identity positions, patriots provide an everyday example of why identity politics should consider both class positionality and racial/gendered/sexual positionality and why an analytic fusion of Marxism and poststructuralism would be prescient, especially in the context of progressive political action.

In this book, I have begun this task by trying to link a driving analytic of identity theory (where you see something from) with a driving analytic Harvey (1998, 2000) identifies (who and where you learn it from and how you learn it). Indeed, in conducting my analysis I see both questions as crucial to an analysis of the Patriot Movement. The first question, the where (or position) of the modern patriot, is a fundamental one. Scholars and journalists interested in identity politics have been right to emphasize that the Patriot Movement is made almost entirely of white men. The stereotypes of "angry white men" aside, the history of this movement, which I detail in chapter 4, demonstrates clearly that the movement's early leaders saw "patriotism" as a convenient category through which to mobilize whites who felt cowed by new, "PC" norms but eager nonetheless to maintain their dominance. Yet, as I note in chapter 4, early patriot agitators were also aware that their message would take greater hold in areas devastated by economic restructuring associated with globalization. And their success relative to left-wing activists indicates that Harvey is on the mark when he chastises the left for its abandonment of class politics at precisely the same time it is so desperately needed. Indeed, left-wing activists during the crisis made this exact point, arguing that many farmers turned to the right because they provided answers the left did not.

When I began my own analysis, I started by asking where Kentucky patriots stood. Sitting on the hard wooden benches at CCK meetings, I could not help but notice that, week in and week out, these meetings were all-white affairs. And, as my time studying the movement progressed, I witnessed increasing invocations to that whiteness in the patriot politics. Yet I also noticed, as I observed the cars people drove to meetings, the outfits they wore there, and the intonation of their voices, that those assembled, while not poor, were not well-off, either. Rather, they were workers—auto mechanics, restaurant workers, the self-employed. And even those with white-collar jobs and good educations seemed to be only one generation removed from the working class and frequently invoked their humble, rural roots. Where they saw it from, I concluded, depended on what part of their social position you focused on. Mention the General Agreement on Tariffs and Trade (GATT) or NAFTA at a CCK meeting, for example, and you would hear various complaints about "greedy corporations," "the government that sold us out," and "a country in disrepair." Mention the UN, however, and you would be assailed with comments about the quality of American culture and civilization and warned about people from what patriots pejoratively called the "third world." The conclusion I came to was that the patriot category was a proxy for contradictory locations (at once oppressed and dominant) and the viewpoint each provided.

Given the duality of their point of view, I also asked myself *how* patriots had come to see things as they did. Sitting in CCK meetings, it was obvious that by the time I encountered most patriots they had already graduated from "patriot school." When I spoke to patriots one on one, however, I realized that none had been preenrolled in the patriot school of thought. Before their involvement in the movement, many had been apolitical. Others had been liberal. Many had been educated on the battlefields of Vietnam and had chosen at the end of the war to "drop out—to party, have a good time, and forget," as Steve Kelly put it, when explaining his own background to me. At many points during my fieldwork, I could not help but think patriots could have been, and still could be, mobilized through a solid class-based politics instead. Of course, not all would change their views and leave the movement. Its leaders, in particular, would find such a move difficult, not only because their reputations have been staked on the patriot ideology, but also because they have come to wield a great deal of power through the movement. Yet a powerful social movement is always built on the support of its people and, with other options, especially for their class-based needs (which are not substantially addressed in the patriot politics), adherents might move elsewhere.

As the whiteness literature illustrates, however, a class politics in and of itself will not solve the problem of whiteness. Indeed, scholars such as Noel Ignatiev (1995) have identified attachment to whiteness as a key stumbling block to the formation and maintenance of a solid working-class politics in the United States. What to do about attachment to whiteness among the white working class, however, is an open question. Some, like Ignatiev, argue that whites must learn to disidentify—to abandon their whiteness so that they may not only see their fundamental links with workers of other races, but also understand how their attachment to whiteness oppresses their working-class brethren of other races. Others argue that whiteness must be reconstructed and note that white workers will not altruistically abandon their whiteness just because "race traitors" tell them to do so.

After spending time in the patriot field, I believe that disidentification is not a viable strategy. As LaClau and Mouffe (1985) note, differentiation is a fundamental part of human identity formation. Trying to do away with one moment of differentiation will not abolish its role in identity formation. Nor will it address the real problem, which is not differentiation, but differentiation that is crafted antagonistically. I also believe white workers will not disidentify without something, as Kincheloe and Steinberg (1998, 21) put it, for them "to rally around or to affirm" in place of their old identity. As a variety of scholars note, working-class politics is in serious disarray in many quarters and severely limited in others. Most importantly, I believe, disidentification does nothing to address the problem of white elitism. The whites most capable of disidentifying are those who can afford to abandon their racial identity because they have their wealth, and the status they derive from it, to fall back on. The political implications of this are obvious. As Jim Goad succinctly noted in a 1998 interview he gave with Darius James in *Transitions,* "I think people in power realize that if the dialogue is confined to race and gender issues, you can keep the underclass fighting among themselves for seats on the bus, while the bus driver remains the same" (Goad 1998, 215).

As I note in chapter 3, however, attempts to reconstitute whiteness have been heretofore problematic. Some attempts, like Reeder and Kipnis's performance art character, White Trash Girl, end up fetishizing the very working-class whites they hope to reconstruct. Others, like Goad, attempt to liberate the "redneck" by validating his anger, but the antagonism that drives his reconstructed redneck is based on an individualism that contradicts the very collectivist view necessary to reach out across categorical divides.

Given these problems, I believe the left should consider other categories for reconstruction. And in assessing what category (or categories) to reconstruct, I believe it would be fruitful to examine how white workers themselves are currently articulating their varied (and contradictory) concerns. As my analysis of the Kentucky Patriot Movement indicates, patriots are comfortable with broad, umbrella categories. Using the patriot category, for example, the movement in Kentucky has addressed a variety of issues, including industrial hemp, biospheres, gun rights, and gay rights. These issues give testimony to the multiple positionality of patriots and to the diverse concerns that derive from them. And given the success they have had with the category of "patriot," I would suggest that it is as good a category as any with which to begin a project of reconstruction. Indeed, co-opting the category of patriot from the right would work to undermine the current power of the category, which not only thwarts class-based concerns but buttresses cultural anxieties, providing a palatable venue for their expression.

Traditionally, of course, the left has shunned the category of nation. They have proffered scathing criticism of nationalism and in many cases have called for an end to the nation-state itself. They have done so with good reason. The historical record on the nation-state provides a stark picture of the scale of violence enacted under its auspices. As Giddens (1985) now long ago remarked, the nation-state is the quintessential power container, affording human history its bloodiest century on record. Yet trying to get rid of the nation has proven an unwieldy task. Indeed, even as the forces of neoliberalism have undone many of the traditional powers of the nation-state, people from across the globe have invoked "nation" as a symbolic lever against those who would dismantle the state.

It is for this reason that LaClau and Mouffe first suggested in 1985 that we not abandon broad categories such as the "nation." It is also why they argue for "reconstructing" the nation rather than destroying it or replacing it with other identities. As Mouffe (1995, 264) puts it: "The struggle against the exclusive type of ethnic nationalism can only be carried out by articulating another type of nationalism, a civic nationalism expressing allegiance to the values specific to the democratic tradition and the forms of life that are constitutive of it."

The question that begs to be answered, of course, is *how* a national project may best encapsulate difference. As the above quote implies, LaClau and Mouffe see the recognition and support of difference as a fundamental element. As I note in chapter 2, their conception of hegemony is intricately tied to this view. Rather than view hegemony as centered in institutions, they locate it in the power to define and, rather than viewing hegemony as counter to democracy, they view its *agonistic* expression as crucial to the project. As Mouffe (1995, 265) argues, agonistic pluralism

> is anchored in the recognition of the multiplicity within oneself and of the con-
> tradictory positions that this multiplicity entails. Its acceptance of the other
> does not merely consist of tolerating differences, but in positively celebrating
> them because it acknowledges that, without alterity and otherness, no identity
> could ever assert itself. It is also a pluralism that valorizes diversity and dissen-
> sus, recognizing in them the very condition of possibility, of a striving demo-
> cratic life.

For LaClau and Mouffe, only through these processes may varied constituencies be linked through a democratic chain of equivalence that will inhibit antagonism and thus violence.

Others, however, find fault with the idea that an unfettered ability to differentiate will, by itself, lead to a progressive politics. In his new book, *Spaces of Hope*, David Harvey takes this viewpoint to task, arguing that any politics that revels in particularity without addressing the need for universals is doomed to compete with a capitalist social order that will invoke universals, and to its own benefit. As he explains,

> Dialectics here is useful. It teaches that universality always exists in relation to
> particularity: neither can be separated from the other even though they are dis-
> tinctive moments within our conceptual operations and practical engagements.
> The notion of justice, for example, acquires universality through a process of
> abstraction from particular instances and circumstances, but becomes particular
> again as it is actualized in the real world through social processes. But the
> orchestration of this process depends upon mediating institutions. . . . . These
> mediating institutions "translate" between particularities and universals and
> (like the Supreme Court) become guardians of universal principles and arbiters
> of their application. They also become power centers in their own right. This is,
> broadly, the structure set up under capitalism with the state and all of its institu-
> tions (now supplemented by a variety of international institutions such as the
> World Bank and the IMF, the United Nations, GATT and the World Trade
> Organization) being fundamental as "executive committees" of capitalism's
> systemic interests. Capitalism is replete with mechanisms for converting from
> the particular (even personal) to the universal and back again in a dynamic and

interactive model. . . . No social order can, therefore, evade the question of universals. (Harvey 2000, 242)

Harvey's argument for universals (which he reminds his readers are always "socially constructed, not given"; Harvey 2000, 247) resonates with my findings presented here. Indeed, what is remarkable about the Patriot Movement in (and out) of Kentucky is its ability to use the very democratic structures available to it to exclude and in some cases physically threaten its "others." Patriots' use of the legislature has been phenomenal, covering topics as broad as the Second Amendment, biospheres, and gay rights. They have also shown adroitness at moving back and forth between particularist and universalist arguments to frame their various positions, invoking local sovereignty to fight the LBL Biosphere, yet opposing local control when enacted for the benefit of the GLBT community.

After spending five years studying the Patriot Movement (in the midst of it and from a distance), I can say that I agree with Harvey when he argues, "The contemporary 'radical' critique of universalism is sadly misplaced. It should focus instead on the specific institutions of power that translate between particularity and universality rather than attack universalism per se" (Harvey 2000, 242). It is here, in Harvey's call for shifting progressives' focus to society's "mediating institutions," that I think LaClau and Mouffe's agonistically constructed chain of equivalence (held together by the category of citizenship) may be matched with Harvey's calls for a return to universalism. Indeed, it is not a coincidence that in the Patriot Movement the state has become the enemy. In a globalizing world, the state is in many ways the new mediating organization. The state is increasingly to international organizations (the International Monetary Fund, the World Trade Organization, the World Bank) and transnational corporations what bodies like the courts, the National Labor Relations Board, and the Farm Bureau were to the state during the heyday of the welfare state.

And while patriots call for the state's destruction, I believe, as I note in chapter 6 with particular reference to tobacco farming, there is room for the left to make a counterargument for a reconstructed state—one that is no longer discursively articulated vis-à-vis capital, but vis-à-vis its citizens, who are workers, producers, housewives, and the like. As I look back at my very first interview with Gatewood Galbraith, I realize that this is exactly what the Patriot Movement is proposing to do. As Gatewood explained it to me during our first interview:

I'm trying to go back to the roots of what government's role is. I sent a letter to Bill Clinton when he got elected. I sent him a three-page letter and I said, "Dear Mr. President, you were elected on the theme of bringing change. That's what you said—there was going to be a change when you got elected. You didn't give us any plan for that change, or set out, or enunciate a paradigm for how you're gonna bring that change about. So may I suggest that you assume the paradigm of renegotiating the New Deal." And here's why. . . . Everybody agreed we needed the New Deal back in 1937, but government's gotten too big and too bloated and too many agencies have gotten too fat off it. So let's sell it to the people as renegotiating the New Deal. This being the theme of it, only this time, instead of just business and government, we're gonna include the people, the Bill of Rights, and Mother Earth.

I heartily agree with Gatewood that the citizens and Mother Earth, instead of capital, should be at the heart of such a renegotiation. However, in the absence of a progressively articulated project, built (however temporarily) around some universal categories, Galbraith's attempts to renegotiate the New Deal become, as I have documented in this book, regressive. Indeed, when I look on the horizon of leftist politics, I see few examples anywhere. But there are, amid the haze, a few bright spots (see McPhail 2002; Wilson 1999).

The Reverend Jesse Jackson's Rainbow Coalition's recent forays into mostly white Appalachian towns provides one such ray of hope. Indeed, the coalition's rallying cry, "Leave no one behind," embodies a nationalistic politics quite different from that of the militias. The coalition rallies are a complex attempt to foster class consciousness among the poor whites who live in often desperate poverty, and to build alliances between them and their urban, often black or brown brethren. Jackson's purposeful visits to mostly white towns, however, are more than the passing of an olive branch. Jackson is reaching out to poor whites, not in spite of their race, but because of it. By purposefully choosing impoverished white areas for coalition rallies, Jackson acknowledges that class oppression operates in varied ways—between categories (white and black), through them (wealthy whites and poor whites), and across them (elites and working classes). Furthermore, by trying to build alliances across categories (while remaining aware of the differences between them), workers of all races will be better able to respond to government workers that "There is no alternative" and force government instead to consider alternatives that work for all citizens rather than against them.

Another hopeful example of how broad categories—universally cast—can bring together workers of different races can be seen in William Julius Wilson's call for *affirmative opportunity*. Wilson argues that, for affirmative action to survive, it must be discursively rearticulated. This is necessary because at present calls for support of affirmative action divide rather than unite workers of different races. Indeed, for working-class whites, in particular, affirmative action has come to signify handouts given to "undeserving" minorities at the expense of whites. As Wilson (1999, 111) explains it,

Unlike "preferential" racial policies, opportunity-enhancing programs have popular support even among those who express anti-black attitudes. For all these reasons, *to make the most effective case for affirmative action programs in a period when such programs are under attack from many quarters, emphasis should be shifted from numerical guidelines to opportunity.* The concept I would use to signal this shift is *affirmative opportunity.* . . . It echoes the phrase *equal opportunity,* which connotes a principle that most Americans still support, while avoiding connotations now associated (fairly or not) with the idea of affirmative action—connotations such as quotas, lowering standards, and reverse discrimination, which most Americans detest. (emphasis in the original)

As the above quote indicates, Wilson cites the numeric guidelines that undergird the implementation of many affirmative action programs as the crux of the problem because they differentiate, for example, between workers or between students, along the lines of race. In criticizing the numeric basis for affirmative action, however, Wilson does not support an increasingly popular alternative that holds that preferences (e.g., in hiring and school admissions) should only cover those who are economically disadvantaged since people of all races fall into such a category. As Wilson (1999, 116) counters with an example from the world of higher education, universities that have dropped race-oriented preferences for class-based ones have witnessed lower rather than higher minority acceptance rates. In short, while race and class share significant territory, they are not interchangeable with one another. Given this knowledge, Wilson argues that multiracial coalitions should support programs that use "flexible merit-based criteria of evaluation that enlarge the pool of eligible candidates," rather than focusing on those from any given group.

It is also worth noting that Wilson calls for the left to apply different mobilizing strategies at the national and local levels. It is an argument that clearly corresponds to Harvey's argument detailed above. Indeed, Wilson argues that at the local level multiracial coalitions should avoid "addressing race-explicit issues like affirmative action" (115), because such issues are divisive and counterproductive to the attainment of goals that are good for Hispanic, black, and white workers. In contrast, he argues that national multiracial coalitions should not avoid race-explicit issues, noting pragmatically that such coalitions can only attract large numbers of minorities by embracing such issues. As Wilson concludes, for multiracial coalitions working at the national level, the question is how affirmative action "can be framed as part of the broader political agenda designed to benefit all Americans" (115).

GUNS AND CLASS:
SOME TENTATIVE SUGGESTIONS

Although Jesse Jackson's and William Julius Wilson's suggestions are certainly applicable for Kentucky, the left there must also contend with the highly charged issue of guns. As any union organizer will tell you, the gun issue is a major stumbling block for progressive politics in rural areas, whether at the party or social movement level. Indeed, while many commentators of the 2000 presidential election focused on the fact that Al Gore lost his home state of Tennessee, the more significant state was probably West Virginia, that quintessential union state and heretofore Democratic ace in the hole. Yet there West Virginia stood on election night, giving its electoral votes to George Bush instead of Al Gore. In short, many West Virginians chose gun rights, rather than workers' rights, when they cast their votes.

A good portion of their decision is clearly based on Gore's pro-environmental record, which is seen, unfairly or not, as bad for the coal industry. While many claim that Gore's environmental positions have been misrepresented, it is safe to say that even leaving aside Gore's record, the environmental movement is often ambivalent about the effect of their policies on workers, if not in some cases downright hostile to workers. Harvey's comments about environmentalists' reactions to the fire in Hamlet, North Carolina, come to mind. To a lesser degree, so too does the pro-hemp movement. While pro-hemp advocates are a diverse lot, many factions are primarily interested in hemp's environmental benefits. Sustained attempts to link hemp's "green" qualities to its potential benefits for small and medium-sized producers are infrequent. Even Jack Herer's analysis (1995), which blames hemp's outlawing on a corporate-led, state-supported conspiracy, does little to link its potential reintroduction to the class-based issues of small and medium-sized producers that might grow it today. There is no reason, however, why hemp's environmental qualities may not be linked explicitly to class-based issues. Indeed, in its own way, Galbraith's comments, excerpted above, about renegotiating the New Deal make this very point.

The NRA's relative strength over the gun control lobby also contributed to Bush's victory in West Virginia. The roots of the NRA are expansive *and* deep. While the NRA donates millions of dollars to national candidates, it is equally attentive to state and local politics. State legislators such as Bob Damron may count on NRA financial support, while legislators like Kathy Stein find that gun control groups have nothing to give. This is not to say that gun control organizations do not want to fund such campaigns (they do), but their coffers are nowhere near as full as those of the NRA.

In this context, then, I think the progressive left must take a pragmatic approach to the issue of guns. At the level of party politics, I believe Democrats running for office in rural areas, or for statewide elections where rural constituencies are important, have little to gain and much to lose by staking out pro–gun control positions. Indeed, candidates doing so are likely to find themselves the target of nasty campaigns by the NRA and, once depicted as pro–gun control, at a loss to respond, since gun control advocates do not have comparable backup to the legions of Second Amendment groups working alongside the NRA.

The gubernatorial campaign of Mark Warner in Virginia in 2001 provides a good, if far from perfect, example of how Democrats can keep guns from trumping class. Over the past ten years, the Virginia General Assembly has been transformed from a staunchly Democratic stronghold to a staunchly Republican one. The last two governors, George Allen and Jim Gilmore, ran socially conservative campaigns in which pro–Second Amendment stances figured prominently. Their messages resonated particularly in the state's southwestern corridor, which is markedly similar demographically to West Virginia. It was with this recent history in mind that many pundits suggested Warner should write off southwestern Virginia and focus instead on the urban corridor that runs from the suburbs of Washington, D.C., to Norfolk and supporting get-out-the-vote drives among the state's black populace.

Warner's campaign, however, focused a good deal of energy in southwestern Virginia, with new jobs and economic development serving as the campaign's rallying cry there. Warner was also pragmatic about the gun issue, saying he supported Second Amendment rights and had no plans to enact gun control legislation. While his message angered many on the left and rang hollow for both the NRA and Second Amendment groups, his tactic worked. Most striking about his victory was that Warner won a majority of the districts in the southwestern part of the state (Dionne 2001).

None of this is to say, of course, that the left should not be concerned about gun violence and the legal loopholes that make it easy for criminals and dangerous people to get weapons. Nor is it to suggest that the left should just drop the issue of guns altogether (something Warner has been accused of doing). Rather, if the left wants to make gun control an issue (and thus open up a space for candidates such as Warner to do so), it must consider how to make its arguments resonate in the working-class rural areas that overwhelmingly support gun rights. Indeed, while the Democratic Party is silenced (at least temporarily) in national and gubernatorial elections, grassroots activists should move full steam ahead. Moreover, such activists need not be affiliated or even initially linked with larger, national organizations. As I demonstrate in chapter 5, the NRA, and by extension the candidates it supports, have benefited from its work with Second Amendment activists who are unaffiliated with the organization and who are locally oriented. There is, therefore, no reason why the Brady campaign or other national groups could not benefit from similar counterarrangements with grassroots activist groups.

Local activists must, however, reframe the gun issue. Indeed, fairly or not, many rural people see gun control as a "big-city" concern. It certainly does not help when gun control advocates pejoratively label rural people who own guns and like to hunt as "rednecks." In this context, it is elitist and not a little paternalistic to think rural people will accept gun control arguments (even those delivered without the stereotypes) just because its advocates tell them how dangerous guns are. Obviously, groups like the Brady Center do not invoke these stereotypes, but it is a common trope and it must be countered before any sizable headway can be made.

In this regard, I found Representative Kathy Stein's efforts to launch locally based "million mom" marches in Kentucky heartening. When local women organize such marches, it is more difficult for Second Amendment activists to label them as "outsiders," "big city," or "out of touch." I think it would also be useful for activists to work with local law enforcement agencies. Indeed, while law enforcement is not a standard Democratic stronghold, on the gun issue most officers know firsthand the damage guns can do. And for this reason law enforcement agencies tend to support buy-back programs that get guns off the streets. They are also likely to publicly oppose the NRA, Second Amendment groups, and legislators who make gun control efforts difficult. In the 2000 Kentucky General Assembly, for example, law enforcement agencies opposed a bill that would prohibit police departments from destroying weapons bought in gun buy-back programs (Baniak 2000).

Finally, I think it is also important that grassroots activists confront NRA and Second Amendment arguments that "big government" or the UN is coming to take away civilian weapons. As I note in chapter 5, there are various strands of leftist thought that oppose disarming the general citizenry for some of the same reasons the right does. This leftist history could be deployed to counter the assertion that it is the right, rather than the left, that is protecting the populace from tyranny.

In a related vein, it is also important that the left expose the cynicism and opportunism behind many patriot-led gun initiatives. Representative Bob Damron's attempt to expand the legal use of deadly force to include burglary, robbery, and "deviate sexual intercourse" provides a good example. Indeed, it would have been useful for progressives to call Damron's "pro-gun" credentials into question by noting that his efforts to expand the legal use of deadly force would have had a greater chance at success if he had not included an antigay clause that was at best a gratuitous overture to opponents of the Fairness Ordinance. While such a point may initially gain little attention, the discursive groundwork it would lay could be built upon when reiterated in similar cases. In short, local activists should consistently remind rural gun owners that they are often pawns in a political game that fills up politicians' campaign coffers, while offering constituents little material gain.

ONE LAST LOOK BACK (AND FORWARD?)

I cannot end this book without returning one last time to Gatewood Galbraith. He has occupied an inordinate number of pages in this book and, while his wit, humor, and charisma lend so much to the text herein, my concentration on him is probably also this book's largest failing. He is just one man, and as an "n" that equals 1, he can hardly represent an entire movement. I cannot, however, help but find him fascinating in his own right and in terms of what he can say (as one patriot) to the progressive left. Indeed, Galbraith is so interesting precisely because he used to be on the left. Admittedly, he never looked much like the identity politics left of today. He was never a cultural warrior and he has never carried an urban sensibility into his political battles. Instead, he was much more of a class warrior with an eye focused intently on the rural context around him and an ear cocked for the first sound that big brother was intruding into our collective "bedroom, bladder, or back pocket." Yet it is easy to see how he could have, or would have, embraced cultural issues if the institutions he tried to work through (e.g., the Democratic Party, the Board of Election) had given him the space he needed rather than shut him out. The same goes for the other patriots and nonpatriots he has tried to represent. Though they may not have Galbraith's political aspirations, they share many of his concerns, and if their efforts were funneled properly, they could be a part of, rather than an enemy of, a state- and social movement–led progressive politics.

Epilogue

March 14, 2002—On the Lam

Researchers tend to think of their case studies in narrative terms. We see them, and by extension the general phenomena we study, as having distinct beginnings, middles, and ends. Of course, in most cases, such a narrative frame, while useful for making sense of events, is just that—a temporal parameter for analysis rather than a neat story line. Thus researchers often find that events in the field defy the temporal parameters they have imposed on them. In short, the story keeps on going and the researcher is left wondering whether it will end and, more importantly, how to present a story without a ready ending. Such was the case with my research on the Patriot Movement.

A STORY WITH LEGS

I finished this book in July 2001 but, almost nine months later, on March 14, 2002, I found myself driving to Kentucky to conduct one last interview with Charlie Puckett and Gatewood Galbraith. My trip was precipitated by recent events: on February 26, 2002 (almost five years to the day after I began researching the Kentucky Patriot Movement), Charlie Puckett was indicted on nine different federal weapons charges (Kocher 2002a). He was detained in the county jail until March 4, when his lawyer, Gatewood Galbraith, persuaded the U.S. District Court judge, Magistrate James B. Todd, to release his client on bail. As a condition of his release, Puckett was required to wear an electronic tracking device around his ankle, obtain permission to leave his property, and sign an unsecured $50,000 bond (Staff Reports 2002b).

Puckett's troubles began on November 27, when agents working for the BATF raided his home in Garrard County, seizing ammunition, several weapons, and his concealed weapons permit. According to Don York, a

BATF spokesman, the agency decided to raid Puckett's home after they learned he was "a felon in possession of firearms" (Vanderhoff 2001). The 1968 Federal Gun Control Act prohibits felons from owning firearms. Puckett's felony dates to 1966, when he and some friends were arrested and later convicted for stealing over $100 worth of food from a Virginia grocery store. The BATF indicated that the felony was nonviolent.

Puckett was not arrested in November, but the BATF hinted that it would submit evidence to the State Attorney General's Office for a possible grand jury hearing. Puckett's response after the raid was defiant. Speaking to the *Lexington Herald-Leader*, he argued that the 1968 Gun Control Act did not apply to his case, since his felony was committed two years prior to the statute.[1] Puckett also suggested that he would go to the attorney general's office and demand the return of his weapons (Vanderhoff 2001). When asked what he would do if the attorney general did not comply, he replied, "Either I get my stuff back or we got a real problem." When asked to elaborate, he replied tersely, "Well, it could turn into anything. Use your imagination" (Vanderhoff 2001).

When I heard in early March that Puckett had been indicted, I decided to return to the field. I was curious what Puckett had to say for himself and what his arrest would mean for the future of the movement. Puckett is certainly not as charismatic as Gatewood Galbraith, but he has been a pivotal figure in the movement nonetheless, respected both inside and outside of his militia. His arrest will, therefore, likely lead to changes, whether organizational, ideological, or some combination of the two. I was also interested in the timing of Puckett's arrest. In particular, I was curious why it had taken the BATF so long to make its move. Not only had Puckett been the leader of the Kentucky State Militia for a substantial period of time (depending upon who you ask, his tenure ranged from seven to twelve years), but he had maintained a relatively high public profile throughout that time. It struck me as odd, therefore, that no prior attempt had been made by either the BATF or the FBI to dig into his background in an effort to find information they could use against him.

My attempts in 1999 to solicit information from the FBI about the Kentucky Patriot Movement, however, indicate Puckett may have managed to fly beneath government radar for quite some time. Indeed, my Freedom of Information Act (FOIA) request,[2] which petitioned the agency for information on both of Puckett's militias, CCK, and a host of other Kentucky patriot groups, turned up absolutely nothing.[3] I was dumbfounded, given that my research was coming in the wake of the 1995 Oklahoma City Bombing, when the movement and the danger it represented were obvious.

Of course, it is possible that the FBI was lying to me. The recent revelation that the FBI withheld thousands of files from Timothy McVeigh's defense attorneys does suggest that such a scenario is at least plausible. Indeed, it is possible that the FBI knew of Puckett's felony but chose not to act on it because it was a minor, nonviolent offense. It is also possible that Puckett's weapon stockpiling was a relatively recent affair that caught the attention of the BATF agents in the area. Another feasible explanation is a communications gap between the FBI and the BATF—two agencies notorious for their intelligence turf wars. Nonetheless, the possibility that there was no credible intelligence on Puckett cannot be discounted. Indeed, it is worth noting that Puckett *passed* the federal background check all applicants for the state's concealed deadly weapons permit must undergo.[4]

It is impossible to know why the BATF acted when it did and not sooner. The only response Don York, the BATF's spokesman, gave to the press about the initial November raid was to say that the agency had received information that Puckett was a felon possessing firearms. And given that the case has not yet gone to trial, the agency is unlikely to explain its timing any time soon.

Under these circumstances, all a researcher can do is make educated speculations about the timing of the indictment. After reading about the raid on Puckett's house in November 2001, my initial sense was that the FBI and BATF may have learned about Puckett's felony indirectly the previous month, when agents interviewed him about Steve Anderson. As the reader may recall from chapter 5, Anderson is an Identity adherent who ran a communications seminar at the April 2001 biannual patriot gathering on Norm Davis's farm. A little more than a month before the November raid, Anderson engaged a Bell County police officer in a firefight after the officer had pulled him over on a routine traffic stop. Anderson fled the scene and has eluded capture ever since. Puckett has publicly denied any knowledge of Anderson's whereabouts and has said on several occasions that he had recently kicked Anderson out of the KSM (Kocher 2002a). It is possible that the FBI's investigation into Anderson led it to dig more thoroughly into Puckett's past (or to take more seriously existing information about him), thereby leading to his arrest.

ON THE LAM

As I drove to Kentucky, I thought about what I wanted to glean from my interview with Charlie and Gatewood. I knew that any inside information was unlikely to be forthcoming. With the trial yet to commence, Gatewood had to protect his client's interests, whether by concealing damning information or reserving a useful story line for the courtroom. Thus I knew that I was most likely to get a calculated spin on recent events. While I would have loved the opportunity to get inside information, I realized the spin I would hear from Gatewood was what the movement's foot soldiers were likely to hear and react to. As such, this spin would be important to analyze in its own right.

In particular, I was interested in what the two would say about John Ashcroft, especially in light of both Puckett's arrest and the post-September 11 Justice Department crackdown on civil liberties. Indeed, initially George Bush's choice of John Ashcroft for attorney general was widely praised among patriots. Ashcroft's avid support of gun rights and a right-wing social agenda made him a popular choice, even among patriots who were opposed to Bush. During my third interview with Gatewood Galbraith in January 2001, for example, he briefly interrupted our interview to do a phone interview with a local radio talk show host about Ashcroft's impending confirmation hearing.[5] In that interview, I recall Galbraith telling the host that John Ashcroft was being demonized, adding that he was an "all-right guy" and a "good choice." Given the Justice Department's crackdown on civil liberties broadly, and its work with the BATF in Puckett's arrest more specifically, I was especially interested in whether the movement's antigovernment stance, which is often targeted against Democrats at the national level, would shift to the Republican Party.

I was also interested in how the movement would respond to the American public's newfound patriotism, which despite the ardent flag waving associated with it is markedly different from that of the Patriot Movement. Indeed, September 11 put the movement in an interesting and somewhat awkward position. On the one hand, the movement finally received what it had long hoped for—a populace resolute in its pro-Americanness. On the other hand, as a variety of commentators have noted, September 11 paved the way for a distinctly pro-government form of patriotism in which questioning the actions of the Bush administration is labeled unpatriotic. The movement, however, was built on a deep distrust of (rather than blind support for) the federal government.

Unfortunately, while I pondered these thoughts, Charlie Puckett had other things on his mind. Sometime in the early morning of March 14 (the day I was driving to Kentucky), Charlie Puckett slipped out of his tracking device and disappeared. Later that day, a message entitled "Charles Puckett, Last Testament" appeared on a militia bulletin board. In it, Puckett denied the charges against him and issued a message to the BATF: "It is my last testament that I have NOT committed ANY criminal acts, nor will I donate years of my life for something that I have NOT done" (Puckett, quoted in Kocher 2002b). Interestingly, Puckett's message also reiterated his claim that he did not know the whereabouts of Steve Anderson.

Of course, I was unaware of all of these fast-moving events during my nine-hour drive to Kentucky. When I arrived in Lexington later that evening, a good friend in town called to tell me the news. I was taken aback. In the five years I had followed the Kentucky Patriot Movement, I had grown accustomed to the movement operating above board and through legitimate channels. The leaders, as I encountered them, insisted on it. Indeed, according to Dan Wooten, Puckett had been instrumental in kicking Rick Tyler out of CCK precisely because his polygamy reflected poorly on the movement.

Despite Puckett's disappearance, I showed up for my interview the next morning. It was scheduled at 9:00 A.M. in Gatewood's downtown law office. When I arrived, Gatewood was there, although a television crew was swarming around his desk, asking questions about his now fugitive client. I listened outside as he held court. One reporter wanted to know how Puckett slipped out of the tracking device. Galbraith replied that he had no idea how he had done it. Another wanted to know why the authorities had taken so long to respond to the signal from Puckett's tracking device,[6] suggesting that Puckett's escape was possible because the command center where the signal was transmitted was too far from Puckett's home. Again, Gatewood responded that he did not know. Still another reporter wanted to know if Galbraith thought Puckett had committed suicide, given that his purported web message was entitled "Last Testament." Gatewood shook his head, saying "No" several times.

After the television crew left, Gatewood waved me in. Smiling broadly, he told me he had to head to the courthouse in thirty minutes to meet with Puckett's wife, but he was happy to chat with me until then. I began by asking Gatewood to clarify the details surrounding Puckett's arrest. He handed me a copy of the indictment, telling me that of the nine counts Charlie was accused of, eight of them were related to the fact that he was a felon. That is, the weapons and ammunition he possessed would be legal for nonfelons. As I flipped through the indictment, I was surprised to learn what an average citizen can legally own in the way of firearms. One of the charges, the possession of almost thirty-five thousand rounds of ammunition, is only illegal for Puckett because he has a felony on his record. I was also disturbed by the second count, accusing Puckett of possessing unregistered "destructive devices," which the indictment described as an elaborate set of pipe bombs built around his house, each with "a spring-loaded activator designed to expel a 12 gauge round of ammunition."[7]

While the full copy of the indictment suggests that six, rather than eight, counts are related to Puckett's prior felony, Galbraith's larger point was that Puckett was being unfairly targeted because he was in the militia. Indeed, while I was skimming the indictment, Galbraith began proudly recounting how he had gotten Puckett released on bail. His strategy, he explained, was to discredit the BATF's assertion that Puckett was dangerous because he was in the militia. In particular, he deployed a well-worn patriot trope, arguing that Puckett's militia membership made him no more dangerous than any other man, since technically all men are already, by default, a part of the militia. As he recounted his argument to me:

The ATF agent got on the stand for an hour and a half and read from a nine-page prepared statement of nineteen things that Charlie had done that made him a danger to the community. . . . [A]bout ten of them had nothing to do with him, but with the Kentucky State Militia, . . . the crux of it being that the agent said that anybody who is a member of the militia cannot be trusted. So, my first question to the agent was, "Do you feel like anybody who holds themselves out as being a member of the militia has taken a step towards the fringe and is no longer a member of the mainstream?" He said, "That's correct." And I said, "Do you feel like a member of the militia cannot be trusted with their word, is that correct?" And, he said, "Yes, that's the way I feel." So, I said, "Then I guess that your last hour and a half worth of testimony is worthless, on the fringe, and can't be trusted—is that correct?" And he said, "What do you mean?" Well, I said, "You're a member of the militia."

Gatewood told me that he then had the BATF agent read aloud from federal statutes stating that all able-bodied men are members of the militia. (Although the case law on these statutes is hardly pro-militia, it is worth remembering that to patriots it is the letter of the law, rather than a case law interpretation of it, that is of utmost importance.) Galbraith told me he concluded his cross-examination by asking the BATF agent, "Who's the most delusional here, agent? Do you see all your ATF buddies out here—they're all members of the militia, too. So, *you've* been running around with a heavily armed group of militia members for seven years!"

Despite Galbraith's success at securing Puckett's release on bail, his escape does not bode well for either Puckett or the movement. Galbraith seemed to recognize that as well. When I asked him to comment on the movement's future, he admitted he didn't know what would happen and he expressed some frustration with Puckett's move:

We had an excellent opportunity to put it [the Patriot Movement] in just the right light with this case here. You know, this case could be used to educate the public about what it is that every able-bodied male, operating at the behest of the government, does. . . . I think that the "federales" are trying to practice a newspeak on the word "militia," just as they have with a lot of other principles. They're dumbing it down. People don't know what a militia is and what it's set up for. . . . What that tells me is that nobody is being educated on the old principles and they're trying to cut us loose from the anchors of those principles and set us adrift in a sea of new world order, where the people are going to be ill-prepared to protect themselves against it.

In light of his comments, I asked Gatewood how the movement's antigovernment "education" would go down in a post–September 11 context, when even supposedly strong allies like John Ashcroft were turning against them. Galbraith's response not only contradicted statements he made about Ashcroft in our previous interview, but also indicated a retreat into well-worn rhetorical territory:

> This liberal legislator asked me, "Don't you find it strange that he's moving against every one of the Bill of Rights except the Second Amendment?" I said "No, I don't find that strange. That's why we arm ourselves under the Second Amendment. We arm ourselves against both the Janet Renos and the John Ashcrofts. We don't trust any of them. The militia and the population out there, they don't trust them, whatever they say. We believe that power corrupts and that power corrupts absolutely, and that whoever gets in there is going to attempt to misuse or abuse the office beyond the bounds.

The question that remains, of course, is how the movement will be able to defend that rhetoric in a context where flag-waving is currently synonymous with unquestioning support for government actors. Indeed, the Southern Poverty Law Center's spring *Intelligence Report* (2002) indicates that membership in hate groups is up 12 percent since September 11 and that the rhetoric of these groups has become more vitriolic and anti-Semitic, as far-right groups have placed the blame for September 11 squarely on the shoulders of Jews and their pro-Israel allies in Congress.

On April 4, almost three weeks after he escaped, Charlie Puckett turned himself in (Taylor and Kocher 2002). Not surprisingly, he will remain incarcerated until his trial. And the potential jail time has increased with a new count lodged against him for fleeing. A few days after turning himself in, Puckett announced through his lawyer that he was resigning from the militia, effective immediately.

What effect his arrest has on the Kentucky Patriot Movement is an open question. After following the movement for five years, I see two possible trajectories for its future. One is that the movement will retreat from the mainstream. On the day that Puckett was arrested, for example, Barry Bright wrote a column on his "Free Kentucky" web site, entitled "BATF Nazis arrest KSM Commander." Using interviews with other militia members, Bright suggested that Puckett's arrest was due to a general cooperative approach in the movement in regard to the media and federal agencies. In particular, Bright suggested that Puckett's arrest was due to KSM's cooperation with BATF agents investigating Steve Anderson and KSM's willingness to assist in a three-part story on the militia conducted by a local television station. Bright's overall conclusion was "to withdraw" from the spotlight and from mainstream channels. The likely by-product of such a withdrawal is a hardening of patriot positions and a move toward the underground, where following the law is no longer a concern.

A second possibility is that the Kentucky Patriot Movement may splinter into smaller groups. With Puckett abdicating his position, the resulting power void provides the perfect conditions for divisions within the ranks of the movement to rise to the surface. These divisions include those between Identity adherents and those opposed to Identity, between politically oriented types and those supporting military "solutions," and between those with libertarian leanings and culturally conservative types. Indeed, research indicates that leaders take on a heightened importance in horizontally organized groups because, if the leaders are successful, they are able to hold together factious elements. Conversely, events that undermine a pivotal leader often lead to fragmentation. At the time of the Oklahoma City bombing, for example, the Michigan Militia was one of the largest and most influential militias in the country. After infighting and serious challenges to Norman Olson's leadership in the bombing's aftermath, however, the movement fractured into several smaller groups. The Theatre Command Militia suffered a similar fate in western Kentucky, when infighting between Identity adherents and more mainstream elements led to the movement's ultimate dissolution. While it is not always the case, such splintering often facilitates the formation of smaller, more hard-core groups.

What is ultimately important about the trajectory of events, however, is the opportunity it presents the left. While Puckett may disappear, the generalized discontent his organization channels will not. The left can and should insert itself, whether they follow the suggestions proffered in chapter nine or develop new approaches altogether.

NOTES

1. The 1968 law does not stipulate that persons convicted of felonies before 1968 are exempt from the ban. The law states that felons are prohibited from possessing firearms unless they file for a reinstatement of their gun rights and are so approved.

2. The FBI is prohibited under the FOIA from releasing information about an individual to a third party before the individual on whom information is requested is deceased. Therefore, I requested information on groups Puckett was affiliated with rather than on Puckett himself.

3. I mailed my FOIA request in August 1999 to the Kentucky bureau of the FBI. I sent my request there, rather than the main office in Washington, D.C., because the FBI's FOIA office suggested I do so. The officer I spoke to explained that, since my request was relevant to one state, it was likely housed in the FBI's state office, in Louisville. The FBI's response informed me that "based on the information furnished, a search of the indices to the central records system maintained in the Louisville office located no records responsive to your request."

4. Galbraith told me in our interview that Puckett approached an FBI agent named Ed Amento before he applied for his permit. According to Galbraith, Puckett told the agent that he wanted to be an up-front member of the militia and to apply for a permit, but that he was worried about his 1966 felony. Amento's reply, accord-

ing to Galbraith, was that he should apply for the permit and let the FBI make that decision.

5. That Gatewood would give an interview while participating in one may seem strange, but as I discovered during my first interview with him, I had to be prepared for diversions and spur-of-the-moment events. And as I discovered during subsequent interviews with him, these sorts of diversions were always informative (and entertaining).

6. In addition to transmitting the wearer's geographic coordinates, such tracking devices also send a signal if the device is tampered with, cut, or removed.

7. The indictment was filed February 13, 2002, in the U.S. District Court, Eastern District of Kentucky, Lexington.

A Note on Method

One of poststructuralism's key contributions has been to open up our understanding of power, to explode its presumed structural moorings and help us to view it instead as the ability to delineate categories of meaning. In keeping with this revised view of hegemony, poststructuralists have also questioned the way research is conducted and have analyzed in particular how people's social positionings, and the power that resides within the categories associated with them, affect the research process.

When I began this study, I took with me a general set of concepts about fieldwork taken largely from poststructural theory. As I discovered the hard way, this approach, while not without its merits, was limited in what it offered my particular study. In this short note on method, I outline a few of these problems. In doing so, it is not my intention to discredit poststructural methodology or to blame it for the mistakes I made during my research. In the end, it is always the researcher who is culpable for errors made during the research process. Rather, my primary goal is to create a road map of the potential hazards that may befall future researchers of the right and, in so doing, help others avoid making the same mistakes I did.

POWER DIFFERENTIAL

One of the key markers of poststructuralism is its focus on oppression that stems from social positions beyond, or in addition to, class. Race, gender, disability, and sexual orientation, for example, have all captured the attention of progressive and left-oriented researchers interested in oppression. Poststructuralism has carried these concerns into the field as well. As any researcher knows, there is often a power differential between the researcher and the researched. In the social sciences, researchers request time and a good bit of personal information from informants, while giving little if anything in return. Poststructuralists have questioned how social positionality is mapped onto this already uneven relationship between researcher and researched. In so doing, they have illustrated how the dominant positionality of researchers (normally white, upper-middle class, and male) affects not only the outcome of the research (positionality frames the kinds of questions asked as well as the conclusions drawn), but the researched themselves (who may later be represented in ways not of their liking). Recognizing this entails dismantling the idea that researchers can present things in a purely objective manner, an approach Rose (1993) has called the "view from nowhere."

These sorts of questions have been especially acute in the so-called imperial disciplines, such as anthropology and geography. To the extent that sociology studies the domestic other, it too has been affected. There is, of course, good reason for this intellectual hand-wringing, which a variety of scholars have aptly termed a "crisis of representation" (see Clifford 1988; Geertz 1983; Marcus and Fischer 1986). Historically, studies from these disciplines normally furthered political and economic agendas, but were shielded from the criticisms such ends might invoke by the legitimizing cloaks of objectivity and science. Early anthropological studies of race are particularly illustrative. In Rwanda, for example, colonial scholars set about to "scientifically" catalogue the differences between the Hutus and the Tutsis. The differences between these two groups were class or caste based, but colonizers racialized them, arguing that Hutus were biologically Hamitic, and thus inferior, while the Tutsis were lost Christians from Abyssina (Ethiopia), and thus members of a superior race (Gourevitch 1998). This "scientific" schema allowed colonizers to divide the populace against itself, while also justifying their political dealings with the Tutsis, who were after all still African and thus in need of rehabilitation, by the mindset of the day.

Facing this dirty history has been difficult for disciplines built during colonialism. It has required its scholars to radically rethink their positionality, both globally and domestically, and to question how these positions structure the kinds of questions they ask and the kinds of conclusions they draw. It has also required them to think how their research may negatively affect their subjects. When geographer Kim England set about to do a study of lesbian geographies in Toronto, for example, she documented her attempt to grapple with these issues, writing,

> I had to ask myself . . . Could I be accused of academic voyeurism? Am I trying to get on some cheap package tour of lesbianism in the hope of gaining some fleeting understanding of, perhaps, the ultimate "other" given that lesbians are not male, heterosexual, not always middle-class, and often not white? I worried that I might be albeit unintentionally, colonizing lesbians in some kind of academic neoimperialism. (England 1994, 84)

England eventually decided to cancel her study, concluding that she would be unable to set aside the biases that came with her white, heterosexual, middle-class positionality. While the England example is an extreme one (most academics do not cancel their research projects), her words give form to the methodological zeitgeist of the day—researchers can no longer afford to go blithely into the field without some serious self-reflection beforehand. And, once in the field, it is important to keep up a dialogue with one's informants, keeping them apprised of findings and sharing with them research notes and, most importantly, the final product, so that they might have an opportunity to set the record straight (Gilbert 1994; Katz 1992, 1994).

As I entered the patriot field, I took the crisis of representation to heart. Indeed, while studying the Patriot Movement does not produce the most sympathetic pool of research informants, I still worried about how to depict them fairly. I knew it would be easy to represent them through well-worn tropes, as "angry white men with guns," as "malcontents," or as otherwise "cracked and loaded." This is how many people view them, even in the academy. I recall going to one academic conference at the beginning of my study, for example, and being cornered by an acquaintance who wanted to talk to me about my new project (academic circles being what they are, gossip travels fast). The fellow, I discovered, was peeved with me. He was worried that because I was studying patriots I had become "one of them." While I had no intention at the time, nor any now, of becoming a patriot, I realized from encounters like this one that most people have a stereotypical image of the movement (patriots are irrational hate mongers with no redeeming value) and thus no desire to consider alternatives for them, preferring instead to write them off. If I was to dispel any of these notions, I knew I would have to be open to listening to my informants and not prejudge them, and that I would have to focus on how and why they saw things as they did, rather than condemning their view up front.

When I approached the field, however, I came to realize, quite slowly and a bit painfully, that opening yourself up to experiencing the movement as it is was not without its pitfalls. And while poststructuralism enjoined me to lay aside my biases (to be open), it did not prepare me to handle the potential consequences. This is so, I contend, because much of the emphasis on self-reflexivity has turned on the idea that most researchers not only want to avoid exploiting their research subjects, but want to forward their political causes as well. The focus on race, gender, and sexuality, for example, has until recently focused largely on studying the race, gender, and sexual orientation of white male heteronormativity's "others" and the resistance struggles each has waged. Indeed, it is this focus on oppressed others that can allow writers to suggest sharing research notes and rough cuts of the final product with one's subjects. It is assumed that, while subjects may agree with the overall project, they should also have oversight over the final interpretation of their struggle. Such an idea seems absurd, however, when applied to the study of far-right and/or potentially violent groups, who could at the least cut off a researcher's access and at the worst retaliate against him or her.

Nothing illustrates this underlying presumption better than the debate that has evolved around the concept of strategic essentialism. As the reader is by now well aware, essentialism has been thoroughly debunked in post-structural circles. Indeed, there is nothing worse in some quarters of the academy than having your work labeled as "essentialist." It means you have not captured the internal diversity, the multiplicity, or the nuances of the group or community you are studying. Yet scholars who want to boost the cause of a given group also realize the power that comes from representing categories as internally consistent and playing down internal disputes and differences in order to afford unity in the face of detractors. This has been an especially apt debate around feminism, where women are all too aware of their differences, but also keenly cognizant of what an airing of feminism's dirty laundry could mean in the male-dominated academy.

When I entered the patriot field, however, I found such debates largely irrelevant. Certainly, a political goal was forming in my mind—to explain through the Patriot Movement why the left should again consider class positioning—but I did not want to further the patriot cause as it is currently constituted. Nor was I prepared for the fact that the patriots I encountered would be interested in using me for their own political ends, ends that I was opposed to.

This became an issue about seven months into my fieldwork, when Dan Wooten called me to ask if I would be willing to interview Charlie Puckett on a patriot television show. I was immediately torn. On the one hand, I felt I had been given an important entrée into the movement's inner circle. I had wanted to interview Puckett since the first meeting, but I had found him difficult to approach. During CCK meetings, he was usually very busy, running here and there getting things organized or handling quick emergencies. When he did stop to chat with someone, it was usually on a one-on-one basis and he normally gave the air of someone not wanting to be interrupted. Getting an invitation to interview him seemed a boon for my research. On the other hand, I was immediately worried that I could become identified with the "patriot cause." Even though I told each potential informant that I was doing academic research and that I was *not* a patriot, my presence at CCK meetings and my laid-back interview manner probably convinced many that I was a sympathizer nonetheless (I worked hard never to put an informant on the defensive, because I wanted patriots to construct their positions as they saw them, rather than in relation to "the enemy"). With my appearance on a patriot television show, such an image could be dangerously solidified.

In response to Wooten's request, I told him I would first have to talk to the university's Institutional Review Board (IRB) and some of my colleagues and get back to him later. The following day, I called the IRB. After explaining my case, the representative informed me that it was fine for me to do the interview as long as it was not me who was doing the filming. As the IRB officer explained to me, since my initial application had not included filming research subjects, I would have to reapply for approval if I wanted to film even this one interview. Generally, gaining permission to film interviews is difficult—institutional review boards usually require a justification for why a tape recorder will not suffice for the researcher's needs.

My colleagues were generally supportive of my doing the interview. They regarded my potential TV interview as a chance to challenge the boundaries of staid academic research conventions, which had limitations, given that I was studying a group largely reviled by the academy. They cautioned me, however, to be certain I would have control over the questions and that I would get a copy of the interview tape. "It's a tough call," one of them told me, "you'll have to make the decision you feel most comfortable with." But at that point I wanted nothing more than for someone else to tell me what to do.

I eventually decided to do the interview, but I stipulated three conditions before finalizing my decision to do so. I told Wooten I wanted to have an opportunity at the beginning of the interview to inform the audience that I was *not* a patriot and that I was doing the interview as a part of my academic research on the movement. I also told Wooten that I wanted "creative control" over the questions and, finally, that I needed a copy of the tape for my research purposes. Wooten agreed to my conditions and we arranged to do the interview. On the day I decided to do the interview, I explained my decision, which is excerpted below, in my research journal. My decision was based mostly on an attempt to lay aside my own biases and to be self-reflective about *why* I was hesitant to conduct the interview. At the time, I perceived my hesitance as biased because I felt that had I been researching a left-wing group, and had they approached me with a similar request, I would have said yes without hesitation. This recognition led me to consider why I thought patriots did not deserve the same response as others:

> I'm still not sure if it is the right thing to do but here are some of the reasons I decided to do it. At first I was worried that I might be breaching some ethical code by agreeing to do the interview. I talked to the IRB, though, and I came to realize that the ethical issue really wasn't a problem for them since their responsibility is only to protect the subjects of research, not the researcher. Basically, if there were an ethical issue it would be with the patriots who would in essence be using me because I'm not your "typical" looking patriot. The IRB, for example, didn't care what I did so long as I wasn't doing the filming (that would require another application), and the interviewee signed the consent

form. Now, while I don't want to be used by the Patriots in such a manner, I started to think that maybe what was nagging me required a little self-reflection. Basically, I was worried about being seen as buying into the Patriot project. And this got me to thinking. If I was interviewing a group on the left neither I, nor most of my peers, would think anything of it if I said I was going to be on a panel with, for example, black women fighting to keep an incinerator out of their neighborhood. Because the group I'm studying is "blacklisted" so to speak by those in the academic left (and I guess in my mind too), participating in a dialogue is frowned upon. Dialogue, however, can never just happen between groups who agree with one another. Hell, they don't necessarily need to talk it out. Given the political nature of this particular Patriot movement (in contradistinction to an underground militia or something) it seems such dialogue is fair, and need not be on my turf only. I also feel that it is a good chance to "grill" or get at some of the basic claims of the movement. Finally, I think it will allow me greater access into the movement since I will potentially be seen as someone who is willing to take the movement seriously enough to talk to them. Of course, with my decision comes angst. Basically, I may be seen as going "native"—something I'd prefer not to happen. Secondly, it might keep me from getting a job because I'm seen as having ties with and/or being sympathetic to radical fringe groups. Finally, there is a chance that the Patriot movement may itself exploit my presence in the movement and use it to their advantage because I am not, as I said earlier, your typical patriot. I am, after all, female, relatively young, and I dress more like a "trendy young geographer" than your stereotypical militia mamma. But perhaps these trepidations also present me with a challenge, that of trying not to let that happen. And in doing so I might myself be able to present the academic left with a challenge. That challenge is to make us rethink not only what and who we study, but why it is that we study the groups we study (and those we don't) in the first place.

Looking back I cannot help but think of myself as truly naïve and a bit of an idiot, as well. The interview went well in a technical sense. No major "TV flubs" by either Puckett or myself. Yet after the interview I somehow felt that, despite my protective measures, I had come across as a sympathizer and that my academic credentials had given the movement legitimacy in the process. I also felt a bit used by Wooten and Puckett, but unjustified at the same time for feeling so, given that I had agreed to do the interview.

The primary problem with the interview, I realized much later, involved my interview style, which I had adopted in large measure from poststructural methodology. As I state above, I approached my interviews not as venues to challenge patriots, but rather as opportunities to draw them out and encourage them to provide the nuances behind the perspectives they took. I found that patriots were more forthcoming when they did not feel they were articulating their cause in a hostile environment. This tactic worked well for me in terms of my ability to get my informants to open up and to really explain themselves. Yet my interview style is not suited for television, especially in a context where objectivity was not the modus operandi and a pro-patriot perspective was. My questions, in this format, looked like softballs designed to legitimate a particular viewpoint rather than attempts to get at the logic behind it. I also realized that when I asked Puckett my questions on television, he was careful to play down internal differences in the movement and to project a unified front. In my other interviews, however, these same questions generated interesting discussions about the internal tensions in the movement, even leading in some instances to patriots making criticisms of their peers or leaders. On the day the episode was filmed I also found myself in a quandary when Puckett told me he wanted to use graphics on the show. In particular, he wanted to show the biosphere propaganda map I detail in chapter 7 (see figure 7.5). It was only the third time I had seen the map (it had been passed around at patriot meetings a few times). I had reservations about the map even then, but my knowledge of its inaccuracies was not concrete, so I felt like I had poor grounds to refuse Puckett's request. It was only much later, after I found the web site of the map's distributor, EPI, and purchased my own copy that I realized the full extent of the map's inadequacies. And I was horrified to realize that I had let the map stand as "correct" on the show I did with Puckett months earlier. It was at times like these that I realized one could never have too much background research under her belt.

To top off a bleak experience, I never received a copy of the interview tape, so I was unable to quote Puckett in this book as I do other patriots. This is not to say that I ascribe nefarious ends to Wooten or Puckett's failure to give me the interview tape. Indeed, a few weeks after the interview Wooten called me to say he was moving to Arizona. At the end of that conversation, I asked him for the tape and he promised to contact Puckett and have him send it to me as soon as possible. That I never received the tape, I put down to the fact that CCK meetings were still on hold at that point, and to general disorganization in the wake of Wooten's departure. And while I cannot prove it, I now suspect that neither Wooten nor Puckett was too worried about the tape, because they assumed the most important thing for me was to help "the cause." As I realized after the fact, my agreeing to do the interview probably sent a message I did not intend to send.

The responsibility for my decision to do this interview, and for the consequences from it, lie squarely on my shoulders. Indeed, while it is tempting to blame my methodological framework for my decision to do the interview in the first place, that would be unfair and incorrect. Rather, I am left with the recognition that the problem (besides my own naïveté) is not so much what poststructuralist methodology says as what it leaves unsaid or unquestioned. Indeed, I believe poststructuralism, while not without its problems, has provided important methodological insight for social scientists like me. I could never have gotten such a detailed view of the Patriot Movement if I had not put aside my biases and agreed to see the world for a brief while as they saw it. Yet the underlying presumption, that we must not only not exploit our subjects, but that we should also aid their cause (they're left, we're left), does nothing to address the complex problems a left-oriented researcher will encounter while doing research on right-wing identity politics.

In particular, researchers of the right need guidelines for their own protection, so that they may preserve their integrity and not become co-opted by their research subjects. In this regard, I have three suggestions. First and foremost, I believe that institutional review boards should protect not only informants, but researchers as well. In the case of social science research, this could entail training researchers how to spot attempts by research subjects to use a researcher for political ends and how to deal with such attempts in a way that allows the researcher to maintain access to the community in question.

Second, while the idea that you can be objective (and distanced) from your research subjects has been debunked of late by poststructuralism—as Rose (1993) reminds us, there is no such thing as a "view from nowhere"—there is, I believe, a place for the researcher that lies between the vista from above and the view from the trenches that a fully imbricated researcher working for the cause can provide. We can, I believe, reassert the researcher as a distanced subject, but do so openly and frankly, telling our research subjects (whether we agree or disagree with them) why we feel the need to have distance. Indeed, even though I lost my interview with Barry Bright because I told him I was a researcher of the movement but not a patriot, I maintained my integrity.[1] And while I did not get an interview that would have provided a perspective I would have liked to have included here, I was not willing to work undercover or under false pretenses to do so. Some information may remain beyond our purview, but that is, I believe, infinitely better than becoming a de facto spy. If I had wanted to be a spy, I would have joined the Central Intelligence Agency.

Finally, I think it is important for people researching the far right to make sure to surround themselves with a circle of mentors, including scholars and lay people. While I was doing my research, I had few people around who were schooled in the complex ethical issues I was facing. Moreover, the driving logic of my academic context was to get the "information" I needed to finish my project. Indeed, in the pressure-cooker world of academe, even scholars who write about such issues often find that the pressures to produce can cloud their perspective. If I had had such a group around, I probably would not have done the interview with Puckett. And, even if I had, I would likely have done so in a way that did not compromise my integrity, which I believe this interview did. With the benefit of hindsight, these suggestions seem obvious, but they were not part of the poststructuralist methodology canon, and in the middle of the process my perspective could have greatly benefited from such cautions.

NOTE

1. I approached all of my potential informants the same way, telling them that I was an academic doing research on the Patriot Movement and that I was trying to get a deeper understanding of the movement. Bright was the only patriot who saw my support for the cause as a necessary precondition for our interview.

Bibliography

Abanes, Richard. 1996. *Rebellion, Racism and Religion: American Militias.* Downers Grove, Ill.: InterVarsity Press.

Aglietta, Michel. 1979. *A Theory of Capitalist Regulation: The US Experience.* Translated by David Fernbach. New York: Schocken.

Aho, James. 1990. *The Politics of Righteousness: Idaho Christian Patriotism.* Seattle: University of Washington Press.

Alvarado, Rudolph, and Sonya Alvarado. 2001. *Drawing Conclusions on Henry Ford.* Ann Arbor: University of Michigan Press.

Anderson, Jack. 1996. *Inside the NRA: Armed and Dangerous.* Beverly Hills, Calif.: Cove Books.

Anderson, Kay. 1991. *Vancouver's Chinatown: Racial Discourse in Canada, 1875–1980.* Montreal: McGill-Queens University Press.

Anti-Defamation League (ADL). 2001. "The Execution of Timothy McVeigh." www.adl.org/mcveigh/mcveigh%5Fprint.html.

Armstrong, Bryan. 1995. "Faces in the News Q & A—Galbraith: Win Back Freedoms." *Kentucky Post,* April 4, 1k.

Associated Press (AP) Wire. 1991. "Primary '91: Galbraith Takes 5 Percent of Vote." *Kentucky Post,* May 29, 10k.

———. 1996. "Poll: KY Majority Opposes Bill to Allow Concealed Weapons." *Lexington Herald-Leader,* February 12, B3.

Baniak, Peter. 2000. "Senate Leader Supports Resale of Weapons Gun Debate." *Lexington Herald-Leader,* February 5, C6.

Barrett, James, and David Roediger. 1997. "Inbetween Peoples: Race, Nationality and the New Immigrant Working Class." In *American Exceptionalism: US Working-Class Formation in an International Context,* ed. R. Halpern and J. Morris, 181–220. New York: St. Martin's.

Batchelor, Ray. 1994. *Henry Ford: Mass Production, Modernism and Design.* Manchester: Manchester University Press.

Becker, Lori. 1997. "Group Claims UN Is Quietly Seizing Land in US." *Lexington Herald-Leader,* June 12, C1.

Bell, Derrick. 1995. "Property Rights in Whiteness—Their Legal Legacy, Their Economic Costs." In Critical Race Theory, ed. R Delgado, 75–83. Philadelphia: Temple University Press.

Berry, Wendell. 1992. Sex, Economy, Freedom, and Community. New York: Pantheon Books.

Bertram, Eva, ed. 1996. Drug War Politics: The Price of Denial. Los Angeles: University of California Press.

Biele, Katharine. 2001. Where It's a Crime Not to Own a Gun. Christian Science Monitor, March 14.

Billington, Ray. 1966. America's Frontier Heritage. New York: Holt, Rinehart and Winston.

Blum, Virginia, and Heidi Nast. 1996. "Where's the Difference? The Heterosexualization of Alterity in Henri Lefebvre and Jacques Lacan." Environment and Planning D: Society and Space 14: 559–80.

Bondi, Liz. 1990. "Feminism, Postmodernism, and Geography: Space for Women?" Antipode 22: 156–67.

———. 1993. "Locating Identity Politics." In Place and the Politics of Identity, ed. M. Keith and S. Pile, 84–101. New York: Routledge.

Brammer, Jack. 2001. "Bill Widens Deadly Force Limit: Includes Burglary, Robbery, 'Deviate' Sexual Acts." Lexington Herald-Leader, January 16, A1.

Braun, Bruce. 1998. "A Politics of Possibility without the Possibility of Politics? Thoughts on Harvey's Troubles with Difference." Annals of the Association of American Geographers 88: 712–18.

Breed, Allen. 1995. "Groups Unite to Push for '96 Passage of Bill Legalizing Concealed Weapons." Lexington Herald-Leader, June 25, B6.

Bright, Barry. 2000. E-mail correspondence. www.freekentucky.com/ksm/militia-faq.htm.

———. 2001. "Race, Cards or Dice." www.freekentucky.com/columns01/race.htm (January 12).

———. 2002. "BATF Nazis Arrest KSM Commander." www.freekentucky.com/stryarch02/arrest.htm (February 26).

Brooks, Joanna. 1998. "Review of the Redneck Manifesto." Race Traitor 8: 101–4.

Brown, Craig. 1997. "Roeding Leads Fight against Intrusive EPA." Kentucky Post, November 4, letters section.

Burke, William. 1995. "The Wise Use Movement: Right-Wing Anti-environmentalism." In Eyes Right: Challenging the Right Wing Backlash, ed. C Berlet, 134–45. Boston: South End.

Bush, George. 1998. "Toward a New World Order." In The Geopolitics Reader, ed. G. O'Tuathail, S. Dalby, and P. Routledge, 136–38. London: Routledge.

Butler, Judith. 1990. Gender Trouble: Feminism and the Subversion of Identity. New York: Routledge.

Callahan, North. 1980. TVA: Bridge over Troubled Water. New York: Barnes.

Castells, Manuel. 1997. The Information Age: Economy, Society and Culture. Volume II: The Power of Identity. Oxford: Blackwell.

Chandler, William. 1984. The Myth of TVA: Conservation and Development in the Tennessee Valley, 1933–1983. Cambridge, Mass.: Ballinger.

Charpentier, S. 1995. "Hemp's Kentucky Movement." *Dollars and Sense* (May–June): 18–20.

Chellgren, Mark. 1999. "Miners Can't Sue: High Court Says They Must Use Workers' Comp System." *Lexington Herald-Leader,* November 19, D1.

Cheves, John. 1998. "KY Farmers Filing Suit in an Attempt to Legalize Hemp." *Lexington Herald-Leader,* May 15, B1.

Christopherson, Susan. 1989. "Flexibility in the US Service Economy and the Emerging Spatial Division of Labor." *Transactions: Institute of British Geographers* 14: 131–43.

Clark, P. 2000. "The Ethics of Medical Marijuana: Government Restriction v. Medical Necessity." *Journal of Public Health Policy* 21: 40–60.

Clifford, James. 1988. *The Predicament of Culture: Twentieth-Century Ethnography, Literature, and Art.* Cambridge, Mass.: Harvard University Press.

Cockburn, Alexander. 1993. "Beat the Devil." *Nation,* October 18, 414–15.

———. 1995a. "Beat the Devil." *Nation,* July 10, 43–44.

———. 1995b. "Beat the Devil." *Nation,* November 27, 656–57.

Cohen, Jeff, and Norman Solomon. 1995. "Guns, Ammo and Talk Radio." In *Eyes Right! Challenging the Right Wing Backlash,* ed. C. Berlet, 241–43. Boston: South End.

Collins, Michael. 1996. "Job Done: Workers' Comp Altered." *Kentucky Post,* December 13, 1k.

Conrad, Chris. 1994. *Hemp: Lifeline to the Future.* New York: Creative Xpressions.

———. 1997. *Hemp for Health: The Medicinal and Nutritional Uses of Cannabis Sativa.* New York: Inner Traditions.

Constitution Party of Kentucky (CPK). 2001. http://mrclint.freeyellow.com/cpky.html.

Cooper, Matthew. 1997. "Shutting Down a Siege." *Newsweek,* May 12, 46.

Cornell, Saul. 1999. "Commonplace or Anachronism: The Standard Model, the Second Amendment, and the Problem of History in Contemporary Constitutional Theory." *Constitutional Commentary* 16: 221–46.

Crane, Nancy. 1995. "Galbraith Joining Talk Show." *Lexington Herald-Leader,* May 30, A3.

Cresswell, Tim. 1996. *In Place/Out of Place: Geography, Ideology, and Transgression.* Minneapolis: University of Minnesota Press.

Cross, Al. 1999a. "Politics and the World Wide Web." *Louisville Courier-Journal,* May 18, local page.

———. 1999b. "Patton Takes on Foes, Voter Apathy." *Louisville Courier-Journal,* October 31, local page.

———. 1999c. "Patton Easily Wins 2nd Term; Low Turnout Clouds Mandate." *Louisville Courier-Journal,* November 3, local page.

Daniels, Jessie. 1997. *White Lies: Race, Class, Gender, and Sexuality in White Supremacist Discourse.* New York: Routledge.

Davidson, Osha. 1996. *Broken Heartland: The Rise of America's Rural Ghetto.* Iowa City: University of Iowa Press.

Dees, Morris. 1996. *Gathering Storm: America's Militia Threat.* New York: Harper-Collins.

Delgado, Richard, ed. 1995. *Critical Race Theory: The Cutting Edge.* Philadelphia: Temple University Press.

————. 1996: *The Coming Race War? And Oher Apocalyptic Tales after Affirmative Action and Welfare.* New York: New York University Press.

Derrida, Jacques. 1994. *Specters of Marx: The State of the Debt, the Work of the Mourning, and the New International.* Translated by Peggy Kamuf. New York: Routledge.

Deutsche, Rossalyn. 1991. "Boys Town." *Environment and Planning D: Society and Space* 9: 5–30.

Diamond, Sara. 1994. "Watch on the Right: The Christian Right's Anti-Gay Agenda." *Humanist* 54: 32–35.

————. 1995. *Roads to Dominion: Right Wing Movements and Political Power in the United States.* New York: Guilford.

————. 1996. *Facing the Wrath: Confronting the Right in Dangerous Times.* Monroe, Maine: Common Courage.

Dionne, E. J. 2001. "Tuesday's Elections Show That Identity Politic Can Be Lethal." *Washington Post,* November 9, A37.

Drug Enforcement Administration (DEA). 1998. "Statement from the Drug Enforcement Administration on the Industrial Use of Hemp." www.usdoj.gov/dea/pubs/pressrel/pr100901.html (March 12).

————. 2001a. "DEA Clarifies Status of Hemp in the Federal Register." www.usdoj.gov:80/dea/advisories/pa100901.html (October 9).

————. 2001b. "Exemption from Control of Certain Industrial Products and Materials Derived from the Cannabis Plant." *Federal Register* 66 (195): 51539–44.

Dyer, Joel. 1997. *Harvest of Rage: Why Oklahoma Is Only the Beginning.* Boulder, Colo.: Westview.

Dyer, Richard. 1997. *White.* New York: Routledge.

Eagleton, Terry. 1997. "Spaced Out." *London Review of Books,* April 24, 22–23.

Edelen, Sheryl. 1997. "Government Cutting away Rights, People at Militia Meeting Assert." *Lexington Herald-Leader,* February 28, B1.

Edwards, Rick. 1993. Rights at Work: Employment Relations in the Post-union Era. Washington, D.C.: Brookings Institution.

England, Kim. 1994. "Getting Personal: Reflexivity, Positionality, and Feminist Research." *Professional Geographer* 46 (1): 80–89.

Environmental Perspectives, Inc. (EPI). 2001. www.epi.freedom.org/.

Estep, Bill. 1999. "Galbraith Sends Message." *Lexington Herald-Leader,* November 3, A16.

————. 1996a. "KY Bill Would Let Adults Carry Concealed Guns." *Lexington Herald-Leader,* January 1, A1.

————. 1996b. "Panel Limits Concealed Weapons Bill, Committee Adds Provisions on Training, Domestic Violence." *Lexington Herald-Leader,* February 1, A1.

————. 1996c. "House OKs Concealed Guns 74–20, Backers Easily Defeat Attempts to Add Limits." *Lexington Herald-Leader,* February 7, A1.

————. 1996d. "Limits Added to Concealed-Weapons Measure, Next Possible Change Could Send Bill to Unfriendly Panel." *Lexington Herald-Leader,* February 28, A1.

————. 1996e. "House Gives OK on Concealed Weapons Bill." *Lexington Herald-Leader,* March 16, C1.

Fanon, Frantz. 1963. *The Wretched of the Earth.* New York: Grove.

Fellows, Will. 1998. *Farm Boys: Lives of Gay Men from the Rural Midwest.* Madison: University of Wisconsin Press.

Fields, Ingrid. 2002. "White Hope: Conspiracy, Nationalism, and Revolution in *The Turner Diaries* and *Hunter.*" In *Conspiracy Nation: The Politics of Paranoia in Postwar America,* ed. P. Knight, 157–76. New York: New York University Press.

Fifth Estate Production. 1997. *Waco: The Rules of Engagement.* Film. Los Angeles: Somford Entertainment.

Fortune, Beverly. 1999. "Move Over, Jesse: It's Gatewood 'The Body' Galbraith." *Lexington Herald-Leader,* July 25, J1.

Frakenberg, Ruth. 1993. *White Women, Race Matters: The Social Construction of Whiteness.* Minneapolis: University of Minnesota Press.

Friedan, Betty. 1963. *The Feminine Mystique.* New York: Norton.

Frye, Marilyn. 1993. "Some Reflections on Separatism and Power." In *The Lesbian and Gay Studies Reader,* ed. H. Abelove, M. Barale, and D. Halperin, 91–98. New York: Routledge.

Gaffney, Edward. 1995. "Constitutional Concerns and Policy Perspectives." In *Armageddon in Waco: Critical Perspectives on the Branch Davidian Conflict,* ed. S. Wright, 323–58. Chicago: University of Chicago Press.

Gallaher, Carolyn. 1997. "Identity Politics and the Religious Right: Hiding Hate in the Landscape." *Antipode* 29: 256–77.

————. 2000. "Global Change, Local Angst: Class and the American Patriot Movement." *Environment and Planning D: Society and Space* 18: 667–91.

Geertz, Clifford. 1983. *The Interpretation of Culture.* New York: Basic.

Geltmaker, T. 1992. "The Queer Nation Acts Up: Health Care, Politics, and Sexual Diversity in the County of Angels." *Environment and Planning D: Society and Space* 10: 609–50.

George, Jefferson, and Geoff Mulvihill. 1999. "Gay-Bias Law Debate Draws Crowd." *Lexington Herald-Leader,* July 2, A1.

Gershenkron, A. 1994. *Bread and Democracy in Germany.* Berkeley: University of California Press.

Gerth, Joseph. 1999. "Reform Candidate Struggles to Change His Image." *Louisville Courier-Journal,* October 2, local section.

————. 2000. "In Fifth Race, Reform Party's Galbraith Predicts He'll Defy Odds." *Louisville Courier-Journal,* October 22, local section.

Gibson, James. 1994. *Warrior Dreams: Violence and Manhood in Post-Vietnam America.* New York: Hill and Wang.

Gibson, Janet. 1998. "Quota Plan Fight Called Threat to Tobacco Bill." *Lexington Herald-Leader,* May 20, A1.

Gibson-Graham, J. K. 1996. *The End of Capitalism (As We Knew It): A Feminist Critique of Political Economy.* Cambridge, Mass.: Blackwell.

Giddens, Anthony. 1985. *The Nation-State and Violence: Volume Two of a Contemporary Critique of Historical Materialism.* Cambridge: Polity Press.

Gilbert, Melissa. 1994. "The Politics of Location: Doing Feminist Research at Home." *Professional Geographer* 46 (1): 80–87.

Gilroy, Paul. 1993. *The Black Atlantic: Modernity and Double Consciousness*. London: Verso.

Goad, Jim. 1997. *The Redneck Manifesto: America's Scapegoats: How We Got That Way, and Why We're Not Going to Take It Anymore*. New York: Simon and Schuster.

———. 1998. "Pale Face, Red Neck: Darius James's Interview with Jim Goad." *Transitions* 7 (1): 204–217.

Goldberg, Suzanne. 1995. "Civil Rights, Special Rights, and Our Rights." In *Eyes Right! Challenging the Right Wing Backlash*, ed. C. Berlet, 109–112. Boston: South End.

Golden Gate Biosphere Reserve (GGBR). 2001. www.nps.gov/ggbr/ggbr.htm.

Goodwyn, Lawrence. 1976. *Democratic Promise: The Populist Moment in America*. New York: Oxford University Press.

Gorov, Lynda. 1995. "False Leads Abound since Disaster." *Boston Globe*, April 29, 10.

Gourevitch, Philip. 1998. *We Wish to Inform You That Tomorrow We Will Be Killed with Our Families: Stories from Rwanda*. New York: Farrar, Straus & Giroux.

Greene, Susan. 2000. "Virgin, Utah: Where Every Household Must Have a Gun." *Denver Post*, December 26, A1.

Gregg, Robert. 2000. *Inside Out, Outside In: Essays in Comparative History*. New York: St. Martin's.

Gregory, Derek. 1994. *Geographical Imaginations*. Cambridge, Mass.: Blackwell.

Greider, William. 1997. *One World, Ready or Not: The Manic Logic of Global Capitalism*. New York: Simon and Schuster.

Halbrook, Stephen. 1984. *That Every Man Be Armed: The Evolution of a Constitutional Right*. Albuquerque: University of New Mexico Press.

———. 1989. *A Right to Bear Arms: State and Federal Bills of Rights and Constitutional Guarantees*. New York: Greenwood.

Hall, Stuart. 1991. "Ethnicity: Identity and Difference." *Radical America* 23: 9–20.

Halpern, Rick, and Jonathan Morris, eds. 1997. *American Exceptionalism: US Working-Class Formation in an International Context*. New York: St. Martin's.

Harris, Cheryl. 1993. "Whiteness as Property." *Harvard Law Review* 106: 1709–45.

Harvey, David. 1989. *The Condition of Postmodernity: An Enquiry into the Origins of Cultural Change*. Cambridge, Mass.: Blackwell.

———. 1996. *Justice, Nature and the Geography of Difference*. Cambridge, Mass.: Blackwell.

———. 1998. "The Humboldt Connection." *Annals of the Association of American Geographers* 88: 723–30.

———. 2000. *Spaces of Hope*. Berkeley: University of California Press.

Havard, William. 1983. "Images of TVA: The Clash over Values." In *TVA: Fifty Years of Grassroots Bureaucracy*, ed. E. Hargrove and P. Conkin, 297–315. Urbana: University of Illinois Press.

Herer, Jack. 1995. *Hemp and the Marijuana Conspiracy: The Emperor Wears No Clothes*. Unpublished booklet. Copyrighted March 1995.

Herod, Andrew. 2000. "Implications of Just-in-Time Production for Union Strategy: Lessons from the 1998 General Motors-United Auto Workers Dispute." *Annals of the Association of American Geographers* 90: 521–47.

Higginbotham, Don. 1999. "The Second Amendment in Historical Context." *Constitutional Commentary* 16: 263–68.

Hobsbawm, Eric. 1996. "Identity Politics and the Left." *New Left Review* 217: 38–47.

Holmes, Charles. 1995. "Attack Looks Familiar, Israeli Authorities Say." *Atlanta Journal and Constitution*, April 21, 6A.

hooks, bell. 1984. *Feminist Theory from Margin to Center*. Boston: South End.

———. 1990. *Yearning: Race, Gender, and Cultural Politics*. Boston: South End.

———. 1992. *Black Looks: Race and Representation*. Boston: South End.

Hopkins, James. 1998. *A History of the Hemp Industry in Kentucky*. Lexington: University Press of Kentucky, 1951. Reprint.

Howard, John. 1999. *Men Like That: A Southern Queer History*. Chicago: University of Chicago Press.

Hull, Anne. 2001. "Randy Weaver's Return from Ruby Ridge." *Washington Post*, April 30, A1.

Hull, Gloria, Patricia Scott, and Barbara Smith, eds. 1982. *All the Women Are White, All the Blacks Are Men, but Some of Us Are Brave: Black Women's Studies*. New York: Feminist.

Ignatiev, Noel. 1995. *How the Irish Became White*. New York: Routledge.

Ignatiev, Noel, and John Garvey. 1996. *Race Traitor*. New York: Routledge.

Jackson, Stevi, and Jackie Jones, eds. 1998. *Contemporary Feminist Theories*. New York: New York University Press.

Jeffords, Susan. 1989. *The Remasculinization of America: Gender and the Vietnam War*. Bloomington: Indiana University Press.

———. 1994. *Hard Bodies: Hollywood Masculinity in the Reagan Era*. New Brunswick, N.J.: Rutgers University Press.

Junas, D. 1995. "The Rise of Citizen Militias: Angry White Guys with Guns." In *Eyes Right! Challenging the Right Wing Backlash*, ed. C. Berlet, 226–35. Boston: South End.

Katz, Cindi. 1992. "All the World Is Staged: Intellectuals and the Projects of Ethnography." *Environment and Planning D: Society and Space* 10: 495–510.

———. 1994. "Playing the Field: Questions of Fieldwork in Geography." *Professional Geographer* 46 (1): 67–72.

Kelly, Jack. 1989. "4 out of 10 in Country Said to Grow Weed." *USA Today*, July 11, A1.

Kentucky Registry of Election Finance. 2000. Financial Report for Kentucky General Election for Robert Damron, 39th House District. 30 Day Post-General Report, Received December 6, 2000.

———. 2000. Financial Report for Kentucky General Election for Robert Damron, 39th House District. 15 Day Pre-General Report, Received October 24, 2000.

———. 2000. Financial Report for Kentucky General Election for Robert Damron, 39th House District. 32 Day Pre-General Report, Received October 11, 2000.

———. 2000. Financial Report for Kentucky Primary Election for Robert Damron, 39th House District. 30 Day Post-Primary Report, Received May 26, 2000.

———. 2000. Financial Report for Kentucky Primary Election for Robert Damron, 39th House District. 15 Day Pre-Primary Report, Received May 11, 2000.

———. 2000. Financial Report for Kentucky Primary Election for Robert Damron, 39th House District. 32 Day Pre-Primary Report, Received April 20, 2000.

Kentucky State Militia 911 (KSM911). 2001. 9th Battalion, 1st Brigade, 1st Kentucky Division, Kentucky State (Citizens') Militia home page. www.militia.clarksriver.com/.

Kenworthy, Tom. 1995a. "Angry Ranchers across the West See Grounds for an Insurrection." *Washington Post*, February 21, A3.

———. 1995b. "U.S. Enters Range War, Suing Nevada County." *Washington Post*, March 9, A3.

Keys, David, and John Galliher. 2000. *Confronting the Drug Control Establishment: Alfred Lindesmith as a Public Intellectual*. Albany: State University of New York Press.

Kincheloe, Joe, and Shirley Steinberg. 1998. "Addressing the Crisis of Whiteness: Reconfiguring White Identity in a Pedagogy of Whiteness." In *White Reign: Deploying Whiteness in America*, ed. J. Kincheloe, S. Steinberg, N. Rodriguez, and R. Chennault, 3–29. New York: St. Martin's.

Kipnis, Laura, and Jennifer Reeder. 1997. "White Trash Girl." In *White Trash: Race and Class in America*, ed. M. Wray and A. Newitz, 113–30. New York: Routledge.

Kirby, Andrew. 1997. "Is the State Our Enemy?" *Political Geography* 16: 1–12.

Kocher, Greg. 2002a. "Militia Leader Held on Weapons Charges: Guns, Pipe Bombs, Ammunition Found in Felon's Home, Office." *Lexington Herald-Leader*, February 27, B1.

———. 2002b. "Militia Leader Missing: Puckett Posts 'Last Testament' on Net." *Lexington Herald-Leader*, March 15, A1.

LaClau, Ernesto, and Chantal Mouffe. 1985. *Hegemony and Socialist Strategy: Towards a Radical Democratic Politics*. London: Verso.

Land Between the Lakes (LBL). 2001a. "About LBL." www2.lbl.org/lbl/AboutLBL.html.

———. 2001b. "Forests." www2.lbl.org/lbl/NRM/NRMForests.html.

Levinson, Sanford. 1989. "The Embarrassing Second Amendment." *Yale Law Journal* 99: 637–60.

Levitas, Daniel, and Leonard Zeskind. 1986. *The Farm Crisis and the Radical Right*. Atlanta: Center for Democratic Renewal.

Lipietz, Alain. 1992. *Towards a New Economic Order: Postfordism, Ecology, and Democracy*. Translated by Malcolm Slater. New York: Oxford University Press.

Lipsitz, George. 1998. *The Possessive Investment in Whiteness: How White People Profit from Identity Politics*. Philadelphia: Temple University Press.

Livingstone, David. 1992. *The Geographical Tradition*. Oxford: Blackwell.

Loprest, Pamela, and Sheila Zedlewski. 1999. "Current and Former Welfare Recipients: How Do They Differ?" Assessing the New Federalism Program, Discussion Paper, 99–17. Washington, D.C.: Urban Institute.

Lovan, Dylan. 2001. "Rep. Perry Clark Speaks to Militia Gathering, Local Lawmaker One of Pair Who Attended Event." *Louisville Courier-Journal*, April 8, local section.

Luke, Timothy, and Gearoid O'Tuathail. 1998. "Global Flowmations, Local Fundamentalisms, and Fast Geopolitics." In *An Unruly World?: Globalization, Gover-*

nance, and Geography, ed. A. Herod, G. O'Tuathail, and S. Roberts, 72–94. New York: Routledge.

Lusane, Clarence. 1991. *Pipe Dream Blues: Racism and the War on Drugs*. Boston: South End.

Malcolm, Joyce. 1994. *To Keep and Bear Arms: The Origins of an Anglo-American Right*. Cambridge, Mass.: Harvard University Press.

———. 1995. "Gun Control and the Constitution: Sources and Explorations on the Second Amendment." *Tennessee Law Review* 62: 813–21.

Marable, Manning. 1981. *Blackwater: Historical Studies in Race, Class Consciousness, and Revolution*. Dayton, Ohio: Black Praxis.

Marcus, G., and M. Fischer. 1986. *Anthropology as Cultural Critique: An Experimental Moment in the Human Sciences*. Chicago: University of Chicago Press.

Marx, Anthony. 1998. *Making Race and Nation: A Comparison of the United States, South Africa, and Brazil*. Cambridge: Cambridge University Press.

Massey, Doreen. 1993. "Power-Geometry and a Progressive Sense of Place." In *Mapping the Futures: Local Cultures, Global Change*, ed. J. Bird et al., 59–69. London: Routledge.

Mayer, Caroline. 2001. "Hemp-Food Firms Fight U.S. Ban, Deny Marijuana Link." *Washington Post*, January 13, A1.

McDowell, Linda. 1991. "Life without Father and Ford: The New Gender Order of Post-Fordism." *Transactions: Institute of British Geographers* 16: 400–419.

McPhail, Mark. 2002. *The Rhetoric of Racism Revisited: Reparations or Separation?* Lanham, Md.: Roman & Littlefield.

Mead, Andy. 1991. "'Gov. Galbraith' No Pipe Dream in Aylesford." *Lexington Herald-Leader*, May 31, A1.

———. 1996. "Natural Born Tiller." *Lexington Herald-Leader*, June 2, A1.

Melucci, Alberto. 1989. *Nomads of the Present: Social Movements and Individual Needs in Contemporary Society*. Philadelphia: Temple University Press.

Militia of Montana. 1999. "Militia of Montana Homepage." www.nidlink.com/~bobhard/mom.html.

Moore, Michael. 1997. *Downsize This!* New York: Harper Perennial.

Morgan, Robin. 2000. *Saturday's Child: A Memoir*. New York: Norton.

Morrison, Toni. 1992. *Playing in the Dark: Whiteness and the Literary Imagination*. Cambridge, Mass.: Harvard University Press.

Mouffe, Chantal. 1993. "An Interview with Chantal Moufee." *disClosure* 3: 87–104.

———. 1995. "Post-Marxism: Democracy and Identity." *Environment and Planning D: Society and Space* 13: 259–65.

Mozzochi, J. 1995. "America under the Gun: The Militia Movement and Hate Groups in America." In *Eyes Right! Challenging the Right Wing Backlash*, ed. C. Berlet, 236–40. Boston: South End.

Mulvihill, Geoff. 1999. "Gay Bias Law Is Adopted 12–3." *Lexington Herald-Leader*, July 9, A1.

Musto, David. 1999. *The American Disease: Origins of Narcotic Control*. 3d ed. Oxford: Oxford University Press.

Nakagawa, Scott. 1995. "Race, Religion and the Right." In *Eyes Right! Challenging the Right Wing Backlash*, ed. C. Berlet, 279–82. Boston: South End.

National Organization for the Reform of Marijuana Laws (NORML). 2001. "Industrial Use." www.norml.org/index.cfm?Group_ID = 3377.

National Park Service (NPS). 2001a. "Denali National Park and Preserve." www.nps.gov/dena/.

———. 2001b. "Everglades National Park." www.nps.gov/ever/.

———. 2001c. "Big Bend National Park." www.nps.gov/bibe/.

Natter, Wolfgang, and John Paul Jones. 1997. "Identity, Space, and Other Uncertainties." In *Space and Social Theory: Geographical Interpretations of Postmodernism*, ed. G. Benko and U. Strohmayer, 141–61. Oxford: Blackwell.

Nazario, Sonia. 1991. "What Is as Versatile as the Soybean but Illegal Anyway?—Hemp Plants Yield Marijuana but Guru Jack Herer Sees Lots of Commercial Uses." *Wall Street Journal*, May 2, A1.

Newitz, Annalee. 1997. "White Savagery and Humiliation, or a New Racial Consciousness in the Media." In *White Trash: Race and Class in America*, ed. M. Wray and A. Newitz, 131–54. New York: Routledge.

Newitz, Annalee, and Matt Wray. 1997. Introduction. In *White Trash: Race and Class in America*, ed. M. Wray and A. Newitz, 1–12. New York: Routledge.

North American Industrial Hemp Council (NAIHC). 2001. www.webcom.com/naihc/index.html.

Offe, C. 1987. "Challenging the Boundaries of Institutional Politics: Social Movements since the 1960s." In *Changing Boundaries of the Political*, ed. C. Maier, 63–106. New York: Cambridge University Press.

Pankratz, Howard. 1996. "Hope Rises for End to Standoff." *Denver Post*, April 7, A1.

Patton, Janet. 1998. "Backbone of the Harvest." *Lexington Herald-Leader*, May 31, A1.

People with a History. 2001. "An Online Guide to Lesbian, Gay, Bisexual and Trans History." www.fordham.edu/halsall/pwh/index.html.

Pertman, Adam, and Peter Howe. 1995. "Bomb Suspect Ordered Held for Grand Jury Inquiry." *Boston Globe*, April 28, 8.

Phelan, Shane. 1994. *Getting Specific: Postmodern Lesbian Politics*. Minneapolis: University of Minnesota Press.

Pickles, John, ed. 1995. *Ground Truth: The Social Implications of Geographic Information Systems*. New York: Guilford.

Pile, Steve, and Nigel Thrift, ed. 1995. *Mapping the Subject: Geographies of Cultural Transformations*. London: Routledge.

Piore, Michael, and Charles Sabel. 1984. *The Second Industrial Divide: Possibilities for Prosperity*. New York: Basic.

Plotke, D. 1990. "What's So New about New Social Movement." *Socialist Review* 20: 81–102.

Poore, Chris. 1995. "Galbraith's Speaking Style Is What Hooks Many Admirers: He Has Toned down His Campaign But Still Expects More Support Than Predicted." *Lexington Herald-Leader*, April 16, A1.

Powell, Cheryl. 1997. "Organizers Plan Meeting for 'Patriots'—Gathering Will Focus on Rights." *Lexington Herald-Leader*, February 26, B1.

Pred, Allan, and Michael Watts. 1992. *Reworking Modernity: Capitalisms and Symbolic Discontent*. New Brunswick N.J.: Rutgers University Press.

Public Broadcasting Service (PBS). 2000. "The Democracy Project Glossary: Do You Speak Campaign?" www.pbs.org/democracy/glossary/.

Pulido, L. 1996. "Development of the 'People of Color' Identity in the Environmental Justice Movement of the Southwestern United States." *Socialist Review* 26: 145–80.

———. 1998. "The Sacredness of 'Mother Earth': Spirituality, Activism and Social Justice." *Annals of the Association of American Geographers* 88: 719–23.

Quinn-Judge, Paul. 1995. "Luggage Said to Yield Items for Bombs; Man Reportedly Lived in Oklahoma." *Boston Globe,* April 21, 27.

Radcliffe, Sara. 1993. "Women's Place/El Lugar de Mujeres: Latin America and the Politics of Gender Identity." In *Place and the Politics of Identity,* ed. M. Keith and S. Pile, 102–116. London: Routledge.

Raitz, Karl. 1998. "The Agricultural Landscape." In *Atlas of Kentucky,* ed. R Ulack, K. Raitz, and G. Pauer, 153–74. Lexington: University Press of Kentucky.

Raitz, Karl, and Richard Schein. 1998. "Historical and Cultural Landscapes." In *Atlas of Kentucky,* ed. R Ulack, K. Raitz, and G. Pauer, 47–77. Lexington: University Press of Kentucky.

Reed, Adolph. 1995. "Assault on Affirmative Action." In *Eyes Right: Challenging the Right Wing Backlash,* ed. C. Berlet, 283–88. Boston: South End.

Reed, Steven. 1995. "Oklahoma City Tragedy: Bread Crumbs, Thin Trail of Clues Led Police to Track Rental Site, Suspects." *The Houston Chronicle,* April 30, A1.

Reynolds, Glenn. 1995. "A Critical Guide to the Second Amendment." *Tennessee Law Review* 62: 461–512.

Richardson, James. 1995. "Manufacturing Consent about Koresh." In *Armageddon in Waco: Critical Perspectives on the Branch Davidian Conflict,* ed. S. Wright, 153–76. Chicago: University of Chicago Press.

Robinson, Rowan. 1997. *The Hemp Manifesto: 101 Ways That Hemp Can Save Our World.* Rochester, Vt.: Inner Traditions International.

Roediger, David. 1991. *The Wages of Whiteness: Race and the Making of the American Working Class.* London: Verso.

———. 1994. *Towards the Abolition of Whiteness.* New York: Verso.

Rose, Gillian. 1993. *Feminism and Geography: The Limits of Geographical Knowledge.* Minneapolis: University of Minnesota Press.

Ross, Loretta. 1995. "White Supremacy in the 1990s." In *Eyes Right! Challenging the Right Wing Backlash,* ed. C. Berlet, 166–81. Boston: South End.

Schaver, Mark. 1999. "Legalizing Hemp Back in Spotlight." *Louisville Courier-Journal,* October 15, local section.

Scherer, Ron. 1999. "NRA Gun Safety Mascot Ruffles Feathers." *Christian Science Monitor,* July 7, national page.

Schlosser, Eric. 1995. "In the Strawberry Fields." *Atlantic Monthly* (November): 1–30.

Schneider, Cathy. 1998. "Racism, Drug Policy, and AIDS." *Political Science Quarterly* 113: 427–46.

Sedgwick, Eve. 1993. "Epistemology of the Closet." In *The Lesbian and Gay Studies Reader,* ed. H. Abelove, M. Barale, and D. Halperin, 45–61. New York: Routledge.

Shugar, Dana. 1995. *Separatism and Women's Community.* Lincoln: University of Nebraska Press.

Sibley, David. 1995. *Geographies of Exclusion.* London: Routledge.

Slaughter, Thomas. 1986. *The Whiskey Rebellion: Frontier Epilogue to the American Revolution.* New York: Oxford University Press.

Snell, Will, and Stephen Goetz. 1997. *Overview of Kentucky's Tobacco Economy.*

Factsheet of the University of Kentucky Cooperative Extension Service. Lexington: University of Kentucky Cooperative Extension Service.

Southern Poverty Law Center (SPLC). 1998. "The Patriot Movement: Fewer, but Harder, Patriot Groups in 1997." *Intelligence Report* (Spring).

———. 2001. www.splcenter.org/splc.html.

———. 2002. "The Year in Hate." *Intelligence Report* (Spring).

Sparke, Matthew. 1998. "Outsides inside Patriotism: The Oklahoma Bombing and the Displacement of Heartland Geopolitics." In *Rethinking Geopolitics*, ed. S. Dalby and G. O'Tuathail. New York: Routledge.

Staff Reports. 1995. "Galbraith, Hammond to Re-enter Race." *Lexington Herald-Leader*, October 30, B3.

———. 2002a. "Black Lung Benefits: Patton to Seek Less Restrictive Standards for Miners to Receive Payments." *Lexington Herald-Leader*, January 6, B7.

———. 2002b. "Militia Leader Freed with Tracking Device." *Lexington Herald-Leader*, March 2, C3.

———. 2002c. "House Gives Final OK to Black-Lung Benefits Bill." *Lexington Herald-Leader*, April 2, B3.

Staten, Pat. 1987. "The Economic Climate for a Banking Crisis." In *The Embattled Farmer*, ed. J Staten, 133–48. Golden, Colo.: Fulcrum.

Steinberg, Philip. 1997. "And Are the Anti-Statist Movements Our Friends?" *Political Geography* 17: 13–19.

Stern, Kenneth. 1996. *A Force upon the Plain: The American Militia Movement and the Politics of Hate*. New York: Simon and Schuster.

Stock, Catherine. 1996. *Rural Radicals: Righteous Rage in the American Grain*. Ithaca, N.Y.: Cornell University Press.

Stone, Alan. 1993. "Report and Recommendations Concerning the Handling of Incidents Such as the Branch Davidian Standoff in Waco, Texas." Washington, D.C.: U.S. Justice Department.

Storper, Michael, and Allen Scott. 1992. *Pathways to Industrialization and Regional Development*. London: Routledge.

Takaki, Ronald. 1990. *Iron Cages: Race and Culture in 19th Century America*. New York: Oxford University Press.

Taylor, Louise, and Greg Kocher. 2002. "Wanted Militia Leader Surrenders." *Lexington Herald-Leader*, April 5, A1.

Tennessee Valley Authority. 2001. "A Short History of TVA: From the New Deal to a New Century." www.tva.gov/abouttva/history.htm.

Thibodeau, David, and Leon Whiteson. 1999. *A Place Called Waco: A Survivor's Story*. New York: Public Affairs.

Thompson, Eric, Mark Berger, and Steven Allen. 1998. *Economic Impact of Industrial Hemp in Kentucky*. Lexington: University of Kentucky Center for Business and Economic Research, Carol Martin Gatton College of Business and Economics.

Tolliver, Thomas, and Jay Grelen. 1992. "Sodomy Law Struck Down: Ruling Called Both Immoral, Victory for Rights." *Lexington Herald-Leader*, September 25, A1.

Touraine, Alaine. 1985. "An Introduction to the Study of Social Movements." *Social Research* 52: 749–87.

———. 1995. *Critique of Modernity*. Oxford: Blackwell.

Turner, William. 2000. *A Genealogy of Queer Theory*. Philadelphia: Temple University Press.

United Nations Man and the Biosphere Programme (UNMAB). 1995. *Statutory Framework of the World Network of Biosphere Reserves*. Paris: UNESCO.

———. 2001. "Biosphere Reserves in a Nutshell." www.unesco.org/mab/brfaq.htm.

U.S. Senate. 1995a. Judiciary Committee. Subcommittee on Terrorism, Technology, and Government Information. Hearings on Militias, June 15, 1995 (Part 2). Washington D.C.: Government Printing Office.

———. 1995b. Judiciary Committee. Subcommittee on Terrorism, Technology, and Government Information. *Report on Ruby Ridge*. Washington, D.C.: Government Printing Office.

Valentine, G. 1993. "Negotiating and Managing Multiple Sexual Identities: Lesbian Time-Space Strategies." *Transactions of the Institute of British Geographers* 18: 237–48.

Vanderhoff, Mark. 2001. "Feds Seize Guns from Militia Leader: Felony Conviction from 1966 Is Cited." *Lexington Herald-Leader*, November 28, B1.

Virginia Coast Reserve. 2001. "Virginia Coast Reserve Long-Term Ecological Research." http://atlantic.evsc.virginia.edu/.

Vise, David. 2000. "Davidian Raid Whistle-Blower Indicted on Obstruction Charges." *Washington Post*, November 9, A2.

Voth, E., and R. Schwartz. 1997. "Medical Applications of Delta-9-Tetrahydrocannabinol and Marijuana." *Annals of Internal Medicine* 126: 791–98.

Wagar, Kit. 1995. "Galbraith Arrested after Parade Protest, Two Men Charged in Demonstration against U.N. Theme." *Lexington Herald-Leader*, July 5, A1.

Watkins, John. 1998. "Population." In *Atlas of Kentucky*, ed. R Ulack, K. Raitz, and G. Pauer, 79–99. Lexington: University Press of Kentucky.

Wieseltier, Leon. 1993. "The True Fire: A Defense of Spiritual Strangeness." *New Republic* 208: 25–27.

Williams, David. 1999. "Galbraith Won't Support Gay Proposal." *Letter* 10 (10): 8.

Williams, Raymond. 1989. *Resources of Hope*. London: Verso.

Williamson, E., and F. Evans. 2000. "Cannabinoids in Clinical Practice." *Drugs* 60: 1303–1314.

Wilson, William Julius. 1999. *The Bridge over the Racial Divide: Rising Inequality and Coalition Politics*. Berkeley: University of California Press.

Wolfe, Charles. 1996. "Patton Bets Workers' Comp Reform Will Boost Kentucky." *Kentucky Post*, December 26, 4k.

Wolfson, Andrew. 2001. "Two Legislators to Speak at Militia Rally: Critics Say Action Gives Legitimacy to Extremist Group." *Louisville Courier-Journal*, April 6, local page.

Woodward, Comer Vann. 1938. *Tom Watson: Agrarian Rebel*. New York: Macmillan.

Wren, Christopher. 1999. "Bird Food Is a Casualty in the War on Drugs." *New York Times*, October 3, 1999.

Wright, Stuart. 1995. "Introduction: Another View of the Mt. Carmel Standoff." In *Armageddon in Waco: Critical Perspectives on the Branch Davidian Conflict*, ed. S. Wright, xiii–xxvi. Chicago: University of Chicago Press.

Zeskind, Leonard. 1985. *Background Report on Racist and Anti-Semitic Organiza-*

tional Intervention in the Farm Protest Movement. Atlanta: Center for Democratic Renewal.

Zewe, Charles. 1997. "Secessionists Fighting for Texas: State Considers Group a Growing Threat." www.cnn.com/US/9701/11/republic.texas/.

Zinn, Howard. 1980. *A People's History of the United States.* London: Longman.

———. 1990. *Declarations of Independence: Cross-examining American Ideology.* New York: Harper Collins.

Index

Note: Page numbers for figures appear in italics.

About the Author

Carolyn Gallaher is assistant professor of geography in the School of International Service at American University in Washington, D.C. She teaches courses on political violence and critical geopolitics. She has published numerous articles on the religious right, violent social movements, and progressive politics. Her work includes case studies from the United States, Mexico, and, most recently, Northern Ireland.